www.wadsworth.com

wadsworth.com is the World Wide Web site for Wadsworth and is your direct source to dozens of online resources.

At *wadsworth.com* you can find out about supplements, demonstration software, and student resources. You can also send email to many of our authors and preview new publications and exciting new technologies.

wadsworth.com
Changing the way the world learns®

Anthology for Musical Analysis

Sixth Edition

Charles Burkhart

Aaron Copland School of Music at Queens College
and Graduate Center
City University of New York

THOMSON

SCHIRMER

Australia • Canada • Mexico • Singapore • Spain
United Kingdom • United States

THOMSON

SCHIRMER

Publisher, Music: *Clark Baxter*
Development Editor: *Sharon Adams Poore*
Assistant Editor: *Julie Yardley*
Editorial Assistant: *Eno Sarris*
Technology Project Manager: *Jennifer Ellis*
Marketing Manager: *Mark D. Orr*
Marketing Assistant: *Kristi Bostock*
Advertising Project Manager: *Brian Chaffee*
Project Manager, Editorial Production: *Emily Smith*
Print/Media Buyer: *Rebecca Cross*

Permissions Editor: *Kiely Sexton*
Production Service: *Buuji, Inc.*
Copy Editor: *Robin Gold*
Autographer: *Paul Nicholson*
Compositor: *Buuji, Inc.*
Cover Designer: *Cuttriss & Hambleton*
Cover Image: *© PhotoDisc/Getty Images*
Text Printer: *Quebecor World/Dubuque*
Cover Printer: *The Lehigh Press, Inc.*

Printed in the United States of America

1 2 3 4 5 6 7 07 06 05 04 03

For more information about our products, contact us at:
Thomson Learning Academic Resource Center
1-800-423-0563

For permission to use material from this text, contact us by: **Phone:** 1-800-730-2214
Fax: 1-800-730-2215
Web: http://www.thomsonrights.com

Library of Congress Catalog Card Number:
2003102453

ISBN: 0-15-506218-2

Wadsworth Group/Thomson Learning
10 Davis Drive
Belmont, CA 94002-3098
USA

Asia
Thomson Learning
5 Shenton Way #01-01
UIC Building
Singapore 068808

Australia/New Zealand
Thomson Learning
102 Dodds Street
Southbank, Victoria 3006
Australia

Canada
Nelson
1120 Birchmount Road
Toronto, Ontario M1K 5G4
Canada

Europe/Middle East/Africa
Thomson Learning
High Holborn House
50/51 Bedford Row
London WC1R 4LR
United Kingdom

Latin America
Thomson Learning
Seneca, 53
Colonia Polanco
11560 Mexico D.F.
Mexico

Spain/Portugal
Paraninfo
Calle/Magallanes, 25
28015 Madrid, Spain

Contents

PART TWO
Baroque Compositions   **43**

PART THREE
Classical Compositions   135

INTRODUCTION   135

PART FOUR
Romantic Compositions   289

Preface

This edition of *Anthology for Musical Analysis* is, like its predecessors, a collection of complete musical compositions and movements ranging in time from the Middle Ages to the present that is designed to provide theory and analysis classes on all levels with a large and varied body of music for study. Besides providing ample material for both a full-year course in the analysis of musical forms and a one-semester course in twentieth-century techniques, the book offers first- and second-year theory classes a wealth of illustrations of chords, voice-leading techniques, and forms, plus some material for figured-bass realization and score-reading. Because it consists essentially of music, and because it takes no theoretical position, the book is adaptable to any theoretical approach and to any type of curriculum, including those that combine theory study with music literature and the history of musical style. Though the book is not primarily a historical anthology, its chronological arrangement, together with the many opportunities it affords for comparison of the same form or procedure by different composers and from different periods, can teach much of an historical nature.

CONTENTS

The choice of music in this book favors those periods, composers, and genres most useful to theory and analysis courses. Such a selection will naturally emphasize music from the common-practice period to the present and will contain considerable keyboard and vocal music. Nonetheless, the book offers some earlier music and a fair number of works for instrumental media other than keyboard. There are, for example, seventeen works or movements for small ensembles and nine orchestral works given in full score; also, eleven different non-keyboard instruments are represented in pieces that feature them solely or prominently throughout.

The 208 pieces by 69 composers are grouped in five parts, each devoted to a major historical period. Two additional groups—a collection of examples of jazz, and a collection of chorale harmonizations—are placed in appendices. Although many examples are chosen to display a progression from simple to complex, the book as a whole is not intended to be studied in a particular order. On the contrary, its chronological arrangement, being neutral, leaves instructors free to choose the order that best suits their needs.

INDEXES AND OTHER TEACHING AIDS

The most comprehensive of the various teaching aids in the book are two indexes—or, more accurately, *example finders*—which direct the user to elements in the music (not to words in the text). INDEX I is an alphabetically arranged general index that locates examples of forms and genres, as well as of many procedures and devices of tonal and post-tonal music; INDEX II is a systematically arranged locator of chords, sequences, and modulations.

Each of the five parts of the book is preceded by an introduction giving a broad view of that part's contents together with suggestions for use. More specific comments, as well as a few questions, precede most of the individual pieces (or groups of similar pieces), and bibliography is frequently cited in footnotes. A final aid (on page 586) is a graded list of pieces suitable *in their entirety* to first- and second-year harmony study. The use of all the aids is, of course, optional.

Because traditional *Formenlehre* is the closest thing we have to a universally understood theory of form, I have employed its terminology in many of my comments, questions, and index entries. Because this traditional approach has undergone considerable refinement in recent years thanks to Schenkerian theory, I have drawn on a number of generally accepted Schenkerian concepts as well, for some of which I am indebted to the well-known textbook, *Harmony and Voice Leading* by Edward Aldwell and Carl Schachter (3rd edition, Thomson/Schirmer, 2003). Also, I have used some rhythm terminology from William Rothstein's widely used treatise, *Phrase Rhythm in Tonal Music* (New York: Schirmer Books, 1989).

FEATURES NEW TO THIS EDITION

Fourteen new composers are represented, of which six belong to the 20th century. Works by Messiaen, and Ligeti fill long-standing lacunae; Takemitsu, Reich, and Adams provide more recent music, and Vaughan Williams is represented by a modal folk-song arrangement (in Appendix B.)

Of the eight other new composers, five are women, greatly increasing the representation of women in the anthology.

Music for small ensembles has been somewhat increased, most notably by movements from three winds pieces—Mozart's *Divertimento for wind sextet*, Stravinsky's *Octet*, and Ligeti's *Ten Pieces for Wind Quintet*. The representation of music for wind instruments is further strengthened by Mozart's clarinet concerto, first movement.

Other important new pieces include the E major prelude and fugue from Book II of Bach's *Well-Tempered* Clavier, the first movement of Haydn's C sharp minor piano sonata, the first movement of Beethoven's second "Rasumovsky" string quartet, six of Brahms's variations on a theme of Schumann, Messiaen's *Quartet for the End of Time*, first movement, two movements from Stravinsky's *Agon*, and an aria from Adams' *Nixon in China*. Two pieces brought back from the fourth edition (because sorely missed) are the first movement of Beethoven's "Spring" sonata for violin and piano, and the scherzo from his D major piano sonata, Op. 28.

In response to many requests, elementary material has been strengthened. Also, the teaching aid listing complete pieces suitable for harmony study has been expanded to include second year (see page 586).

Less common foreign terms in the scores have been translated for the convenience of students (see page 584).

The comments, questions, and indexes have been revised, and references to analytic literature updated.

Though analysis must be mainly concerned with technical matters, I try in my own teaching (and where possible in the questions here) to relate technique to the expressive qualities of the work under study—in short, to what gives it life and the power to move us. And I have sought to promote the approach described by C.P.E. Bach in a letter to a friend dated October 15, 1777:

> In my opinion, in instructing [students] . . . a most important element, analysis, should not be omitted. True masterpieces should be taken from all styles of composition, and the student shown the beauty, daring and novelty in them . . . especially how a work departs from ordinary ways, how venturesome it can be.[1]

ACKNOWLEDGMENTS

I am grateful to those users of the fifth edition who were invited to contribute suggestions for the sixth: John Buccheri, Northwestern University; Gregory D. Carroll, The University of North Carolina—Greensboro; Craig Cummings, Ithaca College; Charles Forsberg, St. Olaf College; David Heinick, State University of New York—Potsdam; Dennis Kam, University of Miami; and Richard B. Nelson, Cleveland Institute of Music. For their generous advice or assistance I am grateful also to my Aaron Copland School of Music colleagues Jimmy Heath, Arbie Orenstein, Drora Pershing, William Rothstein, Carl Schachter, and Joseph Straus, as well as to other musicians and scholars, namely, Carol Henry Bates, Adrienne Fried Block, Per Broman, Chou Wen-chung, Edgar Coons, Richard Crocker, Sylvia Glickman, Alan Hacker, Roger Kamien, Martín Kutnowski, Mark Lindley, Henry Martin, Cary and Marie-Thérèse Plotkin, Nancy B. Reich, Marie Rolf, Giorgio Sanguinetti, Phil Schaap, Stephen Slottow, and Channan Willner. I extend special thanks to Joseph Ponte of the Queens College Music Library, and to my assistant, Katie Franklin.

Belated acknowledgment is due one of my teachers, the late David Kraehenbuehl, composer, and founder of the *Journal of Music Theory*, whose early influence has endured in all editions. I also single out my colleague Leo Kraft, whose wise suggestions and generosity of spirit since the inception of the anthology have been deeply appreciated. And again I especially acknowledge the invaluable contributions of Marian Burkhart, who in so many ways has been co-author of this book.

C.B.
New York, N.Y.

[1] Quoted by William Mitchell in his translation of C.P.E. Bach, *Essay on the True Art of Playing Keyboard Instruments* (Norton: New York, 1949), p. 441.

Part One

Medieval and Renaissance Compositions

Though theory and analysis curricula focus mainly on the music of the common-practice and modern periods, they should not wholly ignore that of earlier times—the source of so many fundamental materials and techniques. Part One (supplemented by several Renaissance examples in Appendix B) stresses the types of early music that most clearly reveal those materials and techniques.

THE CHURCH MODES

The examples of plainchant have been chosen to show the main characteristics of the most important modes. In the excerpts from Hildegard's morality play *Ordo Virtutum,* changes of mode have a dramatic function. Also of modal interest are various of the polyphonic compositions, notably Josquin's *Tu pauperum refugium* and Lassus' two-voice *Expectatio justorum,* both of which are Phrygian, the mode least like major and minor. Appendix B has another example of Phrygian in Hassler's setting of *Aus tiefer Not* on page 561, and one of Mixolydian in the chant-derived *Komm, Gott Schöpfer* (together with Bach's harmonization of it) on page 573.

It is interesting to compare early modality with its reappearance centuries later in modern dress. See, for instance, the opening of the Brahms clarinet sonata, Debussy's *La cathédrale engloutie,* bars 28–40, and the Ralph Vaughan Williams folk-song setting on page 563.

COUNTERPOINT

Sixteenth-century polyphony is stressed in Part One because the tradition of counterpoint instruction based on that model still survives. The Lassus *Duos* and the biciniae within the Josquin motet provide the simplest examples of two-part writing, and both the Lassus and Palestrina pieces show typical two-, three-, and four-part canonic imitations grouped in "points." Strict canon is shown in Josquin's simple but ingenious *Baisés moy.*

Some of these pieces might be compared to later imitative works, especially Bach's *stile antico* fugue in E major. Exactly what is and is not "old style" about this fugue? And do any old-style elements survive in Hindemith's *Fuga prima* and the movement from Bartók's *Music for Strings, Percussion and Celesta?*

HARMONY

One does not usually think of Renaissance music in terms of "harmony," but simple examples can teach much about the construction and connection of chords. Dufay's *Communio* in fauxbourdon contains only the chords $\frac{8}{5}$ and $\frac{6}{3}$. The simplest four-voice writing is in the two Praetorious settings on pages 567 and 569 plus the Gervaise *Pavane* on page 33, all of which can be supplemented by the three early Baroque figured-bass chorales on pages 559, 571, and 581. Only slightly more elaborate are Hassler's *Aus tiefer Not* (page 561) and Heinrich Isaac's *Isbruck* (page 577). More complex figuration and more explicitly tonal harmony are represented by the Gorzanis dance pair and Thomas Morley ballett. Finally, Gesualdo's radically chromatic harmony using only triads is shown in his madrigal *Moro lasso*.

PREEXISTENT COMPOSITIONAL MATERIAL

A range of cantus firmus techniques is represented by the Machaut isorhythmic motet, the Dufay *Communio*, the Josquin canon, and the Palestrina movements, some of which might be compared with those in the Bach organ preludes, especially *Vor deinen Tron*, and in Charles Ives' song "General William Booth Enters into Heaven." Another way of using given material is shown by the compositions on stock basses, or more accurately, stock chord progressions (page 32ff.). Because these compositions elaborate the given chords via *additional* chords of a secondary nature, they are useful for teaching chord "expansion," or "prolongation."

OTHER HISTORICAL COMPARISONS

The Gorzanis dance pair, the earliest example of variation in the anthology, may be compared with the Handel *Air* and the *themes with variations* of Mozart, Brahms, and Stravinsky, as well as with further related examples listed under "Variations" in Index I. Other comparisons might be assigned as special studies to one or more students. For example: How does the treatment of isorhythm in Machaut's motet compare with that in the movement from Messiaen's *Liturgie de cristal?* Or, how does Gesualdo's chromaticism differ from that in, say, Bach's chorales *So gehst du nun* or *O Haupt voll Blut und Wunden* or other works listed under "Chromaticism" in Index I? Another study might compare the Palestrina movements (or other *prima prattica* works) with Monteverdi's madrigal *Lasciatemi morire*, focusing on precisely how the revolutionary *seconda prattica*, so bitterly attacked by the conservatives of the time, differed from the older style in the treatment of voice leading? Or another might compare the early stock basses (page 32) with the "Rhythm changes" of jazz (see Appendix A).

EXAMPLES OF PLAINCHANT

These examples from the great body of Roman Catholic liturgical chant (also called plainchant or Gregorian chant) have been selected to show some of the characteristics of the church modes. In addition to these examples, three more are given on pages 9, 14, and 22. Identify the mode in each case. Consider what factors create the effect of a "tonal center." Does the finalis of the mode always sound like a tonic in the modern sense? Also examine the motivic content and form of each example. The opening Kyrie, in addition to being given in modern notation, is first shown as it appears in the neumatic notation of the *Liber Usualis* (LU).[1]

KYRIE FROM MASS XIII (STELLIFERI CONDITOR ORBIS) (LU 51)

(11th century)

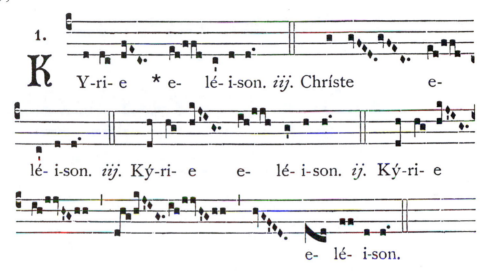

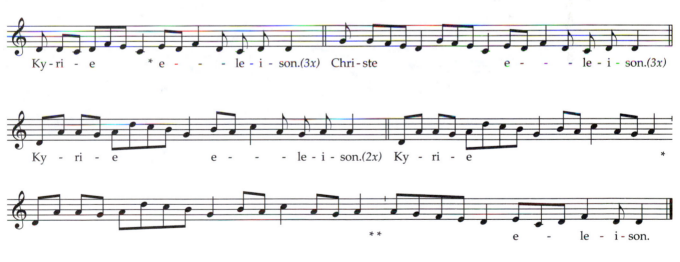

Lord, have mercy.
Christ, have mercy.
Lord, have mercy.

---

[1] Following the title of each chant given here is the page on which it will be found in the *Liber Usualis*, edited by the Benedictines of Solemnes (Desclée, Tournai, 1952). A standard work on chant is David Hiley's *Western Plainchant: A Handbook* (Oxford: 1993). For brief explanations of the church modes, see "Mode" in *The New Grove Dictionary* or *The New Harvard Dictionary of Music.*

■ TONE FOR THE BENEDICAMUS DOMINO (LU 124)

Be - ne - di - ca - mus Do - - - - - - - - - - - - - - - - - - - mi - no.

Let us bless the Lord.

■ HYMN TO ST. JOHN THE BAPTIST (LU 1504)

Ut que - ant lax - is   re - so - na - re fi - bris   Mi - - ra ges - to - rum

fa - mu - li tu - o - rum, Sol - ve pol - lu - ti la - bi - i re - a - tum, Sanc - te Jo - an - nes.

(Four more verses follow to identical music.)[2]

■ HYMN FOR LAUDS, DECEMBER 25 (LU 400)

A so - lis or - tus car - di - ne   Ad - us - que ter - rae li - mi - tem,

Chris - tum   ca - na - mus Prin - ci - pem,   Na - tum Ma - ri - a Vir - gi - ne.

At the rising of the sun, unto the limits of the earth, let us sing Christ the Prince, born of the Virgin Mary.

---

[2] For a translation and comment on the historical significance of this famous hymn, see D. J. Grout, *A History of Western Music* (New York: Norton, 5th ed., 1996, p. 57).

■ ANTIPHON FOR VESPERS, 3RD SUNDAY OF ADVENT (LU 338)

In certain modes B♮ is sometimes replaced by B♭. Consider why the final B is flatted here and why the other Bs are left natural.

Mon-tes et om - nes col - les hu - mi - li - a - bun - tur: et e-runt pra - va in di - rec-ta,

et a - spe-ra in vi - as pla - nas: ve-ni Do - mi - ne, et no - li tar-da-re, al - le - lu - ia.

Every mountain and hill shall be made low, and the crooked shall become straight,
and the rough ways plain (Isaiah 40:4, Douay version). Come, Lord, delay not, alleluia.

■ GLORIA PATRI FOR THE INTROIT OF THE MASS (LU 15)

The singing of a verse from the biblical Psalms occurs at various points in the liturgy. This is usually followed by the "Gloria Patri," the music for which exists in various slightly different versions, depending on the mode of the psalm verse. In which mode is this version?

Glo - ri - a Pa-tri et Fi - li - o, et Spi - ri - tu - i Sanc - to, * Si - cut e - rat in prin - ci - pi - o,

et nunc, et sem - per, et in sae - cu - la sae - cu - lo - rum. A - men.

Glory be to the Father, and to the Son, and to the Holy Ghost.
As it was in the beginning, is now, and ever shall be, world without end. Amen.

ORDO VIRTUTUM (EXCERPTS)
Morality Play (ca. 1151)
Text: Hildegard of Bingen

Hildegard of Bingen (1098–1179)

A person of extraordinary spiritual, intellectual, and artistic gifts, the German Benedictine abbess Hildegard of Bingen is one of the earliest known composers in the history of Western music. More than a musician, she also wrote accounts of mystical experiences, lives of the saints, letters, and medical and scientific works. Much of her music was written to her own poetry. Though it is entirely sacred, monophonic, and largely for liturgical use, its melodic style is generally not typical of Gregorian chant.

Unique among Hildegard's compositions, and quite distinct from her more explicitly liturgical music, is the work excerpted here, the *Ordo Virtutum*, or Rite of the Virtues. Often cited as the earliest preserved morality play, it precedes by several centuries the well-known *Everyman*. An allegory of universal human experience, the work's chief "character" is The Soul (representing every individual human soul), who is tempted, falls, but repents and returns to the community of grace amid general rejoicing. Also personified are some sixteen Christian Virtues, thus the work's title. Another notable character is the Devil, who only speaks, never sings. (Why not?) The *Ordo* was probably performed by the nuns in Hildegard's abbey on festival occasions.

Excerpt *a,* the opening of the *Ordo,* starts with a query from the Old Testament "Patriarchs and Prophets" (who will return at the end, framing the whole). The Virtues' response features d^1-a^1 and d^1-a^1-d^2, motives that frequently recur in the work. Excerpt *b* is the beginning of a long middle section in which each of the Virtues sings individually in turn, their solos separated by passages sung by all the Virtues as a chorus. (Humility's speech contains a reference to Luke 15:8–10—Jesus' parable of the lost coin.) The translations are for meaning only, not for singing.

Analyze the modes employed in the two excerpts. Why do changes of mode occur where they do, and how is "modulation" brought about? In individual phrases, how has the composer achieved a sense of melodic growth and overall coherence?

(a)

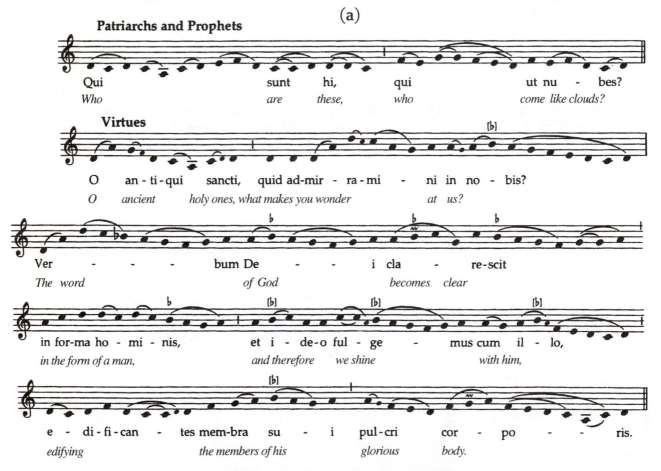

Patriarchs and Prophets

Qui   sunt hi, qui   ut nu - bes?
Who   are   these,   who   come like clouds?

Virtues

O   an - ti - qui   sancti, quid ad-mir - ra - mi - ni in no - bis?
O   ancient   holy ones, what makes you wonder   at   us?

Ver - - - bum De - i cla - re-scit
The word   of God   becomes   clear

in for-ma ho - mi - nis,   et i - de-o ful - ge - mus cum il - lo,
in the form of a man,   and therefore   we shine   with him,

e - di - fi - can - tes mem-bra su - i pul-cri   cor - po - ris.
edifying   the members of his   glorious   body.

(b)

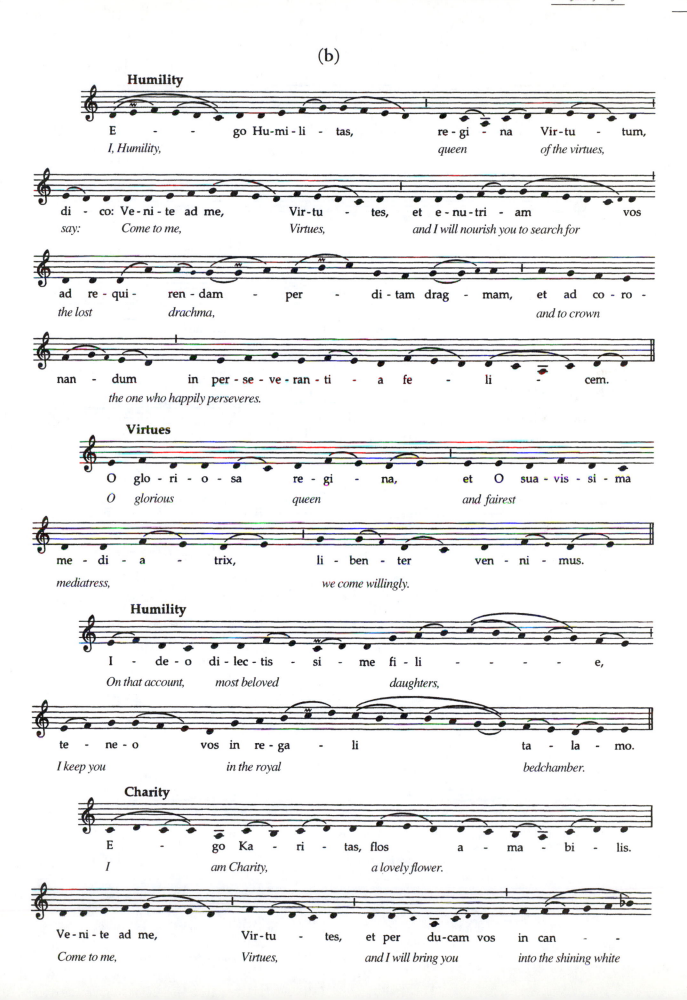

Humility

E - - go Hu-mi-li - tas,   re-gi - na Vir-tu - tum,
I, Humility,   *queen*   *of the virtues,*

di - co: Ve-ni-te ad me,   Vir-tu - tes, et e-nu-tri - am   vos
say: Come to me,   *Virtues,*   *and I will nourish you to search for*

ad re-qui - ren-dam - per - di-tam drag - mam, et ad co-ro -
the lost   drachma,   *and to crown*

nan - dum in per-se-ve-ran-ti - a fe - li - cem.
the one who happily perseveres.

Virtues

O glo-ri-o-sa   re-gi - na, et O sua-vis-si-ma
O glorious   queen   *and fairest*

me-di-a - trix,   li-ben - ter ve-ni-mus.
mediatress,   *we come willingly.*

Humility

I - de-o di-lec-tis - si-me fi-li - - - e,
On that account,   most beloved   daughters,

te - ne-o vos in re-ga - li   ta-la-mo.
I keep you   in the royal   bedchamber.

Charity

E - go Ka - ri - tas, flos   a - ma - bi - lis.
I   am Charity,   a lovely flower.

Ve-ni-te ad me,   Vir-tu - tes, et per du-cam vos in can - -
Come to me,   *Virtues,*   *and I will bring you   into the shining white*

- - di - - dam lu - cem flo - ris vir - - - ge.

light of the flower of the   *branch.*

Virtues

O di - lec - tis - si - me flos,   ar - den - ti

O sweetest   *flower,*   *we run to you with*

de - si - de - ri - o cur - ri - mus ad te.

burning desire.

Fear of God

E - go Ti - mor De - i vos fe - li - cis - si - mas

I, Fear of God, prepare you, most fortunate

fi - li - - as pre - pa - ro, ut in - spi - ci - a - tis

daughters, that you may look upon

in De - um vi - - - vum, et non pe - re - a - tis.

the living God   *and may not perish.*

Virtues

O Ti - mor, val - de u - ti - lis es no - -

O Fear of God, you are exceedingly useful to us;

bis: ha - be - mus e - nim per - fec - tum

we indeed have a   *perfect*

stu - di - um num - quam a te se - pa - ra - ri.

zeal   *never*   *to be separated from you.*

DE BON ESPOIR—PUISQUE LA DOUCE ROSEE—*SPERAVI*
Isorhythmic motet (mid-fourteenth century)
Guillaume de Machaut (ca. 1300–1377)

The isorhythmic motet flourished in France in the thirteenth and fourteenth centuries. Typically in three voices, the lowest voice, or *tenor,* was composed of a series of pitches taken from a particular plainchant. This pitch series, called the *color,* was subjected to an "isorhythm," that is, a reiterated rhythmic pattern, which is called the *talea.* In this motet, Machaut, the most celebrated composer and poet of his day, took the Gregorian introit beginning with the words "Domine, in tua misericordia speravi" (Lord, in thy mercy I hoped)[3] and chose as his color just the eighteen notes covering the word "speravi," as follows.

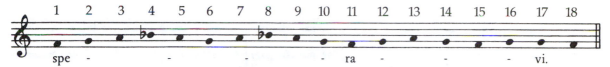

It is a simple matter to locate this series of eighteen pitches in the tenor. How many times is the series repeated? To discover the talea, list the *durations* of the tenor notes and rests (ignoring pitch) until a repeating series of durations emerges. How many durations are there in the series? How do color and talea relate? The upper parts also display considerable rhythmic repetition. Are they, like the tenor, also controlled by an inflexible scheme?

Though the tenor part of such compositions was apparently performed on an instrument, the particular word of the chant from which it is derived is often significant. Here the Latin *speravi*— "I hoped"—is clearly related to the theme of hope—*espoir*—prominent in the first of Machaut's two poems. The whole is a sophisticated union of sacred and secular elements intended for the delectation of highly cultivated persons.[4]

The term "motet" was applied to very different types of composition in the course of music history. A later example is given on page 16. For a twentieth-century realization of the isorhythmic principle, see the work by Messiaen on page 502.

Reprinted by permission of the publisher, Éditions de l'Oiseau-Lyre, Monaco, from *Polyphonic Music of the Fourteenth Century,* vol. 3, ed. Leo Schrade. Copyright 1956. Copyright renewed by Margarita M. Hanson, © 1974. (Some editorial material has been removed.)

[3] See *Graduale Romanum,* first Sunday after Pentecost.
[4] Alec Harman analyzes this motet in his *Medieval and Early Renaissance Music* (Fair Lawn, NJ: Essential Books, 1958, p. 130f).

Triplum

By Good Hope, by Very Sweet Remembrance,
And by Very Gentle Thought has good Love
Oft times been help to me against Desire
When he with utmost strength assailed me;
And the more that Desire has tortured me,
Most gently Hope has reassured me,
And Remembrance showed to me the beauty,
the sense, honor, value, and the goodness
Of the one about whom a tender thought
Came to give comfort to my mourning heart.
Alas! then did Desire e'en more assail,
But strong resistance to him saved me,
Though I was near to losing the comfort
Of Good Hope, which would destroy my courage.

And Mem'ry makes me always remember
When my sad heart would force me to despair.
For Grace, and Love, and Faith, and Loyalty,
Compassion, Learning, and Nobility
In me alone now soundly are asleep;
For Danger reigns above the power of Grace;
And since my lady, to whom I am bound,
Believes in Hardness and proud Refusal,
And wants this, not my love nor my heart,
I cannot leave, whate'er the cost.
Still, since it cannot now be otherwise,
Let her make of me whatsoe'er she will;
In spite of it I'll love her faithfully.

Motetus

Now since the sweet dew
Of humility does not wish to make
Pity bloom until it ripens,
Thanks be I may not achieve
What I so much desire;
For in me is engendered,
By an amorous desire,
An ardor beyond measuring

That Love, by its sweet pleasure,
And my desired lady,
By her most brilliant beauty,
Through grace have aroused in me.
But since thus they be pleased,
I wish humbly to endure
What they will until I die.

(Translated by Margaret Webb)

COMMUNIO
from *Missa Sancti Jacobi* (ca. 1428)

Guillaume Dufay (ca. 1400–1474)

This piece is an example of the fifteenth-century French technique of *fauxbourdon,* in which (1) a cantus firmus (usually sacred) placed in the upper voice is combined with a lower voice that forms sixths and octaves below, and (2) an improvised middle voice that strictly parallels the top a perfect fourth lower is added in performance. The earliest known example of *fauxbourdon* is this *Communio,* which concludes Dufay's mass in honor of St. James. We have notated (in small notes) only the beginning of the improvised middle part, leaving its completion to the student. Can you sing it without writing it out? or while playing the two notated parts at the keyboard, or while others sing them? We suggest a tempo of about 54 to the dotted half note. Are the six quarters of each bar consistently felt as two groups of three, as suggested by the modern time signature?

Examine the relation of the top voice to the chant on which it is based. In the polyphonic setting, notice Dufay's frequent use of octaves. At what point in every phrase did he always write an octave? Why that point?[5]

You, who have followed me, shall sit on seats judging the twelve tribes of Israel.
    (Matthew 19:28, Douay version)

---

[5] *Liber Usualis,* p. 1392.

de - bi -tis   su - - - per

de - bi -tis   su - - - - per

se - - - - des,   ju - di - can - tes   du

se - - - - - des,   ju - di - can - tes du -

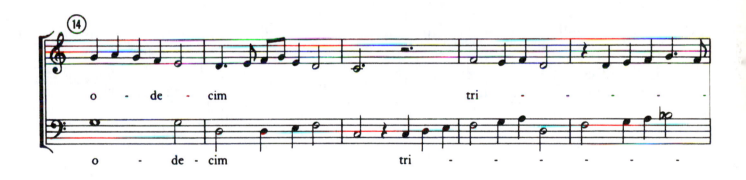

o - de - cim   tri - - - - - - -

o - de - cim   tri - - - - - -

- - bus   Is - ra - - - - - - - el.

bus   Is - ra - - - - - - - el.

TU PAUPERUM REFUGIUM

Motet for four voices (late fifteenth century)

Josquin Desprez (ca. 1440–1521)

Josquin Desprez, the greatest master of the high Renaissance, composed a large body of motets remarkable for their variety and profundity of expression. Many have several more or less independent units. Our example, the second such unit of a large bipartite motet entitled *Magnus es tu, Domine*, forms a complete structural entity and can be performed alone.

Tu pauperum is a rich display of the characteristics of the Phrygian mode. What "key" areas other than E are emphasized? Investigate the sensitively balanced phrases, comparing their lengths. Typical of Josquin is the insertion of two-part passages, or *bicinia*. What is their effect? Might the one at bars 21–27 be painting the text—"path for the wandering?"

The text as a whole falls into two large sections that separate at the turn of bar 34. How does the music reflect this two-part form?[6]

> *Thou art refuge of the poor, alleviator of weakness, hope of the exiled, strength of the burdened,*
>   *path for the wandering, truth, and life.*

> *And now, O Lord Redeemer, to thee alone I flee; I adore thee as the true God, in thee I hope,*
>   *in thee I trust, O Jesus Christ, my salvation. Help me, lest my soul should ever sleep in death.*

[6] Felix Salzer and Carl Schachter give an interesting analysis of this work in *Counterpoint in Composition* (New York: McGraw-Hill, 1969, p. 402f.; repr. Columbia University Press, 1989.)

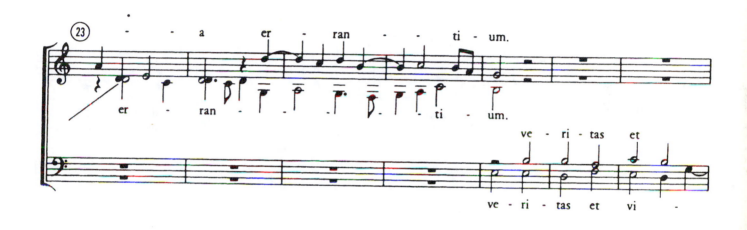

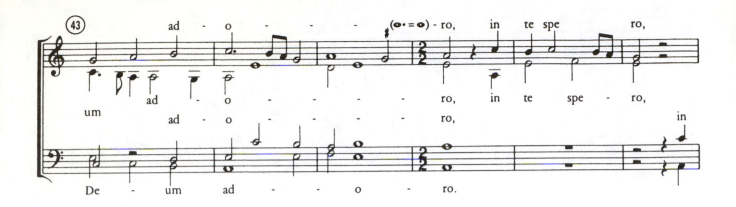

BAISÉS MOY
Double canon (publ. 1502)

Josquin Desprez (ca. 1440–1521)

A master of canon, Josquin could spot at a glance canonic possibilities in a simple folk song, and he wrote settings of many. One such is the following ditty (which you might try turning into a canon before looking at his).

"Bai - sés moy, bai - sés moy! Bai - sés moy, ma doulce a - my - e.

Par a-mour je vous em-pri - e." "Non fe - ray." "Et pour - quoy?" "Se je fai-sois la fol-

li - e. Ma mè-re se-roit mar - ri - e." "Ve - la de quoy! Ve - la de quoy!"

"Kiss me, sweet friend. For love I pray you." "I won't." "And why?"
"If I committed such folly, my mother would be shamed." "That's why."

Now figure out how Josquin's canon works. Notice that only two of the four voices have a signature of one flat. Although the use of "partial signature" is not unusual in Renaissance music (see page 9), the way the signatures are disposed here may mean, among other things, that the canonic imitation should not be tonal, but real—that is, at exactly the same interval throughout. In any event, the editor of our version thought so (see *A Note on the Sources,* page 583). And he has applied this idea to his solution of the *musica ficta* problem. What very unusual combination of notes is produced in bar 36?

An amusing marriage of popular and high art, this little piece was likely written to be performed by instruments, or by a combination of instruments and voices. Take it at a merry clip, two—or even one—to the bar. (Some later canons appear on pages 120 and 360.)

SANCTUS AND BENEDICTUS
from *Missa Aeterna Christi Munera* (publ. 1590)

Giovanni Pierluigi da Palestrina (ca. 1525–1594)

In the Renaissance, composers of masses very frequently based their works on some kind of pre-existing musical material. Of Palestrina's 105 masses, 52 are reworkings, or "parodies," of earlier polyphonic compositions by Palestrina himself or by others; in most of the rest, plainchant provides the preexistent material. Fewer than ten are entirely original.

Of Palestrina's chant-based masses, thirty-four are in a special class in which the given chant, rather than being confined to the tenor voice and explicitly stated there, appears in paraphrased fragments in *all* the voices. The *Missa Aeterna Christi Munera* is such a "paraphrase mass." It is based throughout on a chant which in Palestrina's time was used for the matins hymn for the Common of Apostles (and which has survived in various versions; see, for example, "Nunc Sancte nobis Spiritus," *Liber Usualis,* page 235). We give it here in a version dating from the sixteenth century:

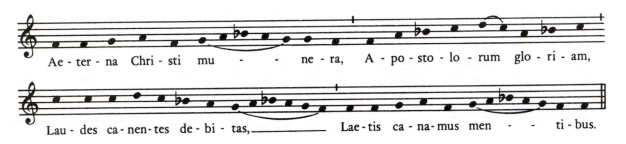

Ae - ter - na Chri - sti mu — ne - ra, A - po - sto - lo - rum glo - ri - am,

Lau - des ca - nen - tes de - bi - tas,_____ Lae - tis ca - na - mus men — ti - bus.

> [Let us sing] the eternal gifts of Christ
> and the glory of the apostles—
> [these,] the praises that we owe,
> with happy minds let us sing.

This music poses several quite different analytic problems. One is to discover the manifold variants of the phrases of the chant that permeate almost every bar. Another is to deduce precisely how Palestrina treated dissonance in relation to rhythm; his style is extremely consistent in this respect.[7] A more general problem is to locate the canonic imitations, noticing their relation to the large sections of each movement and to the text. Finally, consider what aspects of this music might be termed "original."

■ SANCTUS

Reprinted by permission of the Instituto Italiano per la Storia della Musica from *Opere Complete di G. P. da Palestrina*, vol. 15, Raffaele Casimiri, ed.

---

[7] Two classic studies, both by Knud Jeppesen, are *The Style of Palestrina and the Dissonance* (Oxford University Press 1946; repr. New York: Dover, 1970) and *Counterpoint* (New York: Prentice-Hall, 1939; repr. New York: Dover, 1992), the latter a practical work for students.

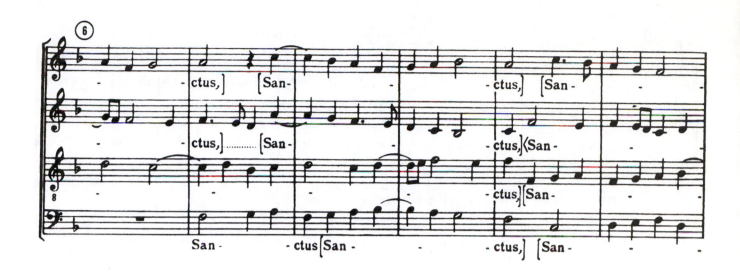

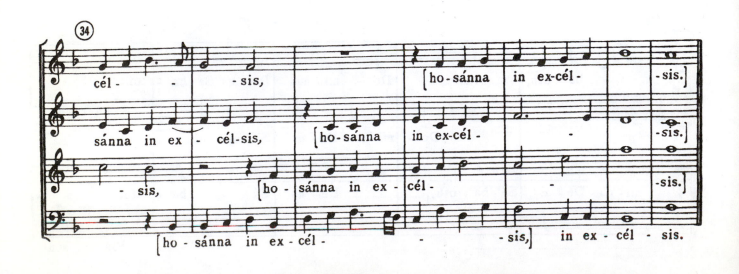

BENEDICTUS

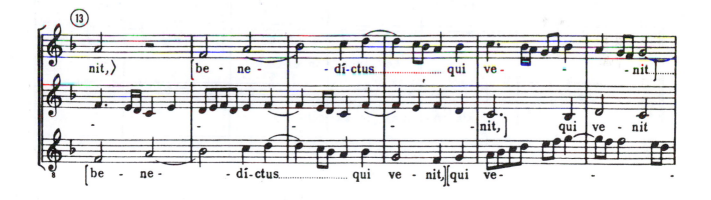

THREE DUOS

Nos. 2, 5, and 12 of *Twelve Duos* (publ. 1577)

Roland de Lassus (1532–1594)

Though Lassus' twelve two-voice motets were apparently written for the instruction of his own pupils, and have long served as models to later students of counterpoint, they are not merely school-book illustrations, but little masterpieces of the genre. Beside providing examples of various kinds of imitation and interior cadence, they may also be viewed as typical of the state of modality in late six-teenth-century sacred music. How close are they to major and minor? What is their "form?" Can you account for the *in*exact imitation in the fourth bar of each of the first two duos? And what is happening at the outset of *Sicut rosa*, which does not begin with imitation at all?

Text-painting is not prominent in these duos, but perhaps there is a little. Our interlinear translations are as literal as possible and purely for study. The text of *Sicut rosa* refers to the Virgin Mary as a "rose"—a common metaphor in medieval religious poetry.

2—BEATUS HOMO

Text: Proverbs 3:13–14

5—EXPECTATIO JUSTORUM

Text: Proverbs 10:28–29

(23) et pa - - - vor his, qui o - pe - ran - - tur, qui o - pe-
but fear   to them who work

ni,   et pa - - - vor his, qui o - pe - ran - - tur,

(28) ran - tur ma - - - - - - - - - - - - - lum.
evil.

qui o - pe - ran - tur ma - - - - - - - - - - - lum.

12—SICUT ROSA

Text: Traditional antiphon

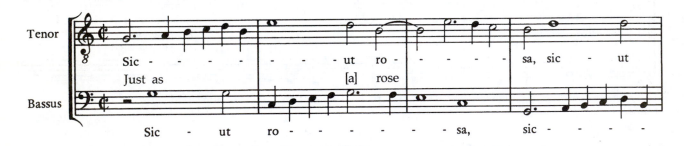

Tenor

Sic - - - - - ut ro - - - sa, sic - ut
Just as   [a] rose

Bassus

Sic - ut ro - - - - - sa,   sic - - -

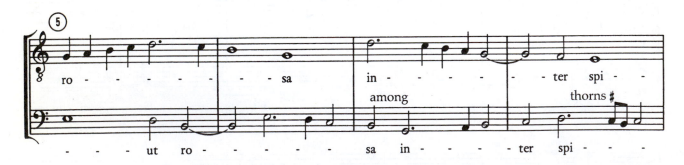

(5) ro - - - - - - sa   in - - - - - - ter spi -
among   thorns #

- - - ut ro - - - - - sa in - - - ter spi -

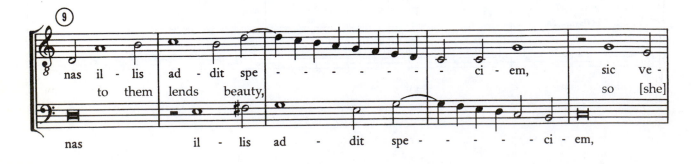

(9) nas il - lis ad - dit spe - - - - - - - - ci - em,   sic ve -
to them lends beauty,   so [she]

nas   il - lis ad - dit spe - - - - ci - em,

nu - stat su - - - - - am Vir - go Ma - ri - a pro -
beautifies   — [the] Virgin   Mary   [does] — her

sic ve - nu - stat su - - - - - am Vir - go Ma -

ge - - ni - em, Ma - ri - a pro - ge - - - - - - - ni - em:
progeny:

ri - a pro - ge - ni - em,   Ma - ri - a pro - ge - ni - em: ger -

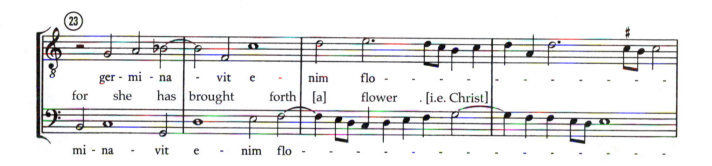

ger - mi - na - - vit e - nim flo - - - - - - - - - - -
for she has brought forth [a] flower . [i.e. Christ]

mi - na - vit e - nim flo - - - - - - - - - - -

rem,   qui vi - ta - - - - lem dat o - do - - - -
            whose fragrance   gives   life.

rem,   qui vi - ta - - - lem dat o - do - - - -

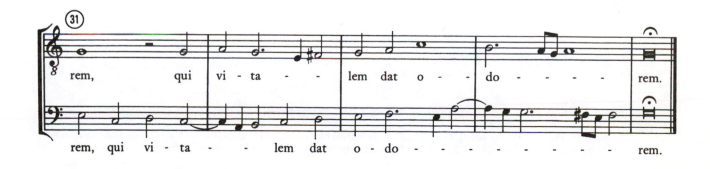

rem,   qui vi - ta - - - lem dat o - do - - - - rem.

rem, qui vi - ta - - - lem dat o - do - - - - - rem.

EXAMPLES OF STOCK BASSES
(late sixteenth century)

An interesting development bridging Renaissance and Baroque was the frequent use by composers in many countries of certain fixed progressions of root-position triads that formed the basis of entire pieces, both instrumental and vocal. These progressions were originally identified by a variety of names in various languages; today they are commonly denoted as shown in Figure A. Though they were closely associated with certain Italian dances, exactly how they evolved is not fully known.[8]

Figure A

passamezzo antico

romanesca

folia

passamezzo moderno

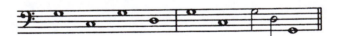

Compositionally, these progressions were treated with considerable freedom. Very often they were fleshed out by the addition of chords of an embellishing nature, including secondary dominants. Thus a given progression could exist as a "framework" consisting of the chords placed on the first beat of a regularly recurring rhythmic unit, such as the first beat of every bar, or of every two bars, and so on.

Examine the following selection of examples and discover for each one the progression on which it is based. Also compare the structural procedures used here with those of the works on pages 56, 95, 545, and 552.

---

[8] Informative treatments of this widely discussed subject are Richard Hudson's "Chordal Aspects of the Italian Dance Style, 1500–1650" (*Journal of the Lute Society of America*, vol. 3, 1970, p. 35), and his articles on "Ground" and "Passamezzo" in the *New Grove Dictionary*.

■ **EXAMPLE 1**

PAVANE PASSAMAIZE

from *Sixième Livre de Danceries* (publ. 1555)

Claude Gervaise (fl. 1540–1560)

A chamber musician at the French court, Gervaise wrote many instrumental dances that were brought out by the publisher Attaingnant between 1545 and 1556. Which progression forms the basis of this pavane? What are the chief soprano tones that go with the chief bass tones?

■ **EXAMPLE 2**

PASSAMEZZO AND SALTARELLO
No. 8B from Libro de Intabulatura di Liuto (1567)

Jacomo Gorzanis (ca. 1520–ca. 1577)

This composition for lute by Jacomo Gorzanis, a lutenist active in the Italian city of Trieste, is an example of a *dance pair,* a very common sixteenth-century genre that was an important predecessor of the Baroque suite. In such a pair, the first dance was often in slow or moderate duple time, the livelier second in triple time, with the note values of the two dances in the proportion of 2 to 3 (for example, ♩ = ♩.).[9]

The present pair is "No. 8B" because it is from a larger (and most unusual) work—a cycle of 24 passamezzo-saltarello pairs, one for every key. (See *A Note on the Sources,* page 583). Which one of the stock basses underlies both dances?

Like most lute music, this work was originally notated in "tablature," that is, a system that uses numbers to specify pitch in terms of the strings of the instrument. Here is the opening of the passamezzo in tablature notation:

Each line represents one string of the six-string lute, which was tuned (in this case) G-c-f-a-d[1]-g[1]. Because Italian tablature indicated the low to high strings in the direction of top to bottom, the top line of the tablature is the low G string. And because tablature indicates exactly where to stop the string, there is no need (indeed, no way) to indicate a key signature. Therefore, we show no signature in the following transcription. What *is* the key?

Tablature has no way of indicating that a pitch once sounded is to continue sounding *beyond* the next pitch sounded. Therefore, polyphony cannot be explicitly notated, only implied. This aspect of tablature is also retained in our transcription. In the passamezzo's bar 3, see the first b[1] and explain its function. And in bar 4, to where does the first c[2] go? And what is the g[1] right under this c[2]? (Does awareness of such matters affect performance?) Gorzanis's tablature also gives no time signature. In the passamezzo the arithmetic of the meter is obvious enough, but today's musicians may find the barring strange. How might a modern composer bar this dance? What is the meter of the saltarello? And how are bars 1–2 rhythmically different from 3–4?

These pieces are readily adapted to the guitar. If you play them on the piano, remember that they sound an octave lower than written, like guitar music. (See also page 550.)

---

[9] For a striking twentieth-century example of proportional changes of tempo, see the tympani piece of Elliott Carter on page 509. Also see Mozart's triple variation of a duple theme on page 000 (but are the tempos proportional in this case?)

Passamezzo

(sounds one octave lower than written)

Saltarello

■ EXAMPLE 3

GREENSLEEVES

Greensleeves was the name of an inconstant lady-love in a popular English song of the late sixteenth century also called "Greensleeves." (Shakespeare mentions the song twice in *The Merry Wives of Windsor,* ca. 1598.) Its tune is still sung, both with its original words and also with a Christmas text beginning "What Child is this?". Because it is so well known, we give only the tune. Which of the stock basses did the tune grow out of?

NOW IS THE MONTH OF MAYING
from *The First Book of Balletts to Five Voices* (publ. 1595)

Thomas Morley (1557 or 1558–1602)

One of the greatest English composers of the Elizabethan period, Morley is particularly esteemed for his cheerful madrigals and balletts, many of which are still popular. The ballett, a type of composition generally lighter than the madrigal and often ending with a "fa-la" refrain, was based on the Italian *balletto* and introduced into England by Morley himself. Singing them from part-books was a very popular social entertainment among cultivated amateurs.

It has often been remarked that Elizabethan secular vocal music generally displays a clarity of harmony that points away from modality and toward the major-minor system. Examine this ballett from that point of view. Are any modal style characteristics still present? How does Tenor II differ from the other parts? And in bar 1, alto part, what kind of note falls on "month"? From bar 10, last beat, into bar 11, are there parallel fifths with the bass?

Now Is the Month of Maying, Thomas Morley ed. Edmund Fellows. © 1913 Stainer & Bell Ltd., London, England. Used with permission. (Dynamics have been removed.)

MORO LASSO AL MIO DUOLO
from *Madrigals for Five Voices, Book VI* (publ. 1611)

Carlo Gesualdo (ca. 1560–1613)

Toward the end of the sixteenth century, the Italian madrigal became in some quarters a vehicle for musical experimentation that anticipated stylistic changes that would soon be identified as the *seconda prattica* (see page 00). A well-known manifestation of this trend is the work of Carlo Gesualdo, Prince of Venosa, whose many madrigals represent an extreme in the use of chromaticism. Notice how "Moro lasso" alternates several times between chromatic and diatonic writing. What words or thoughts in the text inspire this alternation? And how do the large sections of the text relate to the music? Also, consider the music apart from the text. Does it hang together by itself?[10]

I die, alas! from my pain	*I die! alas! from my pain*	*O grievous fate,*
And the one who can give me life,	*And the one who can give me life,*	*The one who can give me life,*
Alas, kills me and will not give me life.	*Alas, kills me and will not give me aid.*	*Alas, gives me death.*

[10] Glenn Watkins makes interesting observations on this work in his *Gesualdo/The Man and His Music* (Oxford: Oxford University Press, 2nd ed., 1991).

Part Two

Baroque Compositions

Though it begins with one of Monteverdi's *seconda prattica* madrigals, Part Two as a whole stresses music written after 1700—that part of the Baroque era most emphasized in theory and analysis courses. Further Baroque examples in the form of chorale harmonizations are given in Appendix B (page 557).

IMITATIVE COUNTERPOINT

Imitative counterpoint by J. S. Bach naturally bulks large here, with two 2-part inventions, one 3-part sinfonia, five fugues, four canons, and a chorale prelude that prominently features *Vorimitation*. The fugues are supplemented by a short keyboard fugue of J. K. F. Fischer, a Corelli violin sonata movement in fugal style, and a choral fugue from Handel's *Acis and Galatea*. Examples of double and triple counterpoint occur within this body of works, and can be located in Index I under "Invertible Counterpoint."

Fischer's fugue is the simplest and might serve as a model for a first attempt at fugue writing. Among the Bach fugues, the F major and G minor from Book I of *The Well-Tempered Clavier* [WTC] have countersubjects and other standard characteristics, while the E major from Book II together with *Contrapunctus VII* from *The Art of the Fugue* feature stretto and other devices. Handel's choral fugue has some unusual attributes, in addition to depicting a highly dramatic situation. All these examples may be compared with those from later periods—the fugato section in the finale of Haydn's "Clock" symphony, and the fugues by Bartók and Hindemith. Double and triple fugue are also represented within the entire cluster of examples.

To enrich the study of the harmonic forces that shape an imitating voice, particularly a fugal answer, see Index I under "Imitation, real and tonal." This group of examples begins with very simple ones from late Renaissance polyphony and continues through the twentieth century.

OSTINATO

Without going into the terminological problems of "passacaglia" versus "chaconne," suffice it to say that the type of piece founded on a reiterated bass melody, or *ground,* is represented in Part Two by *Dido's Lament* of Purcell and the *Crucifixus* of Bach—pieces offering different levels of difficulty and a rich display of Baroque chromaticism. The type based on a reiterated harmonic structure subjected to constant variation is represented by Bach's great D-minor *Chaconne* for solo violin, which displays, among many other things, a wide range of examples of compound melodic line. Related post-Baroque examples will be found in Index I under "Ostinato."

CANTUS FIRMUS

Cantus firmus composition is shown by two Bach chorale preludes and one chorale variation. Though the four selections from *The Musical Offering* are of interest mainly as canons, all are based on a cantus firmus that appears in its simplest form in Canon 2. Some of the techniques in Part Two might be contrasted with Renaissance examples in Part One. Index I gives a complete listing under "Cantus firmus compositions."

OTHER FORMS AND GENRES

Binary form with both parts repeated is amply represented by the pieces from the *Anna Magdalena Notebook,* the Bach suite movements, the E major prelude from *WTC II,* the Corelli *Allemanda,* Purcell's *Lament,* the Handel *Air,* and the Scarlatti sonata, which together show the form worked out in a variety of tonal plans. These examples, together with related ones from other periods, are listed under "Binary form" in Index I. *Bar form* is shown by Bach's *O Gott, du frommer Gott* (as well as by numerous chorales in Appendix B), and *da capo form* by the Bach gavottes and minuets and by the Handel aria, "Where'er you walk." The use of ritornello to create form occurs modestly in this aria and full blown in the Allegro of Handel's B-minor concerto grosso. Related to ritornello is the formal procedure in Couperin's *Les Moissonneurs,* but this work relates more directly to the rondos in Part III. A simple set of *variations* is Handel's *Air,* which should be compared with other variations in the book (again see Index I). Finally, the "one-part form" typical of many Baroque preludes and improvisatory pieces is shown by the Corelli violin *Adagio* (which is given with authentic embellishments), by the *WTC* C-major prelude, and also by Elisabeth Jacquet de La Guerre's *prélude non mesuré*— a piece that strongly invites analysis.

FIGURED BASS

Of the various pieces with figured bass, two—the Handel recitative "Thy Rebuke" and the Corelli *Adagio*—are provided with an empty staff for writing a realization. Also, six chorales in Appendix B are given as a melody with figured bass.

LASCIATEMI MORIRE

from the *Sixth Book of Madrigals for Five Voices* (publ. 1614)
Text: Ottavio Rinuccini

Claudio Monteverdi (1567–1643)

Lasciatemi morire is the first of four madrigals that together form a larger work entitled *Lamento d'Arianna*. Originally the *Lamento* was composed as a monody (for solo voice and continuo) in the opera *Arianna* (1608), a work of which only fragments have survived. Monteverdi later arranged the *Lamento* in madrigal form.

The radical change in musical style that took place in Monteverdi's time is vividly reflected in his own compositions, which he himself distinguished as composed in either the old style (*prima prattica*) or the new (*seconda prattica*). As often happens when traditions are modified, this shift in style gave rise to heated polemics.[1] A characteristic of the new style particularly offensive to Monteverdi's critics was its way of treating dissonance. Examine the use of dissonance throughout *Lasciatemi morire* and compare it with that of compositions typical of the old style, for example, the Palestrina mass excerpt beginning on page 22, or the Josquin motet on page 16.

Another featue of the new style was the intimate relation of the music to the words. Consider *Lasciatemi morire* from this point of view.

> Let me die,
> [For] who could comfort me
>   in my hard fate,
>   in my great torment?

[1] See the famous attack by the conservative theorist, G. M. Artusi, which together with Monteverdi's defense, is given in English translation in Strunk, *Source Readings in Music History* New York: Norton, 1950, pp. 393–412; rev. ed., 1998, pp. 526–544). Artusi's critique is very instructive on certain technical differences between the old and new styles. See also Claude Palisca's informative article, "The Artusi-Monteverdi Controversy," in *The Monteverdi Companion*, D. Arnold and N. Fortune, eds. (New York: Norton, 1968, p. 133 ff).

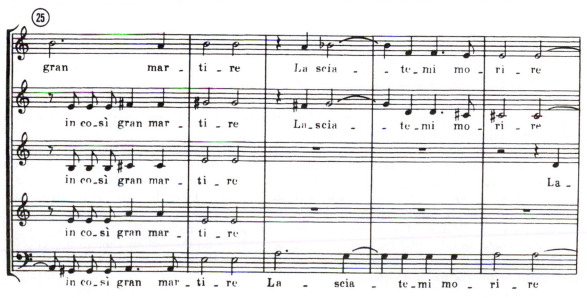

ADAGIO and ALLEGRO
from *Violin Sonata*, Op. 5, No. 1 (1700)

Arcangelo Corelli (1653–1713)

Corelli is remembered both as a violin virtuoso who laid the foundations of modern violin technique and as a composer who contributed much to the early development of chamber music and the concerto grosso. This five-movement sonata begins with a basically slow, improvisatory movement that is followed by two Allegros, then concluded by the two movements given here. The expressive *Adagio* is provided with embellishments attributed (probably rightly) to Corelli himself. Intended to illustrate the correct manner of performance, they are well worth study. How does each one relate to the notes of the unadorned line? (The sign + means trill.)

The performance of this sonata, like virtually all Baroque ensemble music, requires a continuo group. Here the bass line, in addition to being played on a low string instrument, is played also on the harpsichord (*cembalo*) by the player's left hand, while the right realizes the Arabic figures—the "figured bass"—as simple harmonies of an accompanying (not soloistic) nature. For the *Adagio*, an additional staff is provided for writing out such a realization. Not every chord necessarily requires four voices; sometimes just three are effective. (Figures we have added are parenthesized.)

How would you describe the texture of the *Allegro?* How do the various chordal sequences fit into the piece? What harmony following bar 22 is implied over the eighth rest in 23? What rhythmic effect occurs across the bar at 45/46?

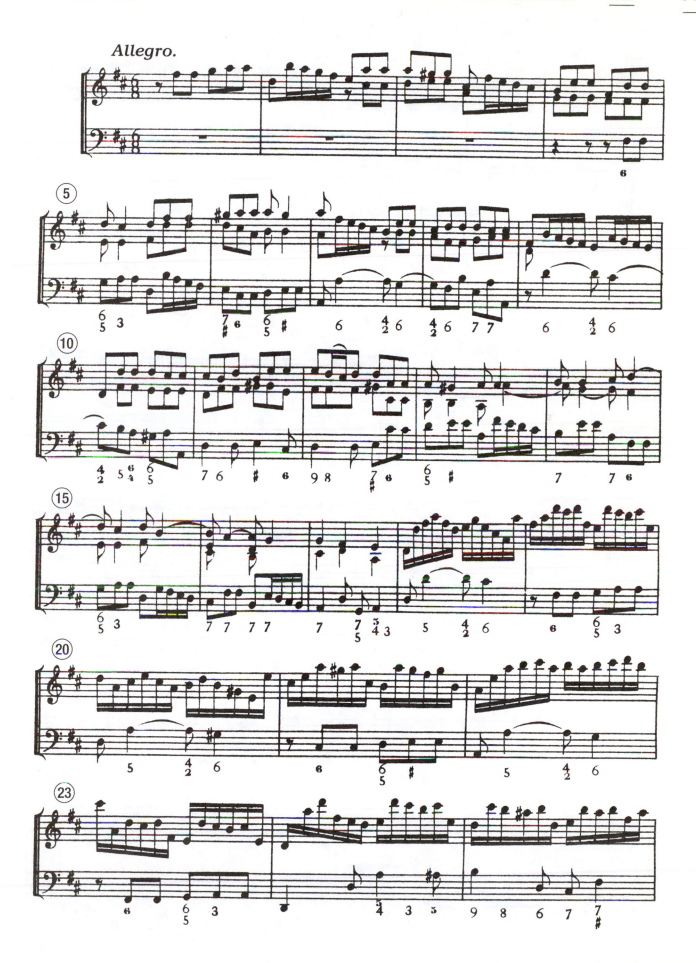

ALLEMANDA
from *Trio Sonata, Op. 4, No. 11* (1694)

Arcangelo Corelli (1653–1713)

The trio sonata was the commonest type of Baroque chamber music. Four players are required—three strings plus a keyboardist, who realizes the figured bass (see comments on the Corelli violin sonata, page 48).[2]

This Allemanda is the final movement of a three-movement sonata and features "walking bass" and suspensions throughout. How are the suspensions produced in bars 5–6? Is there a term for this process? Make one up.

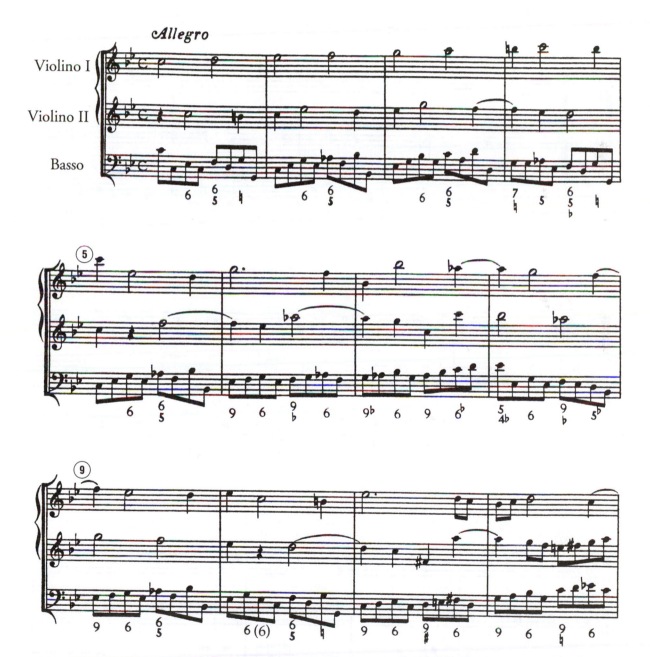

---

[2] Such a texture—two high parts over a bass—also occurs very frequently in other Baroque genres (see for example the Handel concerto grosso, page 69, bar 21ff., and the introductory comments).

DIDO'S LAMENT

from *Dido and Aeneas* (1689)
Text: Nahum Tate

Henry Purcell (ca. 1659–1695)

Near the end of the most celebrated of English operas, the heroine Dido, having lost her beloved Aeneas, elects to die. In this aria she bids a grieving farewell to her lady-in-waiting, Belinda.

What specific musical devices has Purcell used to portray this somber scene? How do the vocal phrases fit with the bass? Where do cadences occur? What is the aria's form? How do the works on pages 95 and 122 compare with this one?

Dido and Aeneas by Henry Purcell, Edward J. Dent, ed. Copyright, 1925, by the Oxford University Press, London. Renewed in U.S.A. 1953. Reprinted by permission.

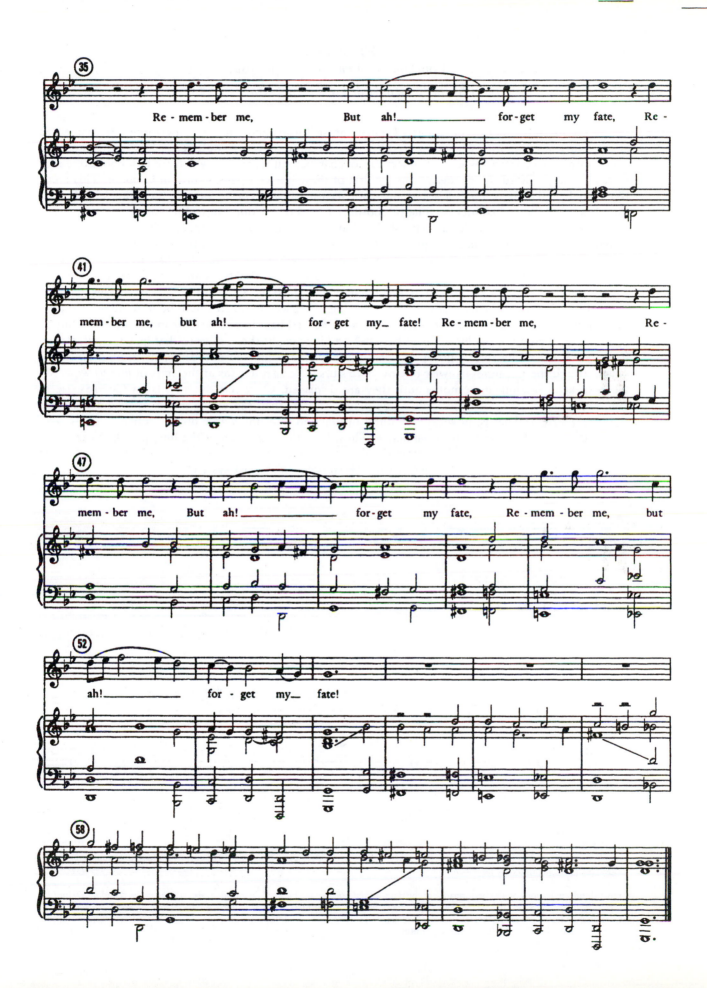

PRELUDE
from Suite II of *Pièces de Clavecin* (1687)

Elisabeth Jacquet de La Guerre (1665–1729)

Elisabeth Jacquet de La Guerre, French harpsichordist and composer, performed from age five at the court of Louis XIV, who supported her musical career into her adult years. Her oeuvre includes many vocal works as well as several collections of chamber music, among which are two books of dance suites for harpsichord. Our *Prelude,* from the first of these books, opens a suite in G minor. This piece is unusual in that it is a *prélude non mesuré*—"not measured"—a type of prelude cultivated by French lutenists (e.g., Denis Gaultier) and harpsichordists from Louis Couperin to Rameau.

Most Baroque preludes are intended to have an improvisatory character, all the more so when, as here, there are no bar lines, regular beats, or fixed note values. It was the practice to notate such pieces mainly in whole notes, but these do not denote duration or tempo. The challenge is to play such a piece with a free, flowing, and persuasive rhythm. Tasteful accelerations and retards are quite appropriate, employed so as to bring out the beginnings, climaxes, and ends of phrases. This requires detailed inspection of the harmony and voice leading. One way to do so would be to write out a reduction showing only the main outer-voice tones, with figured bass to account for inner voices. In line 3, what is the meaning of the high A over bass B♭? And how might the answer to that question affect performance here? A slur over a group of notes (usually an arpeggiated chord) means to hold down the keys through the last note; likewise one or more slurs *following* notes (as at the start of line 5) explicitly mean to keep holding these notes until they are displaced. Of special interest is La Guerre's use of *quarter-notes,* which are not necessarily to be played shorter than the whole notes. Why did she write them as quarters? That is, how do they differ in function from the whole notes? In line 3, the + over the E♭ denotes an appoggiatura from below. Thus, from the beginning of the line, play B♭-G-D-D-E♭. The passage in cut time should be entered and left without a jolt and played with plenty of rubato. At bar 18, the top-line notes B♭-A connect with which notes in the last system?[3]

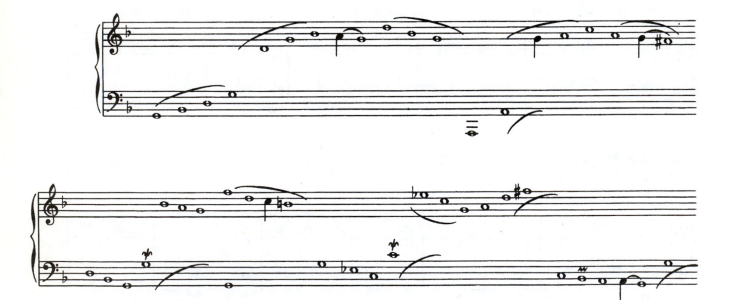

Prelude from Suite II by Elisabeth-Claude Jacquet de La Guerre (pages 16 et 17 of Pieces De Clavecin). Published by Heugel S.A. Copyright 1986. Reprinted by permission.

[3] For helpful suggestions on the performance of the unmeasured prelude, see Howard Ferguson, *Keyboard Interpretation* (London: Oxford University Press, 1975, pp. 20–28). See also Carol Henry Bates, "Elizabeth Jacquet de la Guerre: A New Source of Seventeenth-Century Harpsichord Music," (*Recherches sur la musique classique française* 22, 1984, p. 7–49). Information on recording of La Guerre's music is available at http://www.medieval.org/emfaq/cds/acc90392.htm

LES MOISSONNEURS
from *Pièces de Clavecin, Ordre VI* (publ. 1717)

François Couperin (1668–1733)

Member of a distinguished musical family and one of the greatest French Baroque composers, François Couperin was appointed *claveciniste* to Louis XIV in 1701. His four-volume *Pièces de Clavecin*, which he published between 1713 and 1730, together with his didactic *L'art de toucher le clavecin* (The Art of Harpsichord Playing) of 1716, spread his fame throughout musical Europe and influenced the keyboard style of his younger contemporaries, notably G. F. Handel and J. S. Bach. The *Pièces de Clavecin* consists of twenty-seven suites, or *ordres*, each conceived as a unified whole and comprising approximately eight to ten pieces. The work contains relatively few traditional dances such as allemande, courante, and so forth. Instead, Couperin composed his suites mostly of character pieces to which he gave programmatic titles. *Les Moissonneurs* ("The Reapers"), the first piece in the sixth suite, is an "evocation of the countryside . . . [and of] the swing of the reapers' bodies and the swish of their scythes."[4] It is offered here as an example of a form widely used by Couperin and other French composers of the time.

Couperin's harpsichord music works better on that instrument than on the piano. This is particularly true of its many ornaments, which are integral to the music and generally should not be omitted. Two well-known principles of this complex subject are (1) that ornaments start on, not before, the beat, and (2) that trills start on the upper auxiliary, not the main, note—but there are many exceptions!

---

[4] Wilfred Mellers, *François Couperin and the French Classical Tradition* (London: Dennis Dobson, 1950; new version, 1987, pp. 191 and 400). This is a classic work on Couperin.

For example, in bar 3, the trill should start on the *main* note. Why? Bar 4, first two quarters (and analogous places throughout), are played ♪♫. The symbol ⤙ is the French way of writing the mordent, that is, ♉ (the ornament that begins Bach's familiar *Toccata in D minor*).[5]

Gayement.

1er Couplet.

2e Couplet.

[5] A useful work on these and related matters is Robert Donington's *The Interpretation of Early Music*, new version (New York: St. Martin's, 1992). See also "Ornaments" in *The New Harvard Dictionary of Music*, op. cit., 3rd ed. For general good advice see *Companion to Baroque Music*, ed. J. A. Sadie (London: Dent, 1990, p. 409ff).

3^e*Couplet.*

FOUR PIECES

from the *Notebook for Anna Magdalena Bach* (1725)

It has been conjectured that the *Notebook* of 1725 began as a birthday gift from J. S. Bach to his young second wife. Be that as it may, it grew during the ensuing years into a collection of music of the Bach household, the pieces copied in from time to time by various members thereof. Although the music of Bach himself is well represented in the collection, pieces by other composers, known and unknown, were also included. Several have been attributed to the young Carl Philipp Emanuel Bach. (For later works somewhat similar in idea, see pages 311 and 447.)

The four short pieces given here all have a double bar in the middle. How do they differ in form? What are the harmonies underlying the two-voice texture?

MARCH

In bar 1, second quarter, what is the implied chord? In the same bar, is the C♯ a passing tone or a chord tone?

■ MINUET

■ ARIA

The *Notebook* included some vocal compositions. Here the treble is for the voice, while the bass is to be realized by a keyboard player in the manner of an "unfigured bass." The amusing text, a poem entitled "Edifying Thoughts of a Tobacco Smoker," is translated in *The Bach Reader,* ed. H. David and A. Mendel (New York: Norton, 1945; repr. 1966, p. 97).

So oft ich | mei - ne To-backs - | Pfei - fe, | mit gu - tem | Kna - ster
Zeit - ver - | treib er - grei - fe, | so gibt sie | mir ein

7
1.
an - ge - | füllt, | zur Lust und | *2.* bild | und fü - get | die - se
Trauer -

11
Leh - re | bei, | dass ich der - sel - ben ähn - lich sei. | *1.* | *2.* sei.

POLONAISE

CONCERTO GROSSO No. 12 in B MINOR

from *Twelve Grand Concertos, Op. 6* (1739)
First and Second Movements

George Frideric Handel (1685–1759)

The concerto grosso, the most important Baroque orchestral genre, reached its summit in Handel's *Twelve Grand Concertos,* **Op. 6,** and in J. S. Bach's quite different "Brandenburg Concertos" of 1721. The genre is characterized by the use of a small group of solo instruments called the *concertino,* contrasted with the full string orchestra, or *ripieno.* In Opus 6, Handel followed the Corellian tradition of a concertino composed of two violins and continuo (cello plus harpsichord), the instrumentation of the Baroque trio sonata. He also followed Corelli in employing four or more movements. These movements may take virtually any form. The present example, after the two movements given here, continues with a Larghetto theme with one "variatio," then a brief modulating transition leading to a concluding fugue.

The opening Largo serves as an introduction to the following Allegro, which shows many stylistic traits common to fast movements of concerti grossi. Trace the plan of its various materials. How do they coalesce into a whole?

Among the details of the Allegro are many clear examples of various standard types of sequence. What is the basic progression underlying the sequences in the Allegro's opening three bars?

The score clearly differentiates between concertino and ripieno in the violin parts. The part marked "Violoncello" is for the solo (concertino) cello only. All other cellos, together with the basses, read from the part marked "Bassi."[6]

---

[6] An informative study of Handel's concertos is in Pippa Drummond's *The German Concerto* (New York: Oxford University Press, 1980, pp. 91–180).

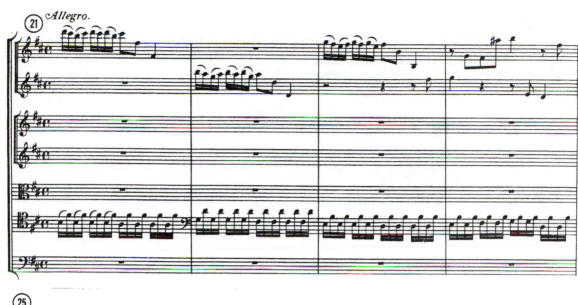

AIR

from *Suite No. 5* (publ. 1720)

George Frideric Handel (1685–1759)

The fifth of Handel's sixteen keyboard suites starts with a prelude, allemande, and courante, then ends with the following tuneful "Air" with its five variations (called *doubles* by Handel). This movement achieved great popularity and in the nineteenth century received the spurious title of "The Harmonious Blacksmith." (It is referred to by this nickname in Dickens' *Great Expectations*.)

What is the basic melodic and harmonic framework that underlies both the theme and all the variations? Are any passages in the variations actually simpler than their counterpart in the theme? Without looking at the score or thinking too hard, listen to someone play the theme, and when you pick up the beat, start conducting in two. Do your downbeats agree with Handel's? His placement of the bar lines is not unusual in Baroque music. Can you think of any reason for it?[7]

---

[7] Heinrich Schenker touches on this phenomenon in his *Erläuterungsausgabe* of Beethoven's E major sonata, Op. 109 (Vienna: Universal Edition, 1913, rev. ed. 1971, p. 4), and in his essay on Haydn's "Emperor Hymn" in *Der Tonwille*, vol. 10 (Vienna, 1924, p. 11). See also bibliography cited below for Mozart's *Andantino*, page 162, n. 3.

Var. 2.

Var. 3.

Var. 4.

Var. 5.

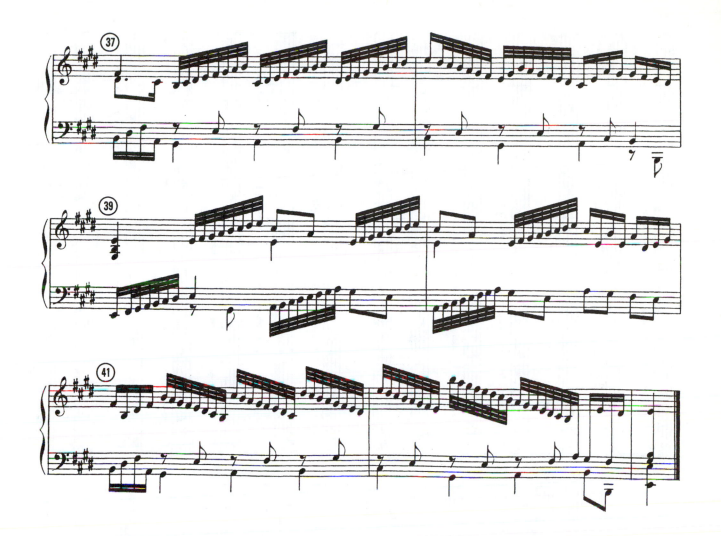

WRETCHED LOVERS
from *Acis and Galatea* (1718)
Libretto chiefly by John Gay (1685–1732)

George Frideric Handel (1685–1759)

Handel's charming two-act masque (a small-scaled dramatic entertainment with costumes and scenery but little or no stage action) was composed for private performance at the palatial residence of his then employer, the Duke of Chandos. It tells the story, drawn from Ovid's *Metamorphoses,* of the mythological lovers whose pastoral idyll is threatened by the one-eyed cyclops, Polyphemus, who has his eye on Galatea. Like Purcell's *Dido and Aeneas* (see page 55), which may have influenced Handel, the work is interspersed with expressive choral numbers. In "Wretched Lovers," Handel treats a well-known genre (what is it?) with typical freedom and a touch of humor. The accompanying instruments are two oboes, two violins, and continuo.

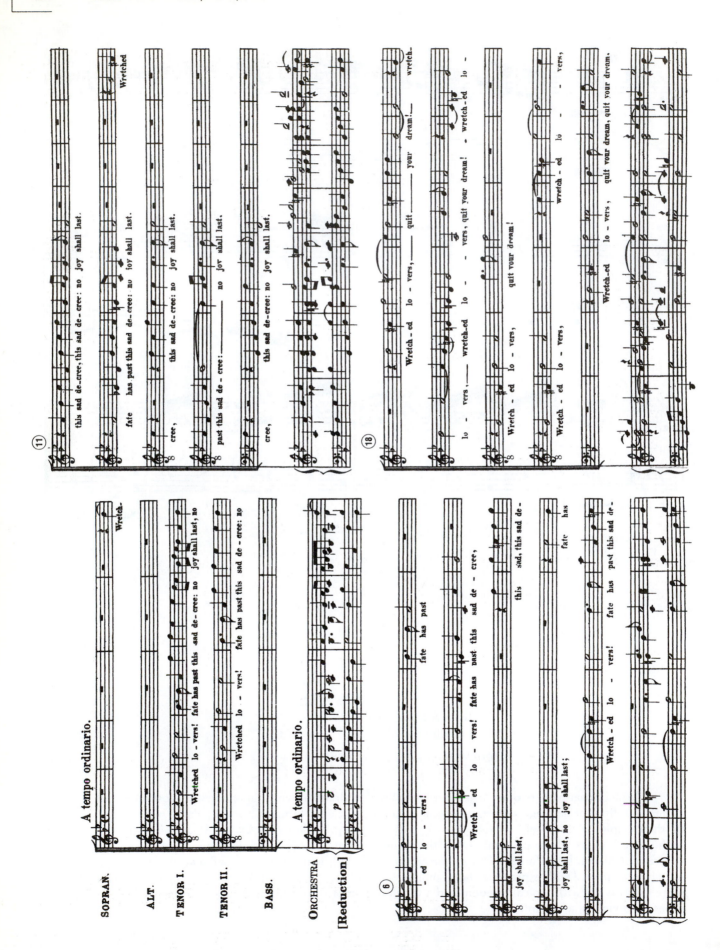

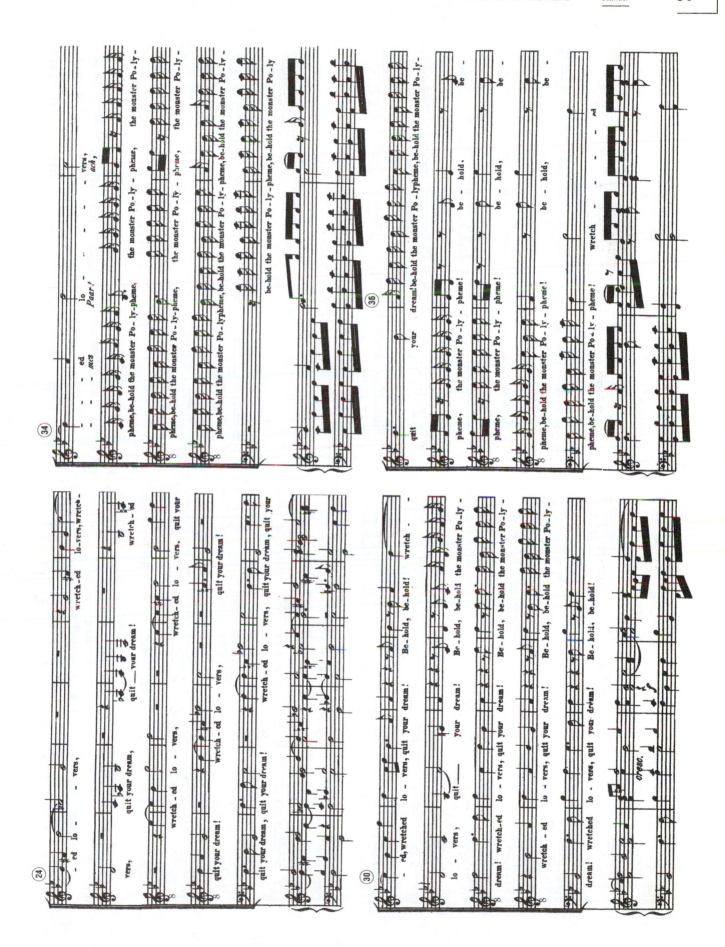

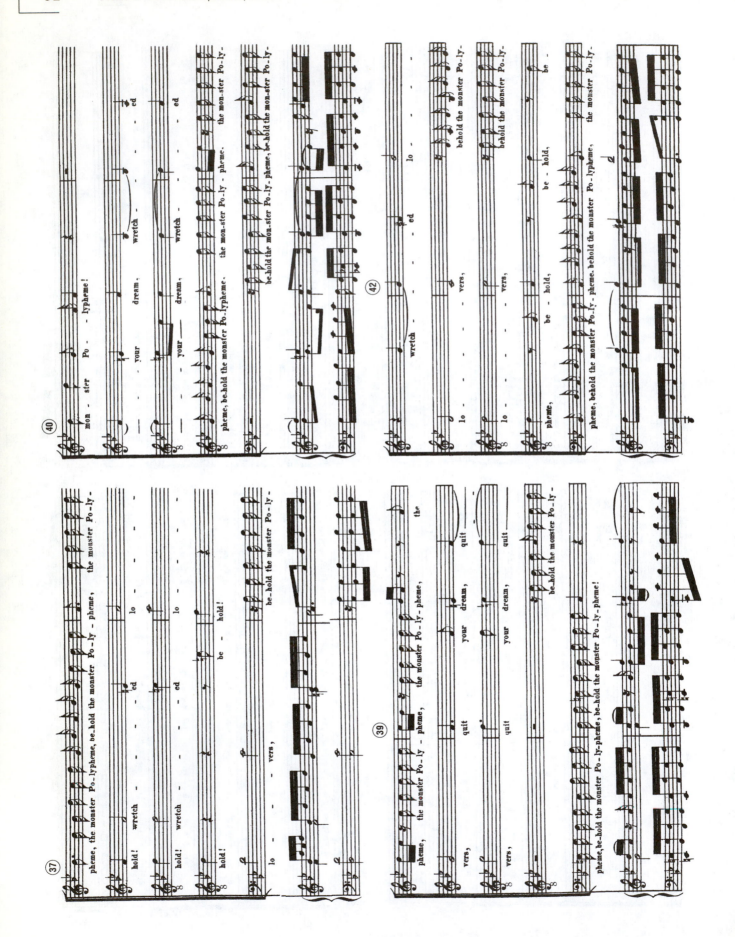

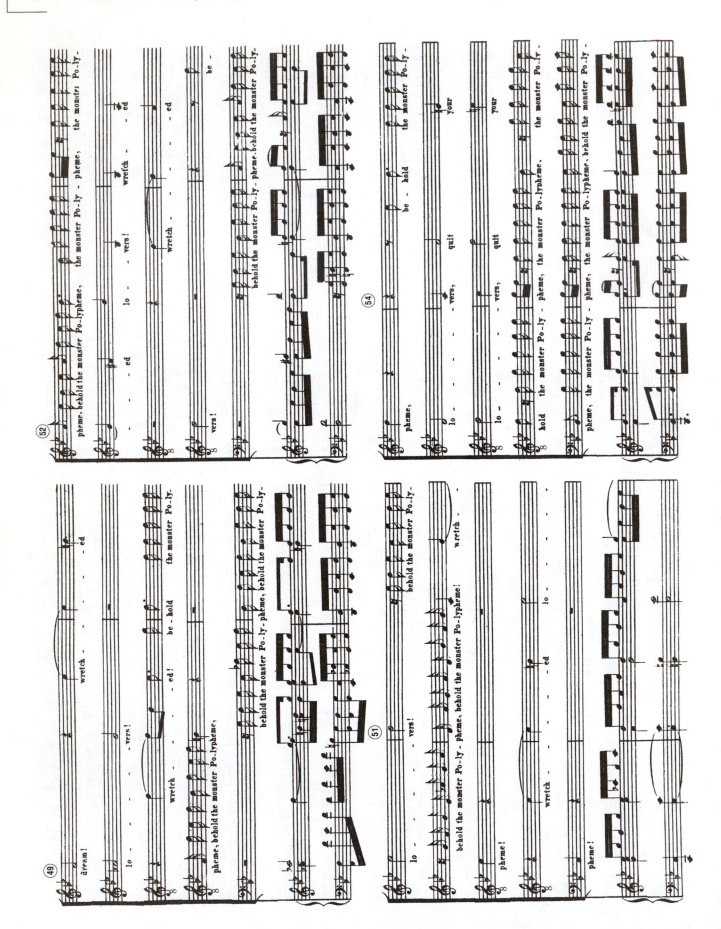

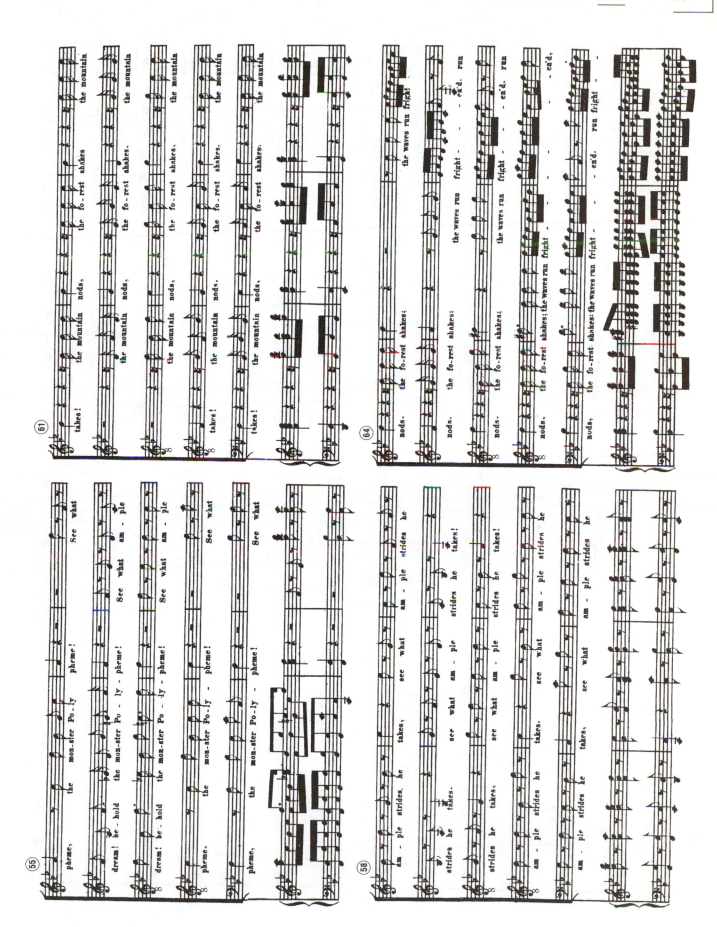

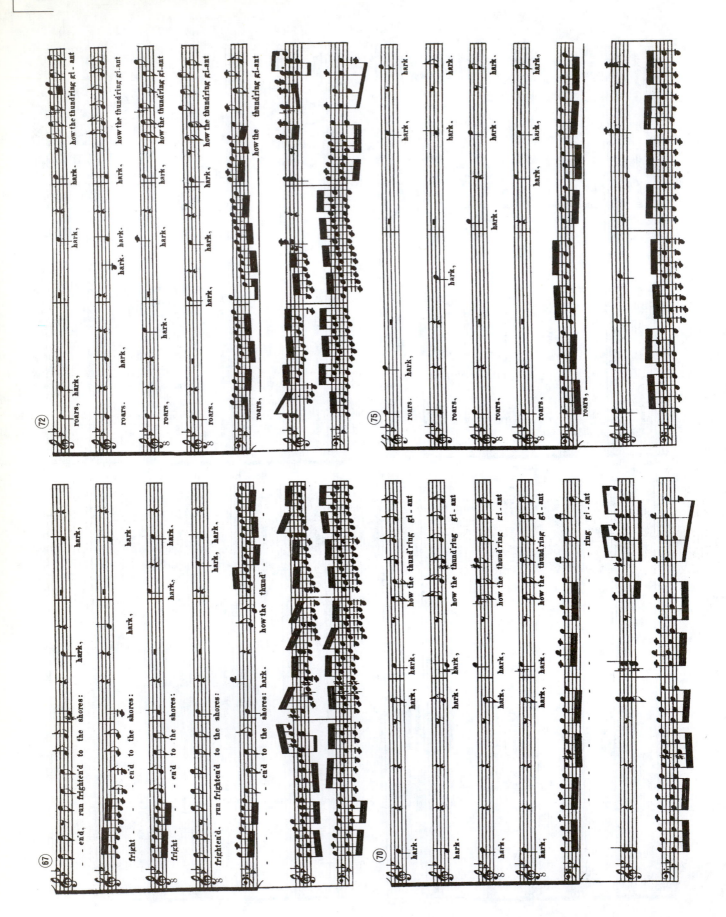

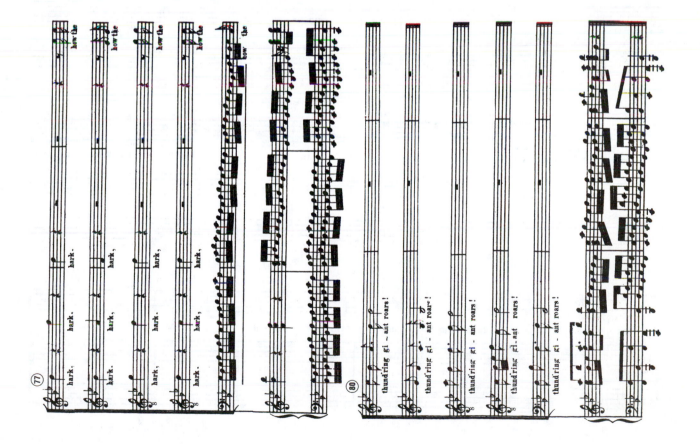

RECITATIVE:
THY REBUKE HATH BROKEN HIS HEART
No. 27 from *Messiah* (1741)
Text based on Psalms 69:20

George Frideric Handel (1685–1759)

This tenor recitative falls between a chorus in C minor, "He trusted in God," and a tenor arioso in E minor, "Behold, and see." It is a particularly effective series of chromatic modulations. Sing the vocal line while playing your realization of the figured bass. (An extra staff is provided for the realization.) How is each modulation accomplished? Which one employs the most radical chromaticism?

WHERE'ER YOU WALK
from *Semele* (1743)

George Frideric Handel (1685–1759)

Not all of Handel's oratorios were sacred; some were based on allegorical or mythological subjects. The latter type is represented by *Semele*, in which Greek gods and mortals figure in a thoroughly human love story. The libretto was by the great comic dramatist, William Congreve, but was modified for Handel by an unknown arranger. In the world-famous tenor aria, "Where'er you walk" (for which the arranger inserted a poem by Alexander Pope), Jupiter conjures up a pastoral paradise for his beloved Semele in which the elements of Nature join to delight and protect her. Why does Handel stipulate "pianissimo throughout"?

What is the genre and the form of this composition? Draw a simple "scheme" representing the largest sections, then, under each section, show the phrases, and under them the sub-phrases. (How does bar 1 fit in?) Below the scheme note the main keys. There is one key relationship (it is between adjacent keys) that can be felt as something of a shock in this gentle song. Do you agree? If you do, what justifies it? What do the string figures symbolize? In bar 21, the voice leaps up a major 7th (g^1-f#^{2})—an interval that can be problematic. Why does it sound so right here?

GAVOTTE
from *English Suite No. 3 in G minor*, BWV 808 (before 1722)

Johann Sebastian Bach (1685–1750)

Without looking at the music, listen to the opening measures and conduct in two. Are you conducting it as notated? (See remarks on page 76.) Study of the harmony and voice leading of *Gavotte I* will reveal that, although the piece has only two parts—treble and bass—it often has three or four *implied* voices. (A simpler example of this phenomenon will be found on page 126). In *Gavotte II,* what harmonies do you hear besides that of the obvious tonic pedal? What is the harmony in bar 46, first half?

■ GAVOTTE I

GAVOTTE II
(ou la MUSETTE)

(*Gavotte I. d. c.*)

MINUETS I AND II
from *Suite No. 1 in G major for Violoncello Solo*, BWV 1007 (ca. 1720)

Johann Sebastian Bach (1685–1750)

In his great six sonatas and partitas for solo violin and six suites for solo cello, Bach manages to imply a polyphonic web of voices by means of a single instrument playing for the most part just one note at a time—a type of texture called "compound (or polyphonic) melodic line." Such a line conveys not only a top voice and a bass, but frequently one or more inner voices as well. In composing this work, Bach sometimes chose to omit one or more notes of a voice, especially a bass voice, but careful listening will usually reveal what is implied.

We recommend starting with Minuet II, which is generally simpler than No. I. However, No. II does contain a famous problem: In the best manuscript source for this work (which happens to be a copy by a hand other than Bach's), bar 27 shows *no flat sign* before the low E, as it should—given the Dorian signature—if an E *flat* were wanted. (Most modern editions, including the one we give here, put in the flat, which certainly sounds right.) But now see bar 31. Here the manuscript does show an accidental next to the low E, but it is a *natural* sign! How does *that* sound? Did the copyist perhaps intend to write a flat here, but by a slip of the pen wrote a natural instead? Or, might Bach have intended the E natural and intended us to hear above it an *implied* tone—a tone following the B♭-C—that would make E *natural* sound right? What would that implied tone be? Can you "hear" it if it isn't actually played? Could Bach be asking more of a listener to this very refined music (which could be just the player alone) than he does of a listener to, say, the Brandenburg concertos?

In Minuet I, the implied harmony of bars 5 and 6 is also quite subtle. What is the implied bass here? For other examples of compound melodic line see the pieces on pages 95, 126, and 383.

▪ MINUET I

▪ MINUET II

Menuet I.
da Capo.

CHACONNE
from *Partita No. 2 in D minor for Violin Solo,* BWV 1004 (ca. 1720)

Johann Sebastian Bach (1685–1750)

This work, the fifth and last movement of a suite, is the most celebrated of Baroque chaconnes. Its composer, though restricting himself to a constantly repeating harmonic scheme (what is it?), has built, within a pitch gamut of only three octaves, a monumental musical edifice as rich in variety as in elements that unify. What holds this piece together? How do its many details group into a single large form?[8]

---

[8] Robert Gauldin discusses this work in his *Eighteenth-Century Counterpoint* (Prospect Heights, IL: Waveland Press, 1988; 1995, p. 252 ff).

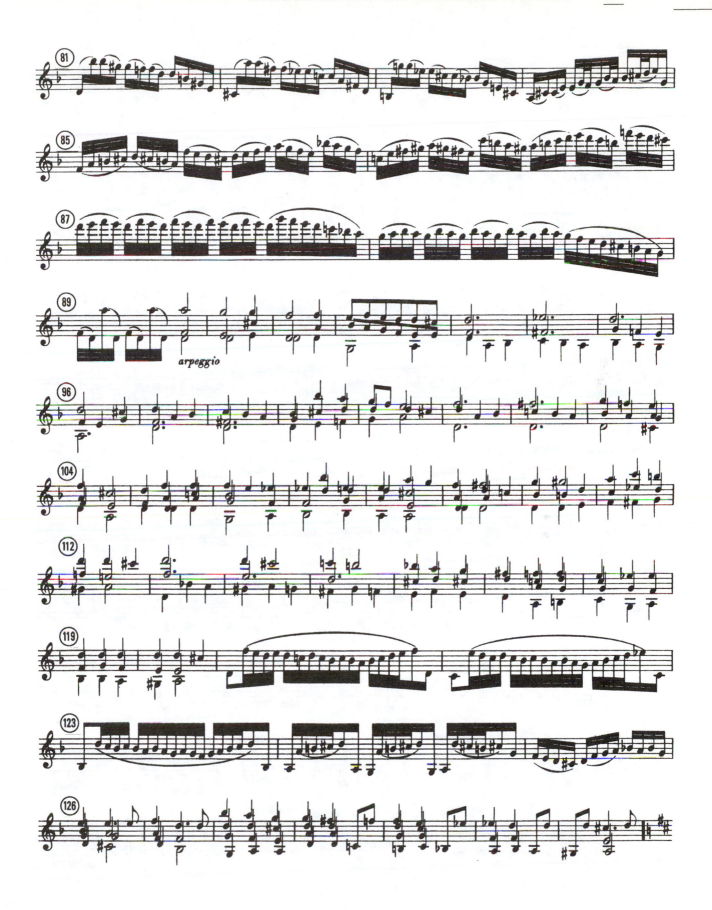

arpeggio

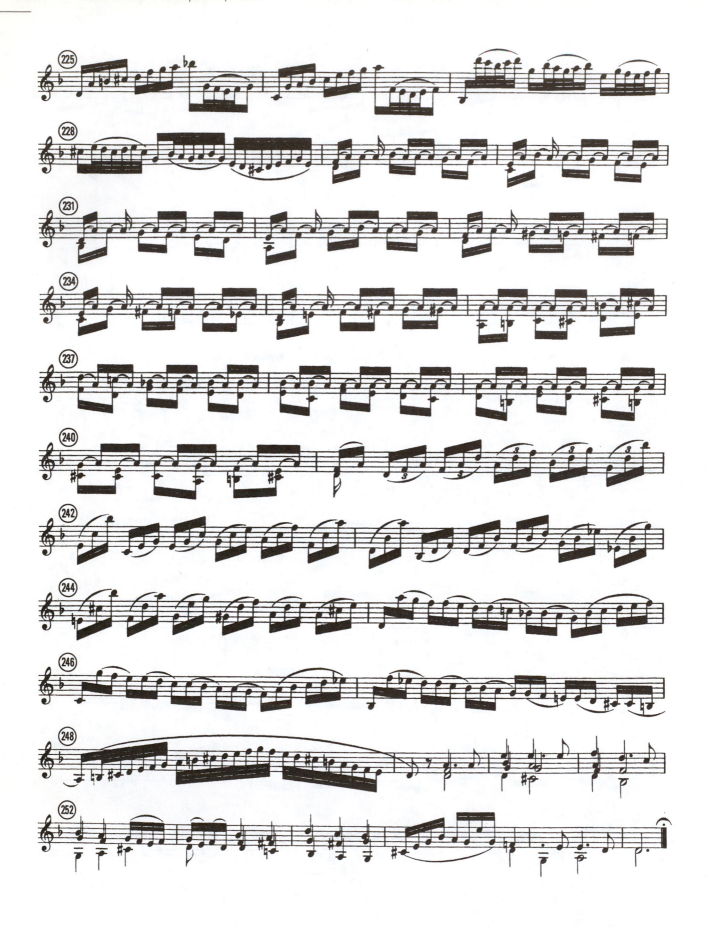

TWO INVENTIONS
(1720–1723)

Johann Sebastian Bach (1685–1750)

These two examples from Bach's well-known set of fifteen *Inventionen,* or "two-part inventions," are constructed in quite different, yet quite typical, ways. In each case, what is the basic melodic material, and how is it treated? How are inventions like and unlike fugues?

■ INVENTION 4 IN D MINOR, BWV 775

INVENTION 12 IN A MAJOR, BWV 783

What is the musical advantage here of the mordents and trills? Are they mere decoration? Does polyphony cease at bar 7?[9]

---

[9] For comment on the metrics of this piece, see Charles Burkhart, "Mid-Bar Downbeat in Bach's Keyboard Music" (*Journal of Music Theory Pedagogy* 8, 1994, p. 12).

PRELUDES AND FUGUES
from *The Well-Tempered Clavier, Books I and II*

Johann Sebastian Bach (1685–1750)

Bach's *Well-Tempered Clavier*, two cycles of preludes and fugues in all twenty-four major and minor keys, is not only a supreme technical achievement, but also displays the widest possible expressive and emotional range. The following selection gives a glimpse of this remarkable variety and provides examples of the chief types of fugue and fugal device. Study might begin with the lively F major or noble G minor fugue (pages 106 and 107), which exhibit many standard characteristics.

The idea for a collection of preludes and fugues in many keys grew out of seventeenth-century experiments with new systems of tuning and was actually first realized by a predecessor of Bach, Johann Kaspar Ferdinand Fischer (c. 1665–1746), who published in 1702 his *Ariadne Musica*, a set of short preludes and fugues for organ in nineteen keys plus the Phrygian mode. (The mythological title denoted that the work was a guide through the "labyrinth" of keys, as Ariadne's ball of thread had guided Theseus.) Bach borrowed not only the plan of Fischer's work, but also a few of Fischer's fugue subjects, writing new and much more elaborate fugues on them. We give here one such example: Fischer's and Bach's E major fugues are placed side by side to facilitate comparison.

For further comparison of fugues in other styles and from other periods, see pages 80, 157 (at bar 189), 452, and 490.

■ PRELUDE 1 IN C MAJOR, BWV 846[10]
from Book I (1722)

The *Well-Tempered Clavier* opens with this simple prelude in an improvisatory style. It is followed by a rather slow four-voice fugue of great dignity.

---

[10] Heinrich Schenker's famous analysis is in *Five Graphic Music Analyses*, ed. Felix Salzer (New York: Dover, 1969, pp. 36–37).

■ FUGUE 11 IN F MAJOR, BWV 856
from Book I (1722)

FUGUE 16 IN G MINOR, BWV 861
from Book I (1722)

Should performers of fugues always bring out the subject? Although it is often appropriate to do so, consider in this fugue—indeed, in all fugues—what *other* elements might here and there be emphasized to achieve an effective interpretation.

FUGUE 21 IN B FLAT MAJOR, BWV 866
from Book I (1722)

Fugues may be said to range between two very general types, "vocal" and "instrumental," the first having a short subject featuring whole and half notes, the second a longer subject featuring eighths and sixteenths. This fugue is clearly of the latter type and shows one fairly common way such a fugue can be built.

PRELUDE AND FUGUE 9 IN E MAJOR, BWV 878 from Book II (1744)

The preludes of the *Well-Tempered Clavier* exhibit as much variety as the fugues. What is the form of this one? (A small detail: At bars 23–24, the right hand part is composed of lines containing numerous syncopations. What do you make of this?) For comment on the fugue, see the Fischer fugue below.

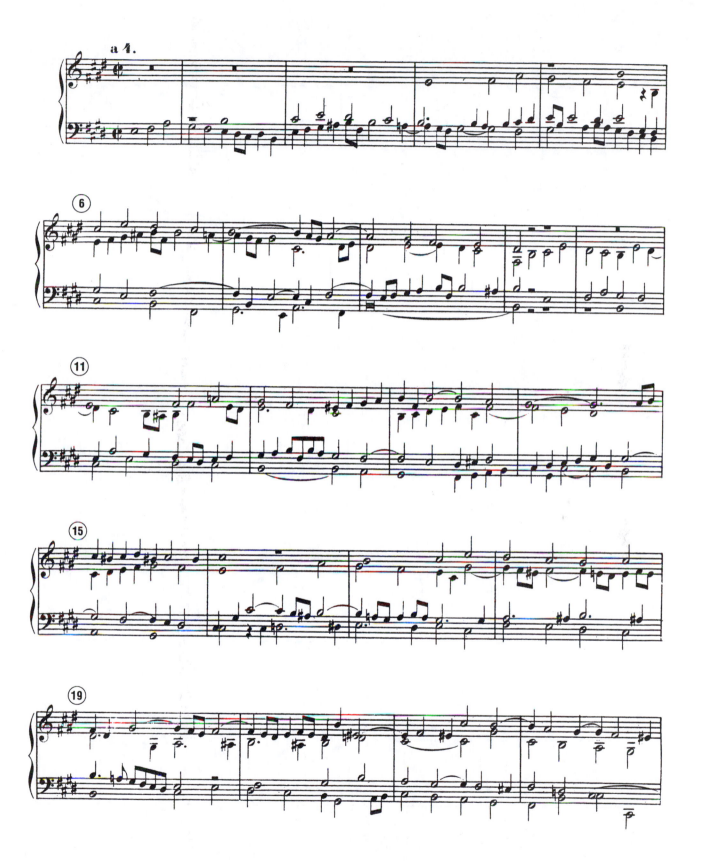

FUGUE IN E MAJOR
from *Ariadne Musica* (1702)

J. K. F. Fischer (ca. 1665–1746)

We append here the fugue that provided the germ of Bach's Book II fugue in the same key (see page 113). The shortness of the subject and the use of long note-values are typical of the so-called *stile antico,* or old style, which had originated in the ecclesiastical vocal music of the seventeenth century to keep alive the style of Palestrina (see page 22). Moreover, instead of composing an original subject for this fugue, Fischer here uses a famous subject that had long been used in the teaching of counterpoint. Bach, writing some forty years later, was perpetuating these venerable traditions, but realized them in a far more highly developed composition. In expanding on Fischer's ideas, what new elements does he introduce? (Other *WTC* examples in the old style are Book I's C♯ minor and B♭ minor fugues.)

CONTRAPUNCTUS VII

from *Die Kunst der Fuge*, BWV 1080 (ca. 1740–1750)

Johann Sebastian Bach (1685–1750)

Bach's *Art of the Fugue,* his great summary of fugal traditions and techniques, is a series of fourteen fugues (each called *contrapunctus*) plus four canons, all based on the following subject:

He worked on it intermittently during his last ten years, but died before he could complete the final fugue (see page 128).

The work begins with a set of four relatively simple fugues, then proceeds to a set of three featuring inversion and stretto. Contrapunctus VII brings this set to a close in a brilliant display of fugal devices. Its two-bar opening is a diminution of the subject, but its next statement (starting in bar 2) has the normal four-bar length (and also is inverted). How many subject-statements occur in the first twelve bars? Now examine the entire fugue. (It can be helpful to mark each statement, depending on length, with a differently colored pencil.) How does Bach get simultaneous statements to sound well together? When he set out to write this fugue down, what did he almost certainly sketch in first? Contrapunctus VII can be very effective on the organ (at which spot especially?).

Because Bach notated The Art of the Fugue in open score, it used to be considered an ensemble work, or even a "theoretical" work not requiring performance. That it is definitely for keyboard is proved by its being entirely playable by two hands on a single manual. (Open scoring had been a conventional notation for polyphonic keyboard music since Scheidt and Frescobaldi.)[11]

---

[11] Donald Francis Tovey's *A Companion to Bach's "Art of Fugue"* (Oxford: Oxford University Press, 1931), is still an invaluable vademecum. See also Christoph Wolff's discussions in his *Bach: Essays on his Life and Music* (Cambridge, MA: Harvard University Press, 1991), and especially his *Johann Sebastian Bach, The Learned Musician* (New York: Norton, 2000).

FOUR CANONS

from *The Musical Offering*, BWV 1079 (1747)

Johann Sebastian Bach (1685–1750)

The term canon comes from the Greek word for rule or law. To musicians it denotes a type of composition in which a leading voice, or *dux*, is strictly imitated throughout by a following voice, the *comes*. For a given canon, the "rule" indicates the intervals of time and of pitch at which the follower is to enter, and the form it is to take, whether an exact replica of the leader, or transposed, or inverted, or what have you. Of the many types of canon, the simplest is the round. Exactly what is the rule governing the performance of "Three Blind Mice"?

The following canons are based on a theme purportedly given to Bach by King Frederick the Great as a subject for improvisation. Bach later sent the king a "musical offering" in which the same royal theme served as the basis of an impressive collection of pieces, many of them canons. In the notation of some of them, Bach carried on the old tradition of the *riddle canon:* The canon is written as one part only, and the reader is left to figure out how it is to be performed.

It is important to distinguish between the rule, which merely indicates how to perform the canon, and the way the canon operates within the tonal system. (For example, what principle governs the construction of "Three Blind Mice"? Why does the round work?) To discover their rules is only one reason—and a superficial one—for the inclusion of these canons here. The real problem is to discover how they are composed. (For other examples, see "Canons" in the General Index.)[12]

■ **1**   How would you go about composing a canon of this type?

■ **2**   Here a two-voice canon is set over a third, non-canonic, line—the king's theme.

---

[12] Solutions by Bach's pupil Johann Philipp Kirnberger (1721–1783) to all the *Musical Offering* canons are given in Volume 31 of the *Gesellschaft* edition of Bach's works.

3   The upside-down clef signifies that the *comes* is to be inverted, but there is no indication of where it is to enter. Instead, Bach gives the Latin for "Seek and ye shall find."

     When inversion occurs in tonal music, it is nearly always *tonal*. This example of inversion is particularly arresting in that it is *real* throughout; that is, it requires not a single alteration in interval size. What particular characteristics of the tonal system does Bach exploit to achieve this *tour de force*? What is the axis of symmetry in this canon? (Twentieth-century examples of symmetrical organization around an axis are on pages 451 and 485.)

CANON A 2. Quaerendo invenietis

4   This amusing example bears the clue, "In whole steps." As in Canon No. 2, the king's theme is played against a canonic duet. The clefs indicate which of the two notated parts is to be performed canonically and at what interval. On reaching bar 9, all parts start again—but what has happened, and how did it happen?

CANON a 2. Per tonos. [Ascendente modulatione ascendat Gloria Regis]

CRUCIFIXUS
from *Mass in B minor*, BWV 232 (1733)

Johann Sebastian Bach (1685–1750)

     In Baroque music, a slow chromatic ground descending from tonic to dominant was traditionally used to symbolize death with its attendant grief. This masterful example is particularly rich in chromatic sonorities. Accounting for them is the problem.[13] The ground is four bars long. Do the upper parts consistently form four-bar phrases parallel with the ground? What factors create the work's several large sections? How do the final five bars relate to the rest of the movement?

---

[13] A start is given in Aldwell and Schachter's *Harmony and Voice Leading* (Belmont, CA: Thomson Learning/Schirmer, 3rd ed., 2002, p. 563).

[He was] crucified also for us under Pontius Pilate.
[He] suffered and was buried.

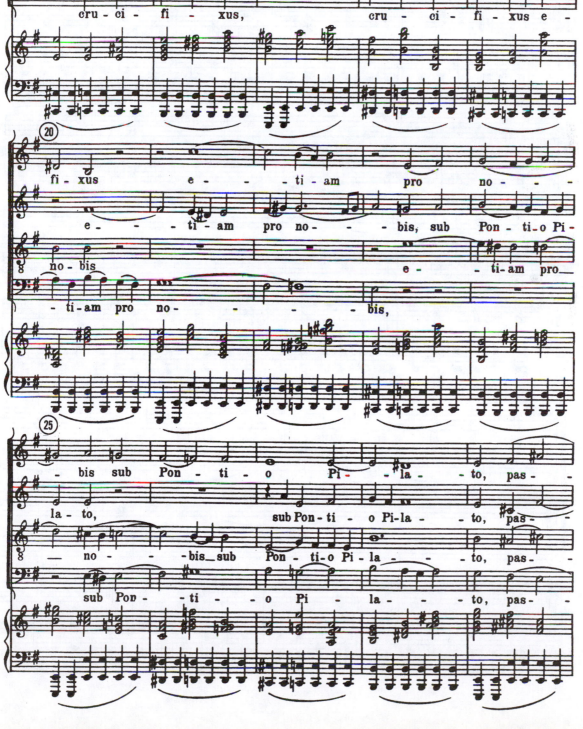

O GOTT, DU FROMMER GOTT
BWV 767 (ca. 1700), fourth variation

Johann Sebastian Bach (1685–1750)

In listening to variations, we appreciate them best when we perceive something of the theme from which they derive. What is the simple tune underlying this piece, the fourth in a set of nine organ variations on a chorale? Write a reduction (in 4/4 time!) that consists of all the essential voices (not just the tune) in their simplest, unembellished form.

TWO CHORALE PRELUDES
Johann Sebastian Bach (1685–1750)

The chorale prelude is an organ composition based on a chorale and performed in the Lutheran service prior to the singing of the chorale by the congregation. The first of the two given here is from the *Orgelbüchlein* (Little Organ Book), an unfinished collection of preludes, in which Bach planned to provide for every occasion of the church year.

WENN WIR IN HÖCHSTEN NÖTEN SEIN, BWV 641 (CA. 1717)

Discover the musical relation between this prelude, "When We Are in Direst Need," and the next, written some three decades later.

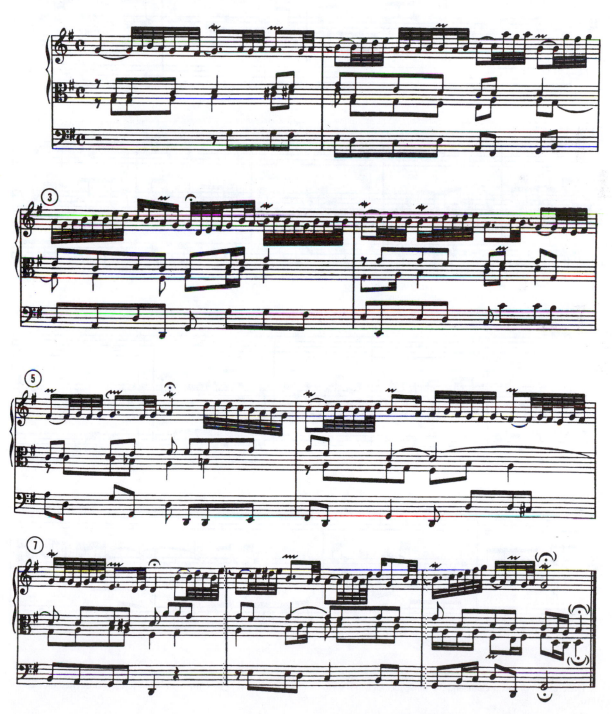

VOR DEINEN TRON TRET' ICH HIERMIT, BWV 668

from *Eighteen Chorale Preludes* (before 1723?–1750)

At some unknown time after composing the chorale prelude given above, Bach had made a revised, and longer, version of it. A few days before his death, and now totally blind and quite ill, he dictated some final improvements to this longer version. Aware that he was approaching his end, he also gave it a new title—"Before Thy Throne I Now Stand." We give the final, improved version here. How does it differ from *Wenn wir in höchsten Nöten sein?*[14]

---

[14] The creation of this prelude and the subsequent legends surrounding it are discussed by Christoph Wolff in the works cited on page 116.

SONATA IN D MAJOR
Kirkpatrick 96; Longo 465 (before 1746)

Domenico Scarlatti (1685–1757)

For his remarkably gifted pupil, Queen Maria Barbara of Spain, the Italian Scarlatti wrote more than five hundred one-movement harpsichord pieces called sonatas. Their originality and expressive range, striking enough in themselves, are the more striking in that nearly all of them are cast in binary form with a double bar and repeat marks in the middle. This witty, capricious sonata, with its opening trumpet calls, is typical of Scarlatti's approach to binary form. How does its form compare with classical sonata form?[15]

Scarlatti's influence on the harpsichord and its technique is comparable to Chopin's on the piano. See the unusual repeated notes at bar 33 (to be played by "changing the fingers"), and the equally unusual octave and crossed-hands passages. (The *"Tremulo di sopra"* at bar 11 means to trill the high notes through bar 16.) This piece frequently imitates the orchestral effect of solo versus tutti. Where do such switches occur? Should they be brought out in performance? If so, how?

[15] Ralph Kirkpatrick's indispensable *Domenico Scarlatti* (Princeton, NJ: Princeton University Press, 1953) discusses this question on page 254 and also contains many references to this sonata.

Part Three

Classical Compositions

Part Three stresses the chief instrumental forms of the late Classical era—sonata, rondo, and compound ternary form—and also contains a typical theme with variations of Mozart, as well as his great C minor fantasia. Two piano sonatas are given complete—Mozart's K. 333 and Beethoven's "Pathétique."

SONATA FORM

Very simple miniature examples of sonata form are the Clementi sonatina and the Mozart Andantino for winds. Standard examples of sonata form proper are, for major mode, the first and second movements of Mozart's K. 333, and, for minor, the first movement of Beethoven's Op. 2, No. 1. (A related form, the "sonata without development," is shown by the second movement of Beethoven's Op. 10, No. 1.) These might be followed by the first movement of Beethoven's "Spring" sonata, Op. 24, for violin and piano, also quite clear in form. The less common "monothematic" sonata form, so typical of Haydn, is shown by the first movement of his C sharp minor sonata. More challenging are three further Beethoven first movements—the "Pathétique," with its slow introduction, the "Waldstein," with its second theme in III# and its extensive coda, and the E minor string quartet, op. 59, No. 2. Also more difficult is the first movement of the Brahms clarinet sonata (in Part Four), with Brahms's typical "third theme" and use of thematic transformation, and the first movement of Mozart's clarinet concerto.

RONDO

Couperin's rondeau *Les Moissonneurs* (in Part Two) can precede study of the Classical rondo, which is represented by five examples. The third movement of Haydn's D major sonata and the second of Beethoven's "Pathétique" progress from elementary to somewhat less so. Increasingly challenging are the last movements of the "Pathétique" and Mozart's K. 333, both sonata rondos, and the finale of Haydn's "Clock" Symphony.

LARGE TERNARY FORM

The term "large, or compound, ternary form" is understood here to cover ABA forms in which A and B are themselves small forms. The clearest examples in our selection are pieces with "trios," the simplest being Haydn's C major minuet and Beethoven's scherzo from Op. 28. These might be followed by three Beethoven movements—the minuet from Op. 2, No 1, the Allegretto from Op. 14, No. 1(with its interesting use of the key of VI and its open B-section), and the Presto from the string quartet, Op. 130—and, finally, the minuet from Haydn's "Clock" symphony. All these might be compared with related pieces in Part Four that can be readily found in Index I under "Ternary form, compound."

Part Three also has two slow movements in large ternary form that have open B sections—the E major Largo from the Haydn string quartet (useful for its chromaticism and for score reading) and the more complex C major Largo from Beethoven's piano sonata, Op. 7.

Fitting a piece into a conventional category is of course only the beginning of analysis. Much more interesting is "how a work departs from ordinary ways, how venturesome it can be" (see Preface, page xvi.) Still, if one has no knowledge of the conventions, can one appreciate the departures?

PIANO SONATA in C SHARP MINOR
Hob. XVI/36 (ca. 1770–75?; publ. 1780), first movement

Joseph Haydn (*1732–1809*)

Of Haydn's forty-seven authenticated keyboard sonatas, most were composed for students or friends to perform at home. The movement given here, from a set of sonatas dedicated to two talented sisters from a wealthy family named Auenbrugger, reveals his characteristic terseness and wit. In exploring it, discover—beyond the customary themes and sections—the ingenious treatment of second theme material in the recapitulation: What is going on at, for example, bars 82–83? And in the development, what does the harmony at bar 43 lead the listener to expect? Then notice that four eighths are often beamed together thus: ♪♪♪♪. Why? In other places they are separated thus: ♪♪♪. What do you make of the latter? Do they tell the performer anything?[1]

[1] For a perceptive discussion, see Roger Kamien's "Aspects of Motivic Elaboration in the Opening Movement of Haydn's Piano Sonata in C♯ Minor," in *Aspects of Schenkerian Theory,* ed. David Beach (New Haven CT: Yale: 1983, p. 77).

PIANO SONATA in D MAJOR
Hob. XVI / 37 (publ. 1780), third movement

Joseph Haydn (1732–1809)

What is the form of this, the closing movement of one of Haydn's most well-known sonatas? In bars 21–40, what do you make of the jumping around between different registers? Is there a double neighbor in bar 61? Haydn's *"Innocentemente"* seems to be authentic; why might he have felt the need for such a word?

PIANO SONATA in C MAJOR
Hob. XVI/3 (before 1766), third movement

Joseph Haydn (1732–1809)

The early Sonata No. 3, whose first two movements are an Allegretto in binary form and a G major Andante in sonata form, ends with this simple minuet—a model example of both genre and form. In bars 10–14, how long should the appoggiaturas be held? In bar 26, why is one note marked staccato?

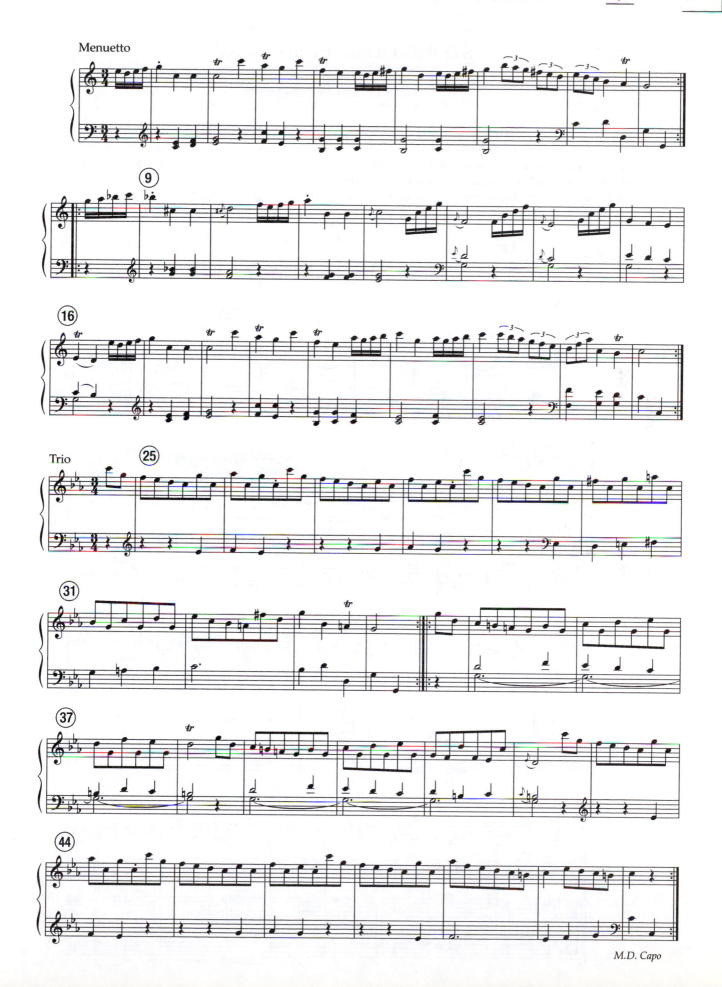

Menuetto

Trio

M.D. Capo

STRING QUARTET in G MINOR
Op. 74, No. 3 (Hob. III / 74) (1793), second movement

Joseph Haydn (1732–1809)

The string quartet reached its first high point in works of Haydn beginning in the early 1770s. This expressive slow movement from a quartet written much later—between Haydn's two London visits—is astonishing first for its choice of key—E major in a work basically in G minor! Its many chromatic chords will reward study. How do you explain what happens in bar 8 and relate that to the rest of the movement? (Later examples of string quartet writing are on pages 277, 481, and 494.)

II

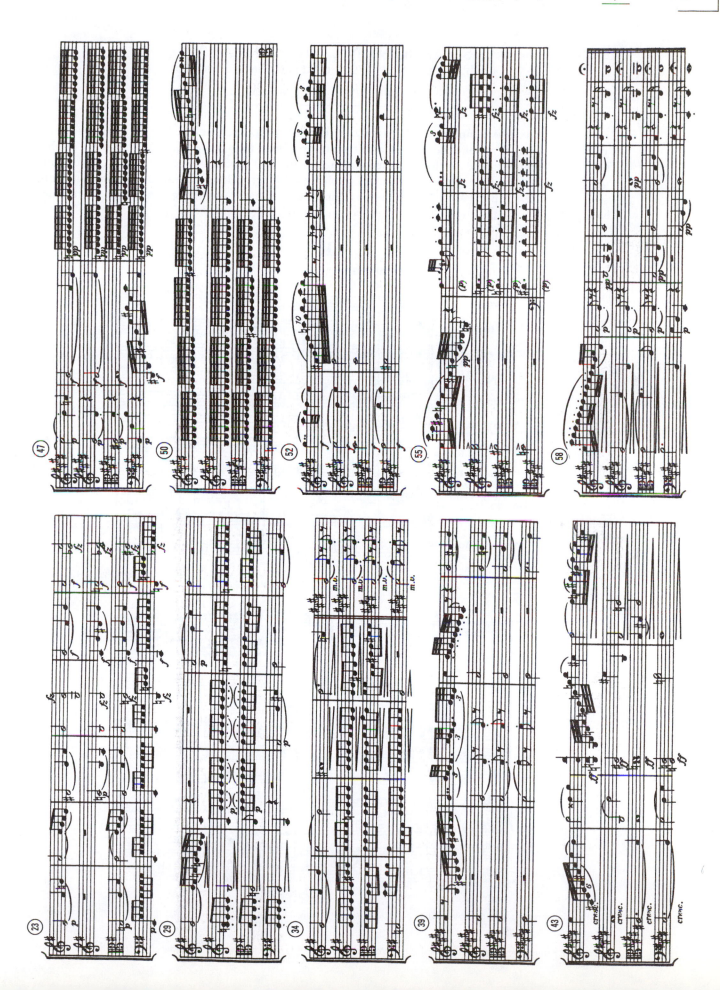

SYMPHONY No. 101 in D MAJOR
Hob. 1 / 101 (1793–1794), third and fourth movements

Joseph Haydn (1732–1809)

Of Haydn's 104 symphonies, the last 12, written in London between 1791 and 1795 for a series of public concerts, represent the summit of his achievements in that genre. No. 101 has been dubbed "The Clock" because of the rhythm of its second movement. The third movement, though conventional in genre, reveals a most imaginative treatment of phrases. (What melody note would a humdrum composer have written at bar 148–150?) In the vivacious fourth, what is surprising about the way the form is handled?[2]

Third movement reprinted from Peters Edition No. 1027e. Reprint permission granted by the publisher, C.F. Peters Corporation, New York.

[2] Leonard G. Ratner gives a comprehensive discussion of the opening section of the minuet in *Classic Music* (New York: Schirmer Books, 1980, p. 203ff).

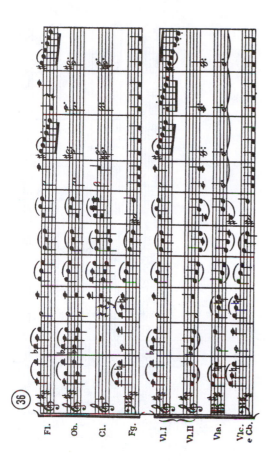

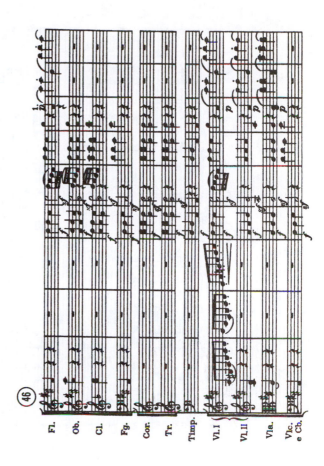

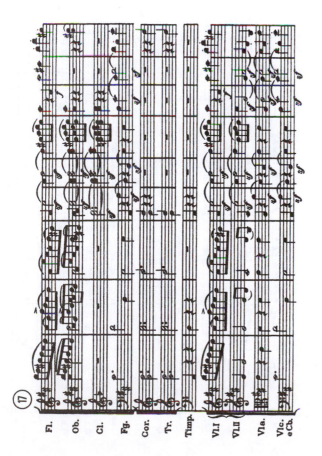

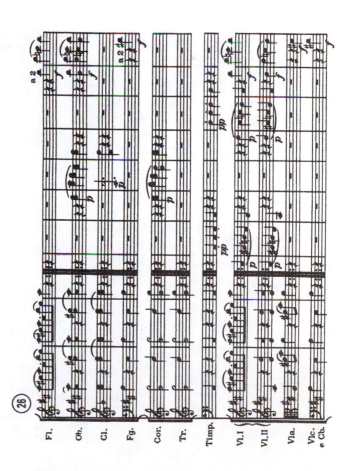

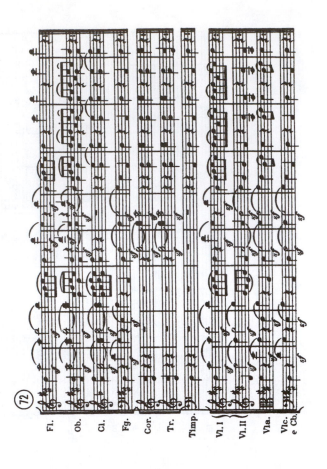

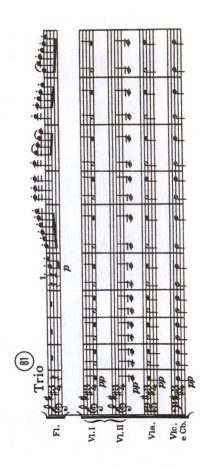

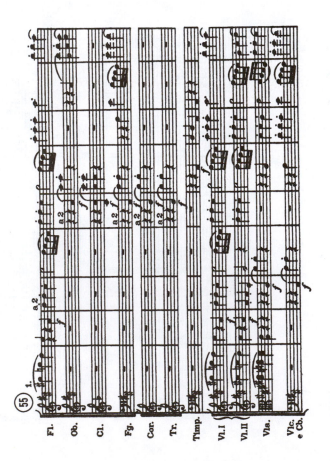

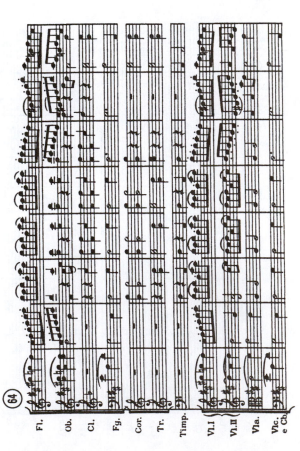

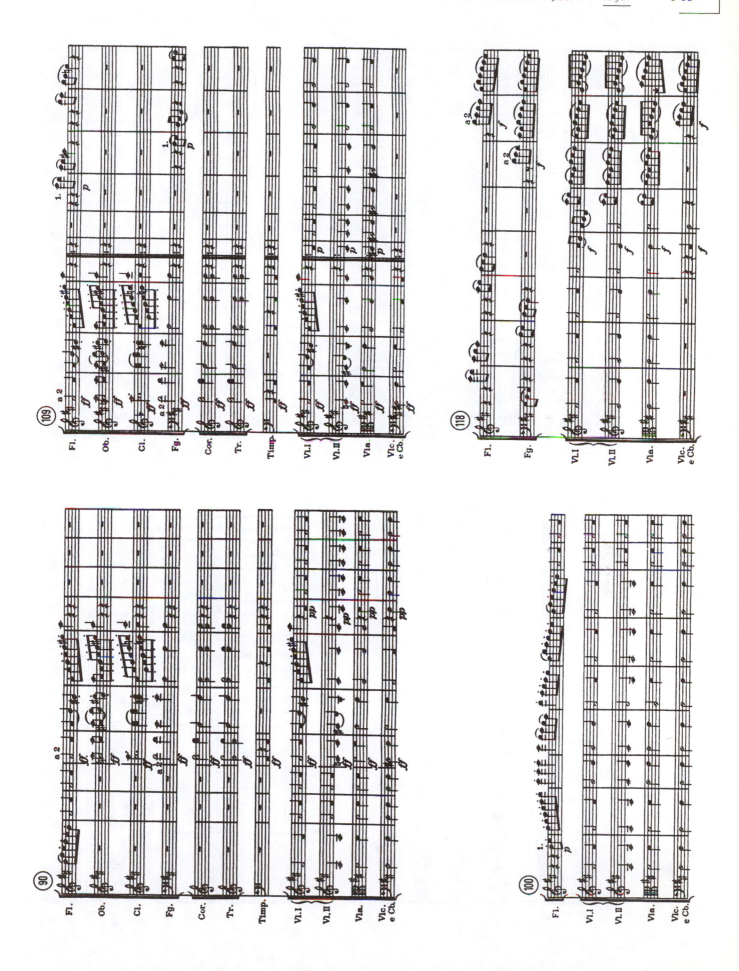

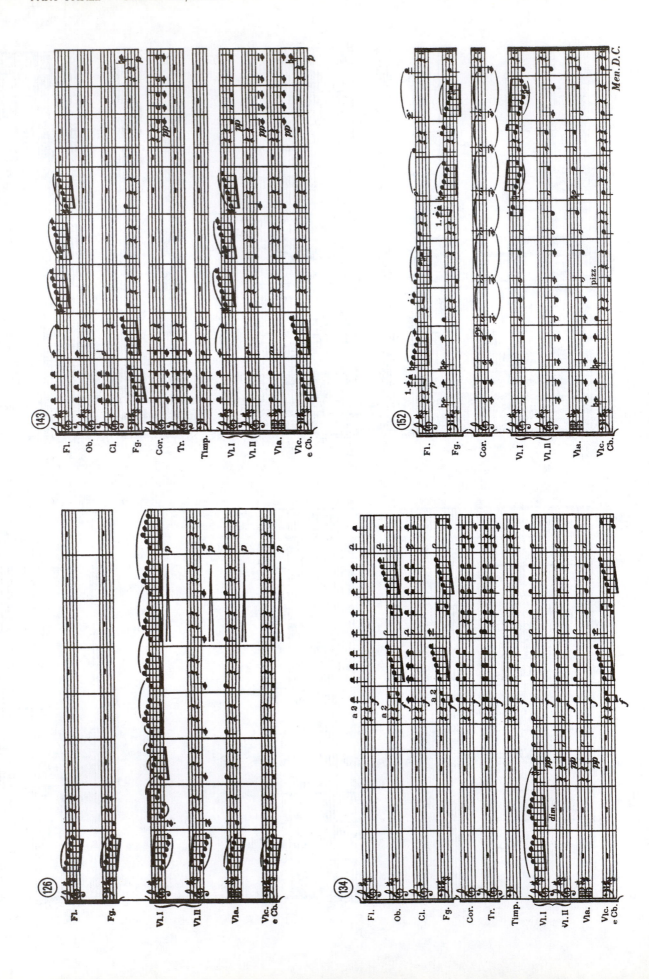

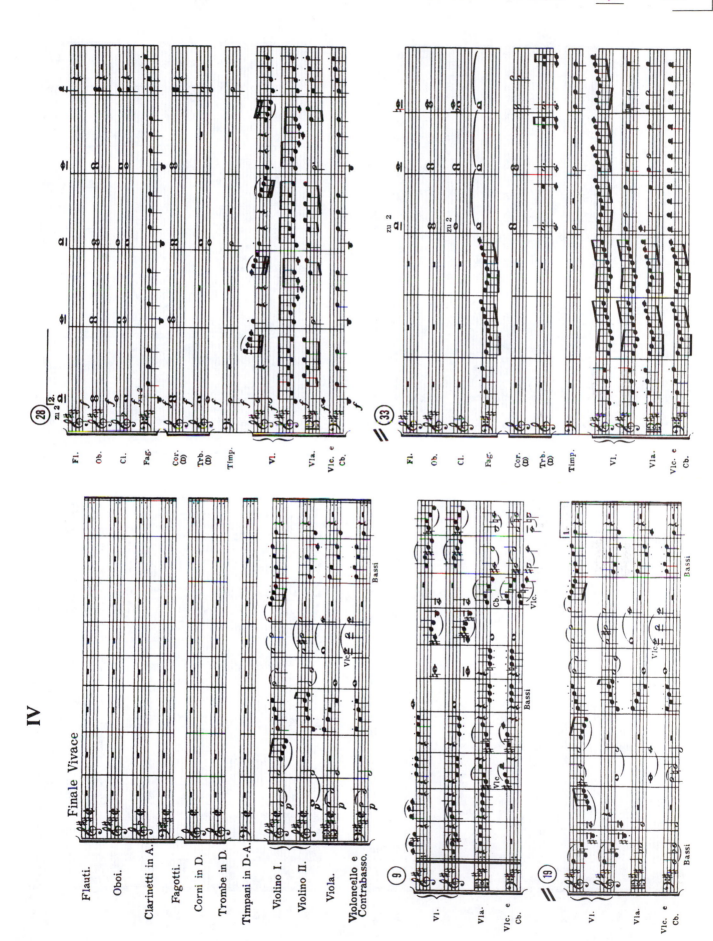

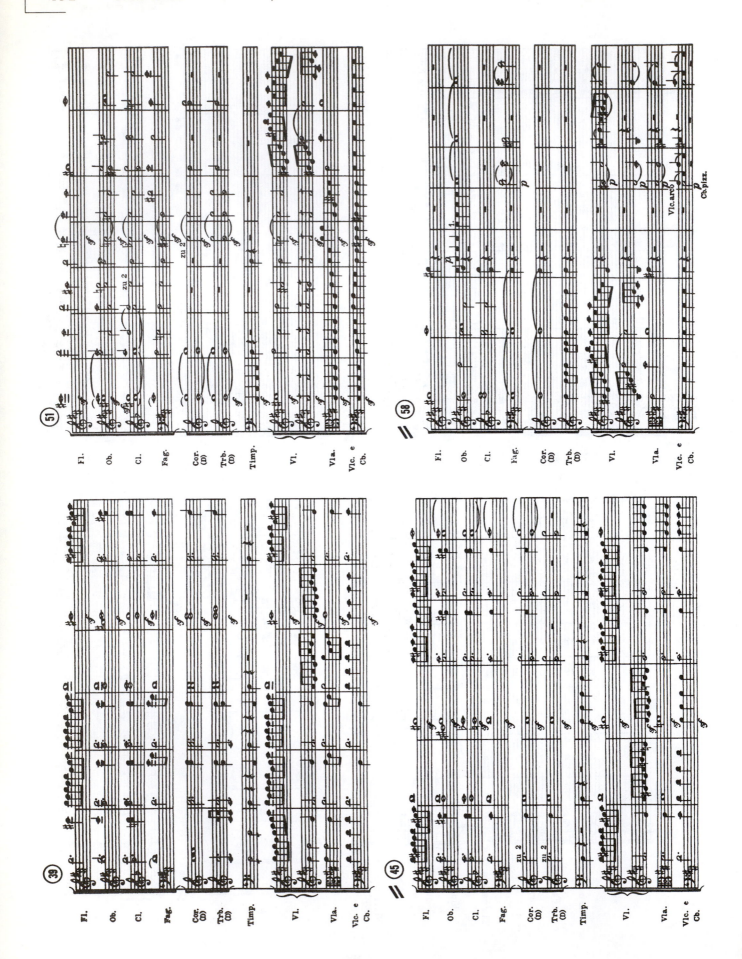

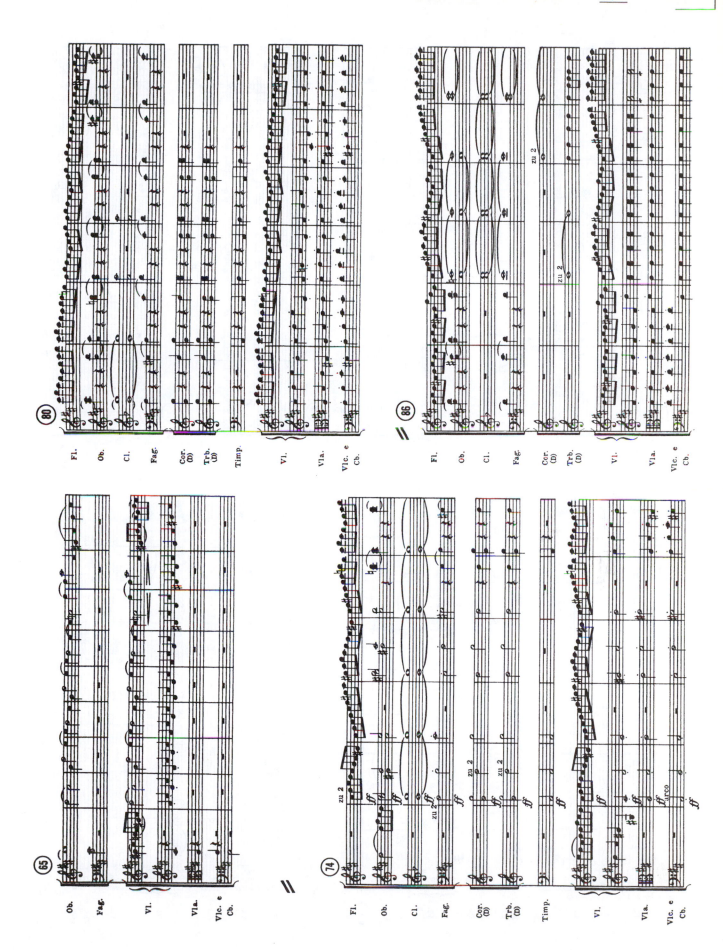

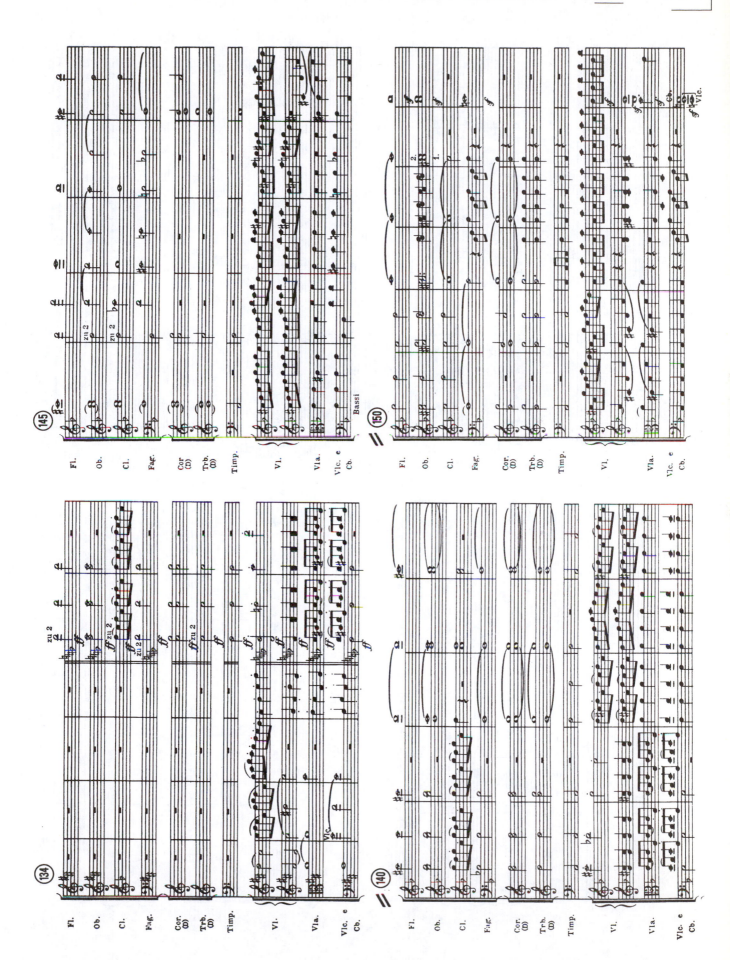

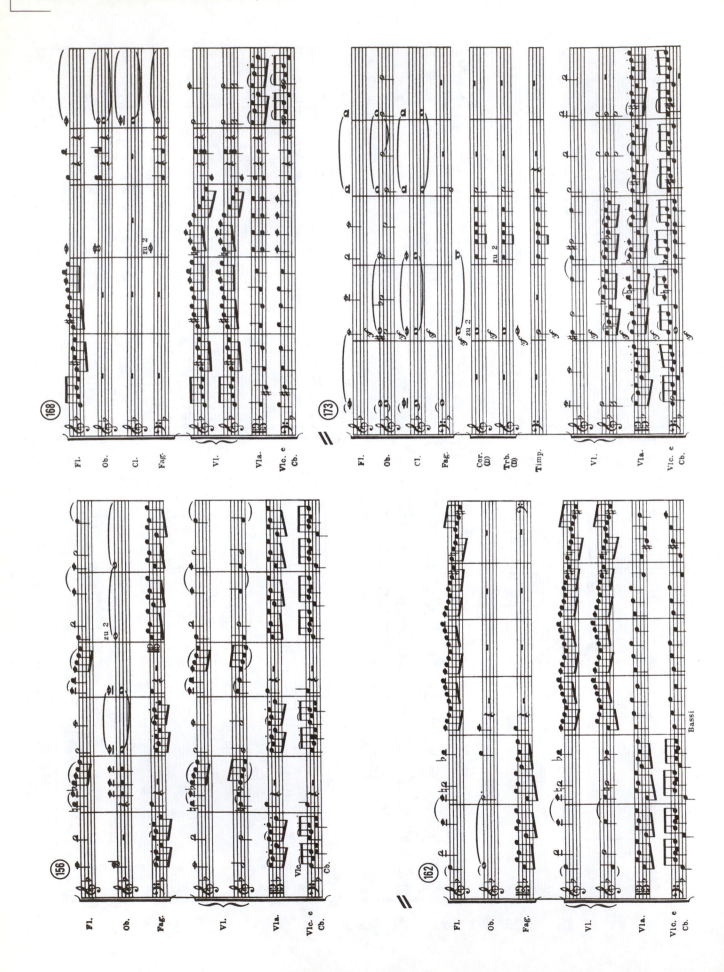

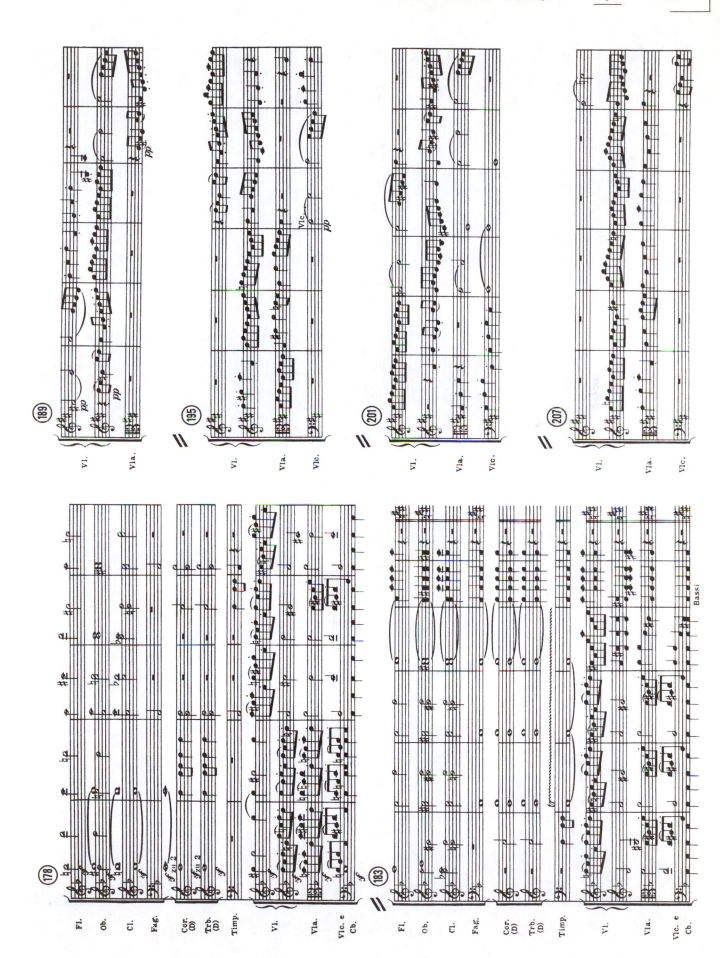

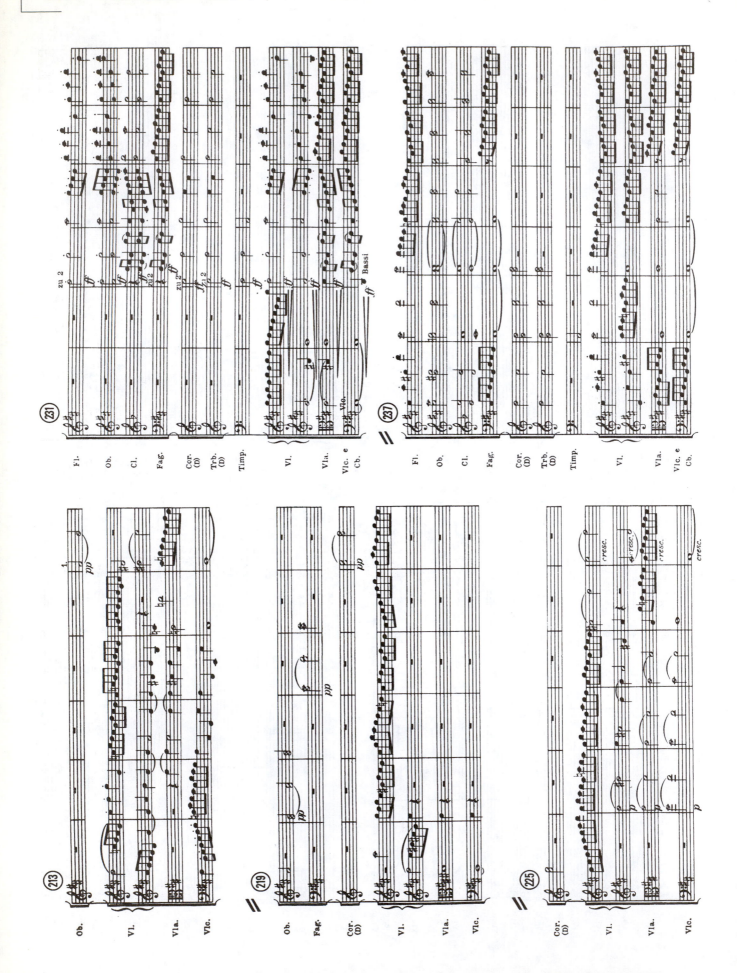

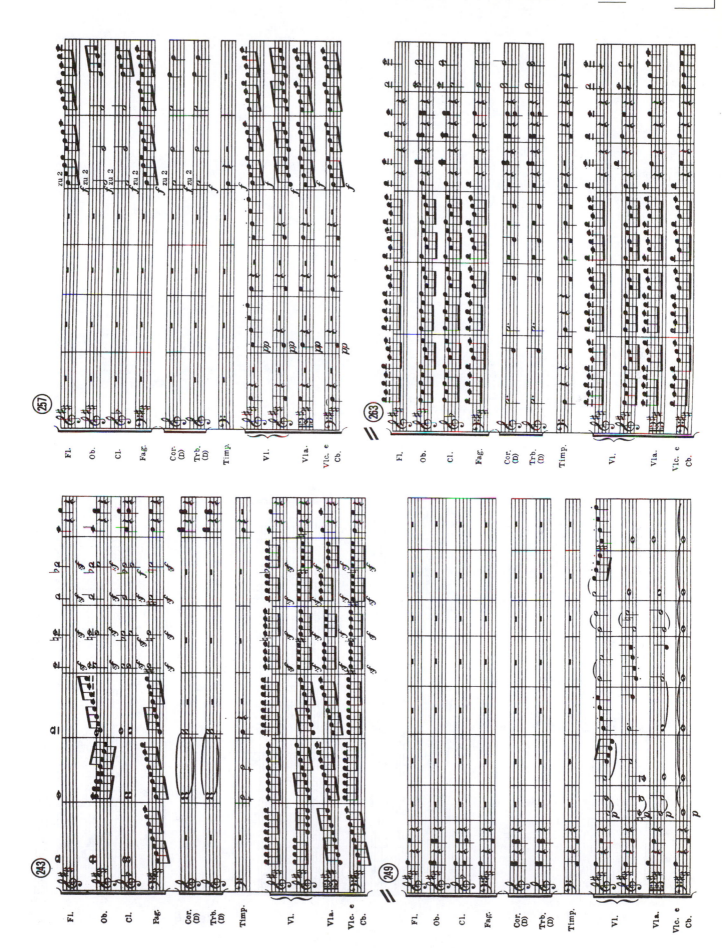

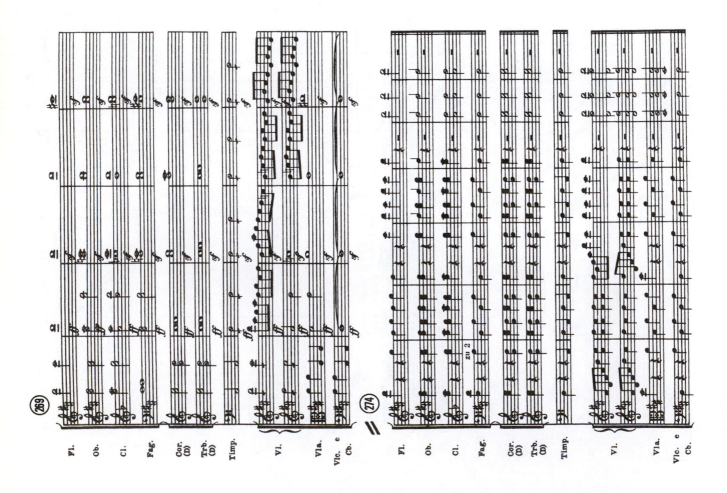

SONATINA in G MAJOR
Op. 36, No. 2 (publ. 1797), first movement

Muzio Clementi (*1752–1832*)

Clementi was a musician of such achievement that in 1781 he and Mozart engaged in a "friendly" pianistic duel. It ended in a draw, but Clementi later altered his playing style in Mozart's direction. Also a great pedagogue, Clementi trained many distinguished pianists of the next generation. His sonatinas are still useful to students. What is the form of the following example? At what point does the piece markedly increase in tonal motion? Compare the D major harmonies in bars 3, 8, 35–36, and 43. All would be correctly labeled as "V." Do they "feel" the same?

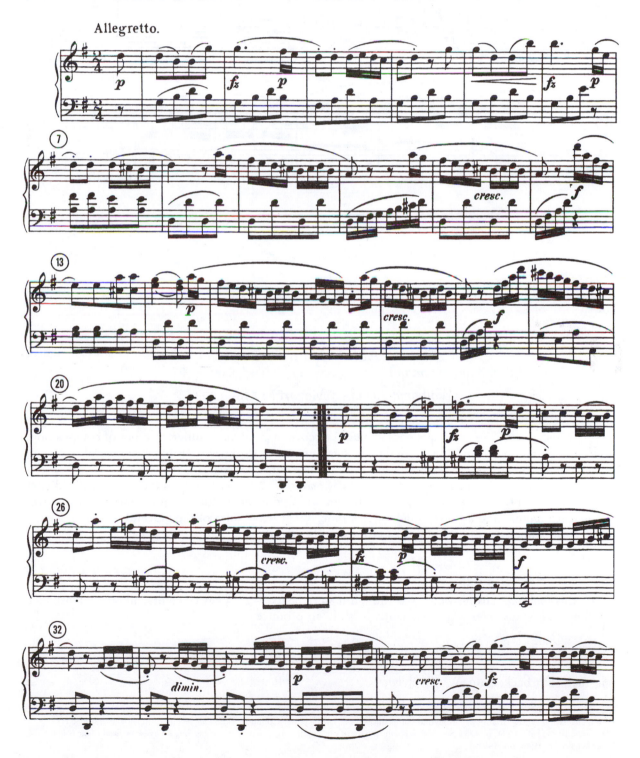

ANDANTINO
Second movement of *Divertimento No. 14 for Wind Sextet*, K. 270 (1777)

Wolfgang Amadeus Mozart (1756–1791)

In the 1700s, the term *divertimento* was used to cover a great many different types of composition. Mozart generally used the term to designate small ensemble works written for some social occasion, but his "divertimenti" still vary greatly and even include some orchestral works.

The four-movement Divertimento in B flat major, K. 270, written to serve as *Tafelmusik* (dinner music), presumably for the Salzburg court, begins with a full sonata form, and for the last two movements has a minuet and a Presto rondo in 3/8 time. What is the form of the graceful *Andantino*?

Notice that the opening motives group *over* the bar, thus:

(Does this feel like "strong-weak"—as though it were beats 1–2? What elements militate against such a feeling?) Now discover where the motives "shift" to produce

and then shift back again. Why just *there*?[3]

---

[3] An illuminating article (that goes far beyond our example) is Floyd Graves's "Common-Time Displacement in Mozart" (*Journal of Musicology*, III /4 [Fall] 1984, p. 423). See also William Rothstein on "conflicting downbeats," in his *Phrase Rhythm in Tonal Music* (New York: Schirmer Books, 1989, pp. 199ff.).

THEME WITH VARIATIONS
from *Piano Sonata in D major, K. 284 (1775)*

Wolfgang Amadeus Mozart (1756–1791)

This set of variations, the third and final movement of a sonata, is based on an original theme. What elements of the theme remain constant from variation to variation? What is being varied? And which measure creates an unexpected rhythmic bump every time? How would you conceive the large "form" that the entire set as a whole creates?

It was Mozart's custom to give the penultimate variation a slow tempo and much embellishment. In this case, we follow the practice of giving Var. 11 in two versions—Mozart's autograph and the first printed edition (by Toricella of Vienna), in which the still more elaborate embellishments are likely authentic.

Variation is one of the most basic of musical techniques and is found in all periods and styles as well as in many non-Western musics. For numerous other examples, see "Variation" in the General Index.

Var. XII.
(Allegro.)

PIANO SONATA in B FLAT MAJOR
K. 333 (1783)
Wolfgang Amadeus Mozart (1756–1794)

This work, given here in its entirety, has been called by Alfred Einstein a realization of the ideal of Mozart's piano sonatas.[4]

Remember that the opening four notes are performed as four sixteenth notes, and that all the small appoggiaturas are generally to be played on the beat. Their length depends on their context. The one in bar 27, for example, is to have the length of an eighth note; the ones in bar 7 of the second movement are thirty-seconds. Are all appoggiaturas written small? What is the advantage of so writing them?[5]

The third movement imitates another type of composition. What is it? And what is the source of the melody in bars 76–80?

---

[4] Alfred Einstein, *Mozart, His Character, His Work* (New York: Oxford University Press, 1945, p. 240). Charles Rosen comments briefly on the first movement's bridge secion in his *Sonata Form* (New York: Norton, 1988, pp. 229–230). For a remark on the third movement, see his *The Classical Style* (New York: Viking, 1971, p. 45).

[5] An informative article on this subject, with many examples, is Ernst Oster's "On the Meaning of the Long Appoggiatura," (trans. by R. Kosovsky), in *Theory and Practice* (Ithaca, NY: Music Theory Society of New York State, August, 1982, p. 20).

II

Andante cantabile

III

Allegretto grazioso

FANTASIA in C MINOR
K. 475 (1785)

Wolfgang Amadeus Mozart (1756–1791)

In the creation of a fantasia, the composer does not adhere to a pre-established form. This is not to say that fantasias are formless but, rather, that each has a unique form. The idea is to control improvisatory flights by means of an overall direction. In this bold, uninhibited fantasia, with its astonishing lack of key signature, how does Mozart achieve unity from such violently contrasting parts.[6]

[6] For an analysis of this fantasia, with a graph showing the bass structure, see Oswald Jonas, "Improvisation in Mozart's Klavierwerken," in *Mozart Jahrbuch* (Salzburg: Internationalen Stiftung Mozarteum, 1967, pp. 179–181). Another is in Felix Salzer, *Structural Hearing* (New York: Dover, 1962, vol. 2, Graph 507).

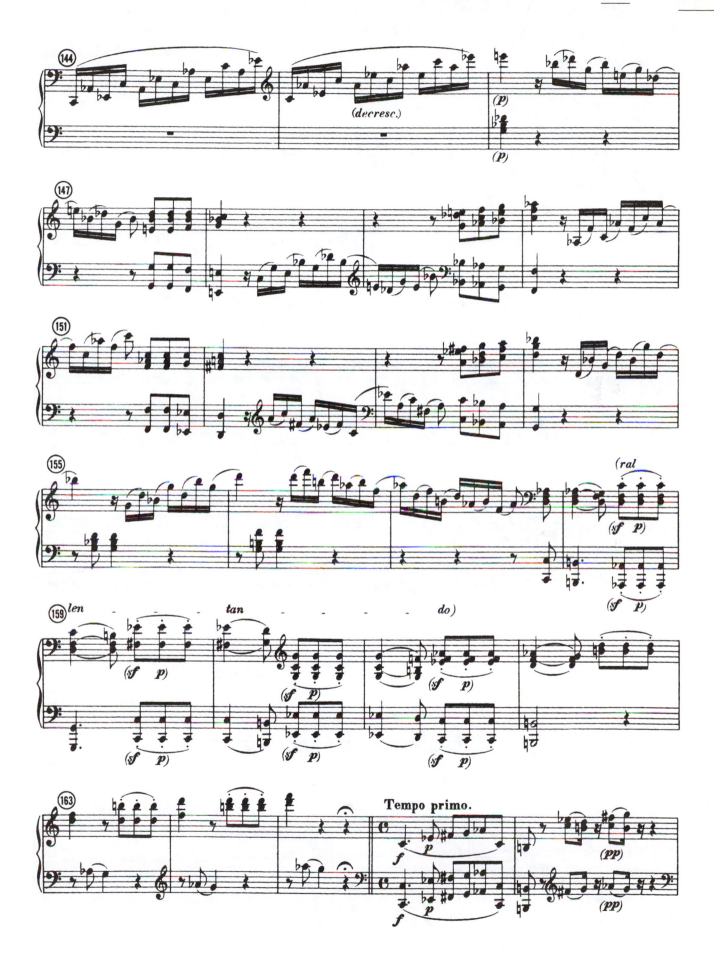

THE BIRD-CATCHER'S SONG

from *The Magic Flute* (1791)
Text: Emanuel Schikaneder

Wolfgang Amadeus Mozart (1756–1791)

Mozart's last opera is a sublime allegory on universal themes, at once comic and serious. In its fairy-tale-like story, Papageno represents the simple ordinary man—the child of nature. His job is catching birds for the Queen of the Night, but what he really wants to catch is a wife. Soon after the opening of Act I, he makes his entrance with this song.

1.

The bird-catcher am I,
and always merry!
As bird-catcher I'm known
by young and old throughout the land.
I know how to lure them,
and make them understand my pipes.
So I'm happy and gay,
for all the birds are mine.

2.

The bird-catcher am I,
and always merry!
As bird-catcher I'm known
by young and old throughout the land.
I'd like to have a net for girls
and catch them by the dozen.
Then I'd lock them up with me,
and all the girls would be mine.

3.

If all the girls were mine,
I'd fetch a fine lump of sugar;
I'd choose the girl I like the best
and give the sugar lump to her.
She'd kiss me then most tenderly,
she'd be my wife and I her man.
She'd fall asleep beside me then;
I'd rock her like a child to sleep.

The music, in popular style and composed of the simplest chords, non-chord tones, and modulations, is unusual for its use of Pan-pipes, which Pagageno plays between phrases. How is this composition saved from four-squareness? (Omitted here is the orchestral introduction, which is identical in form with the song.)

CLARINET CONCERTO
K. 622, first movement (1791)

Wolfgang Amadeus Mozart (1756–1791)

Mozart's concerto for clarinet, written just two months before his death, is the equal of his great piano concertos in scope and depth of expression. He wrote it for his clarinetist friend Anton Stadler, and for Stadler's "basset clarinet," a short-lived instrument with a range down to the second A below middle C—four semitones below the lowest note of the standard A clarinet. Although it is known that certain passages in the work call for these low notes, we can never be entirely certain how all of them went because the manuscript is unfortunately lost, and the best remaining source is an edition published in 1801 in which these passages are modified to fit the range of the standard clarinet. Various bits of secondary evidence have enabled modern scholars to restore some of these passages to their original form, which enhances the effectiveness of the work.[7] But even in its standard version (which we print here), the work is a masterpiece.

In the richly melodic first movement, solo and orchestra are closely integrated, and the latter quite delicately scored. (Find some examples.) Here and there Mozart actually gives to the clarinet alone the *bass* voice of the harmony. (Where?) Rather unusual is the treatment of the bridge, which is quite long and has an important theme of its own. (Where does the "second thematic group" begin?) Also unexpected is the absence of a cadenza. (For what possible reason?) If Mozart had wanted one (and we are glad he didn't), at which bar would it quite probably have been inserted?[8] (If you are not a trained score-reader, an expedient is to read the clarinet part down a third, adjusting it to key and harmony.)

---

[7] See for example the commentary by the clarinetist Alan Hacker given in the Eulenburg score. See also the reconstructed version for basset clarinet given in the *Neue Mozart Ausgabe*, V:14/iv (1977).

[8] For an example of a cadenza, see page 188, bar 171ff.

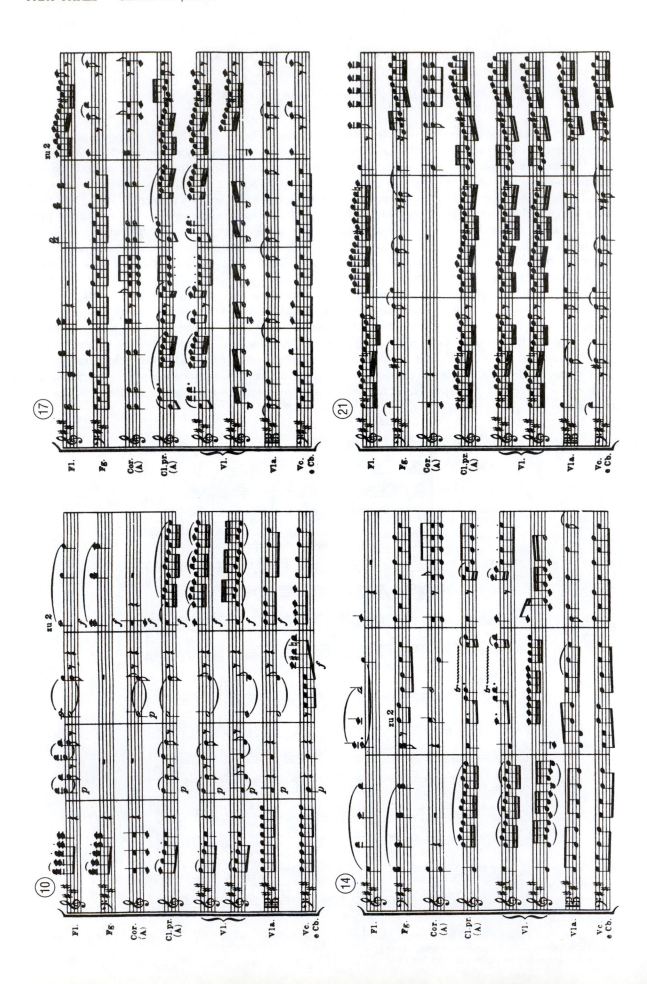

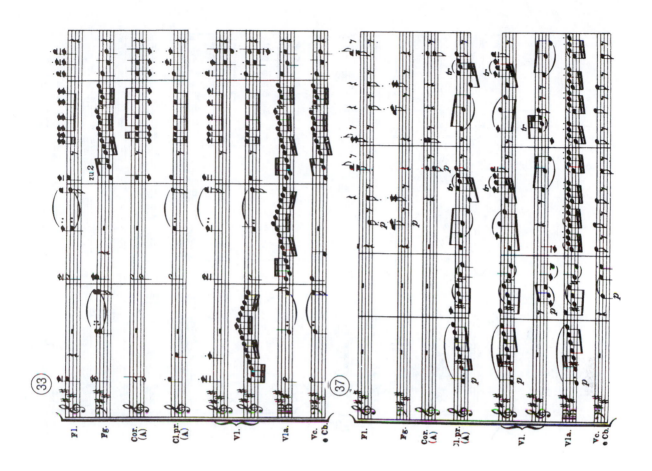

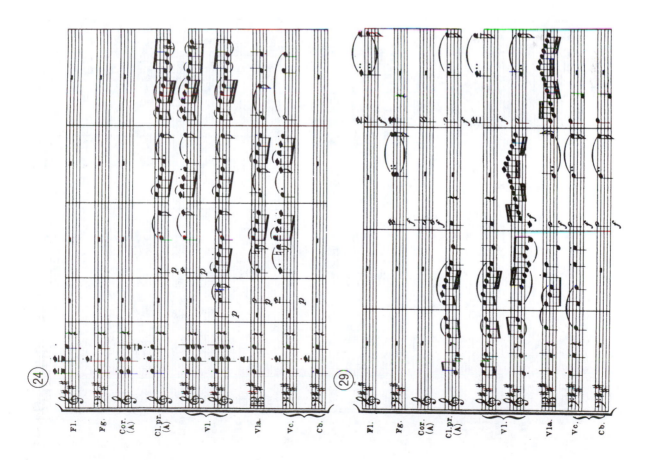

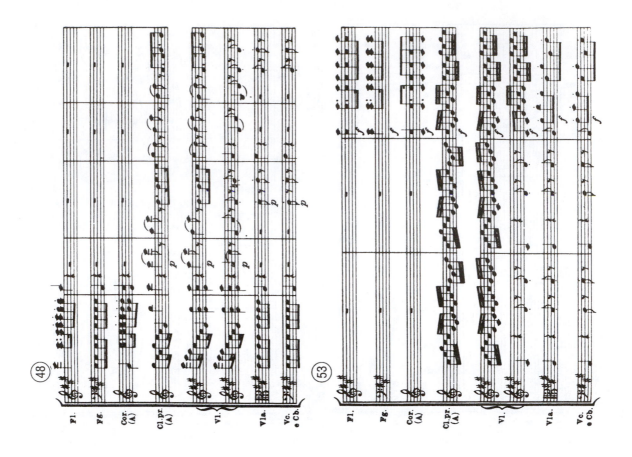

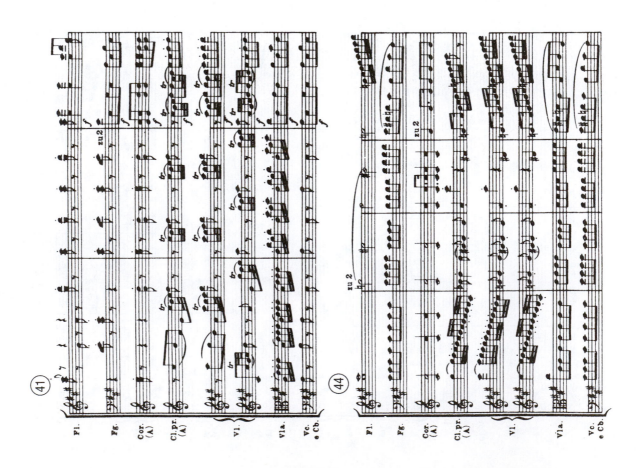

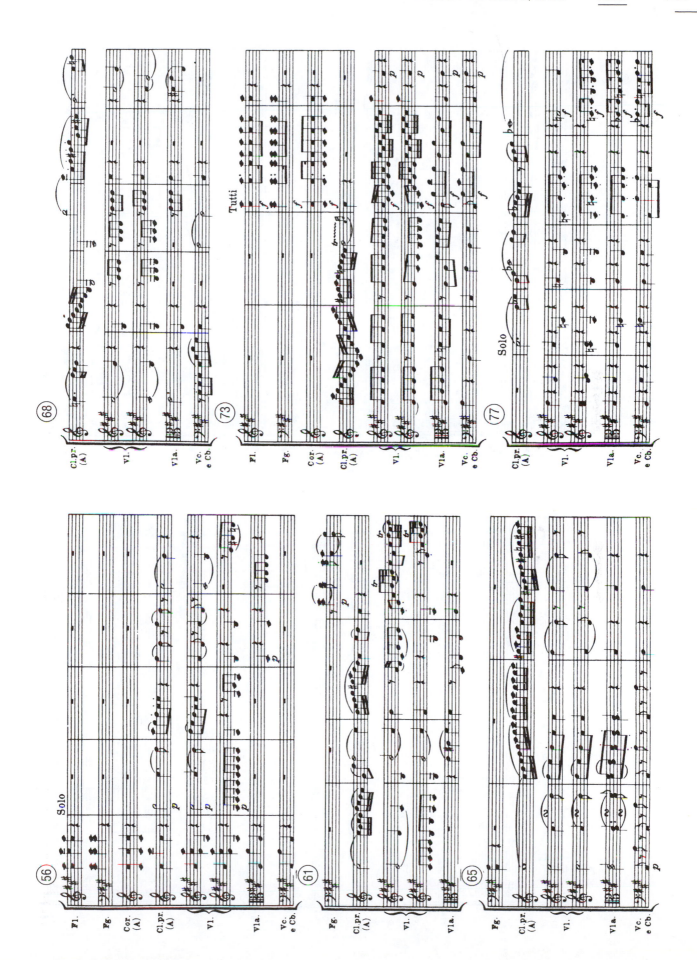

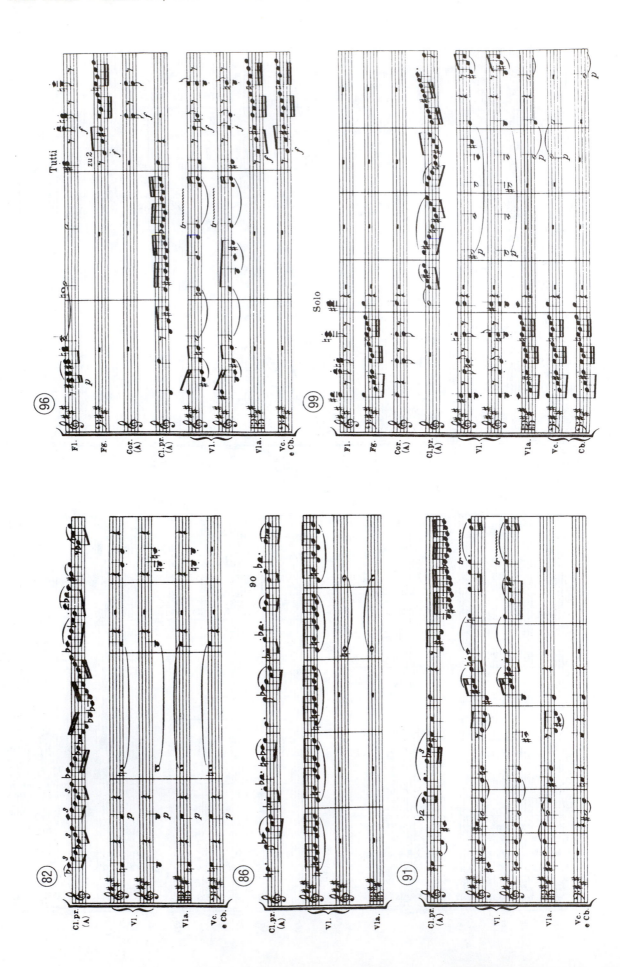

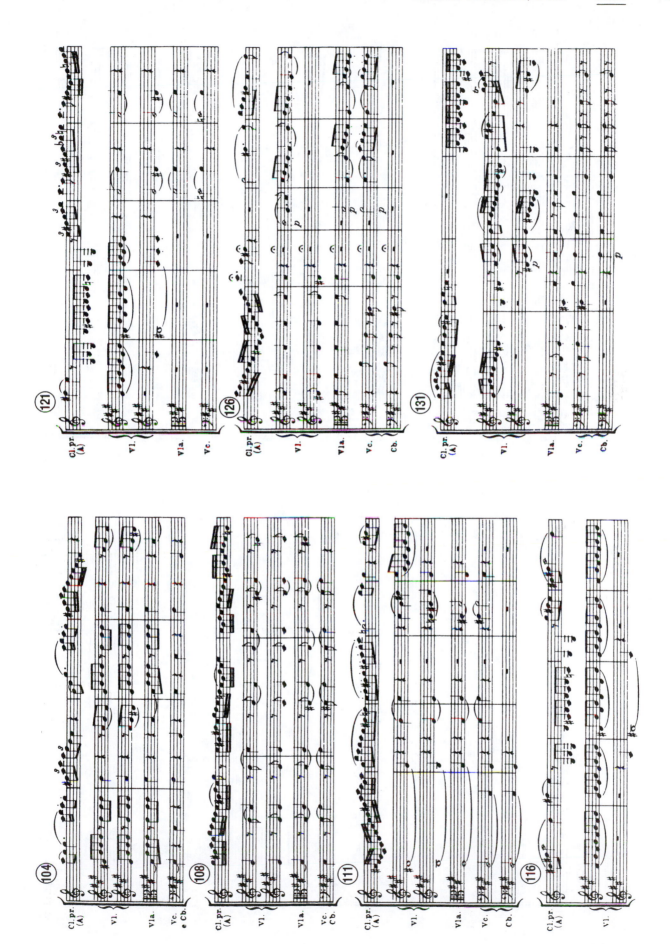

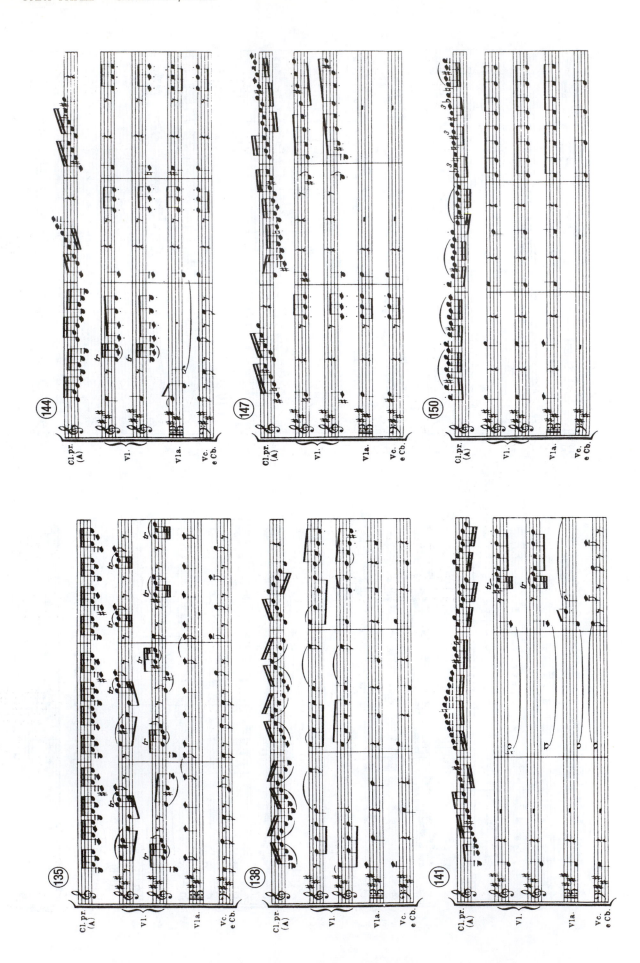

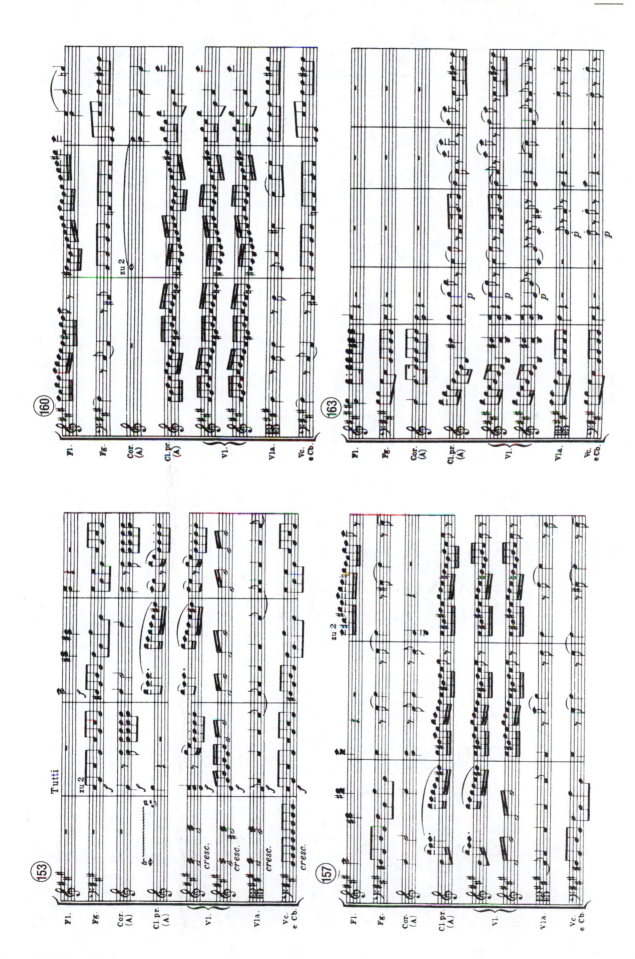

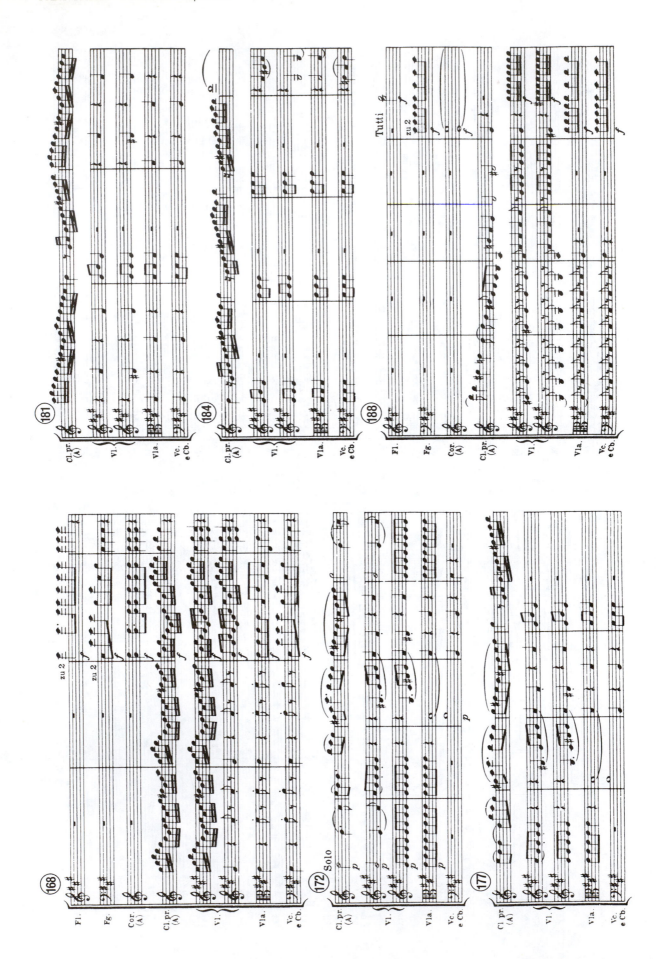

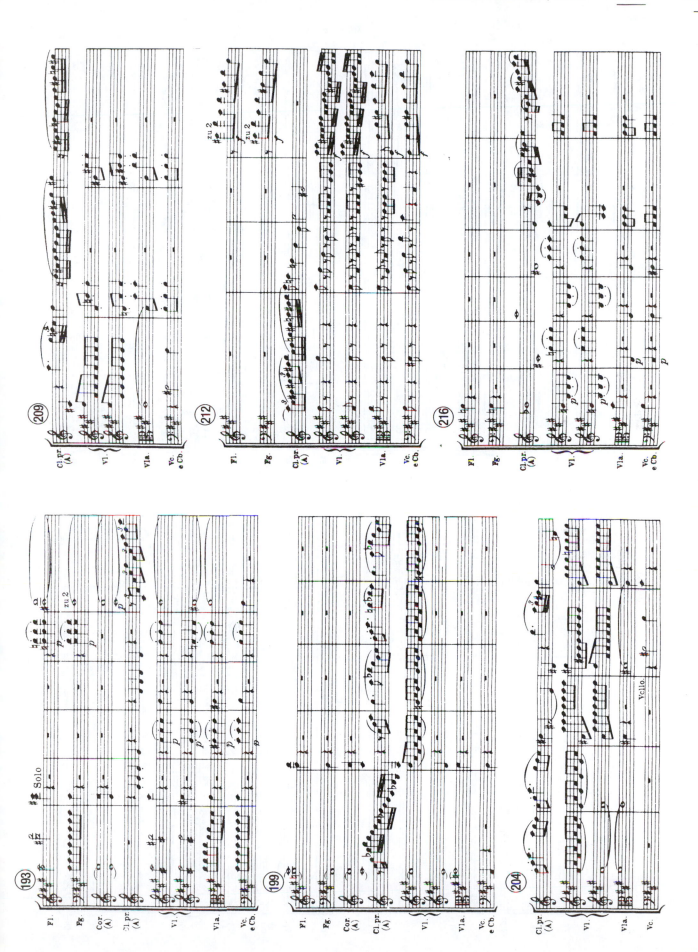

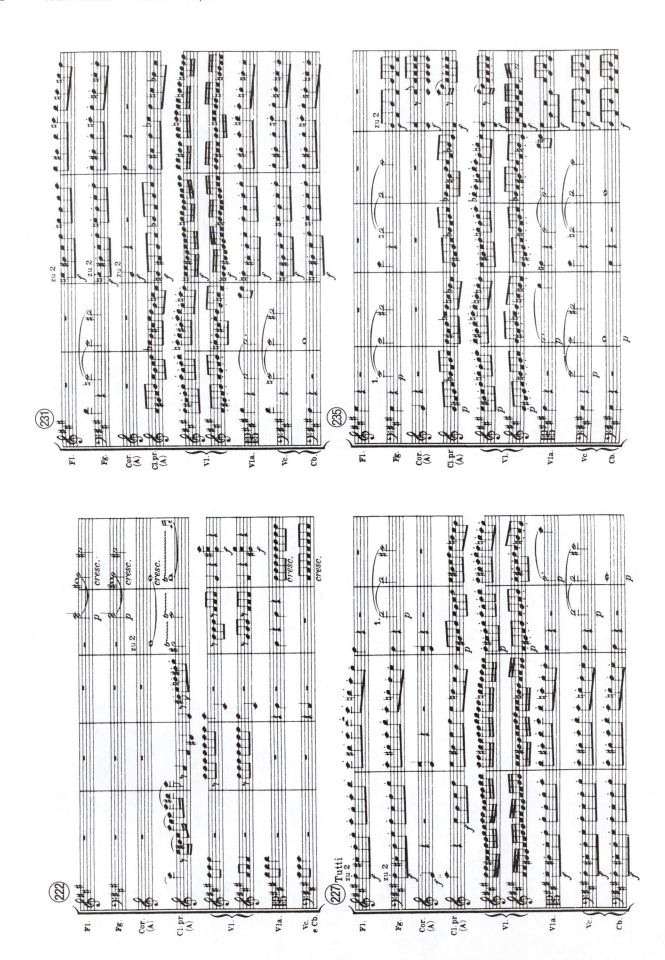

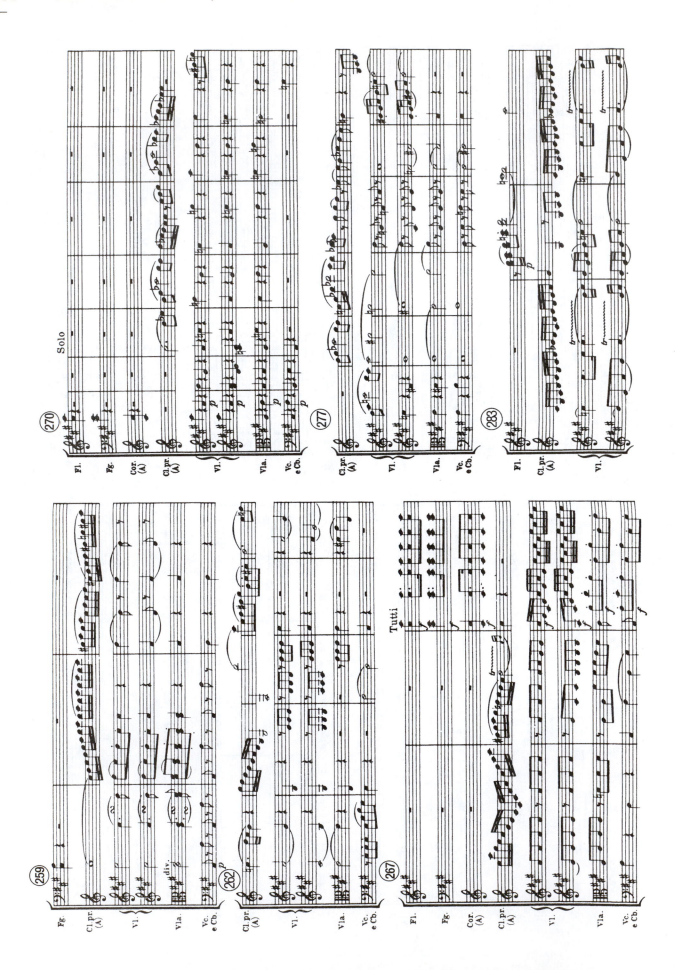

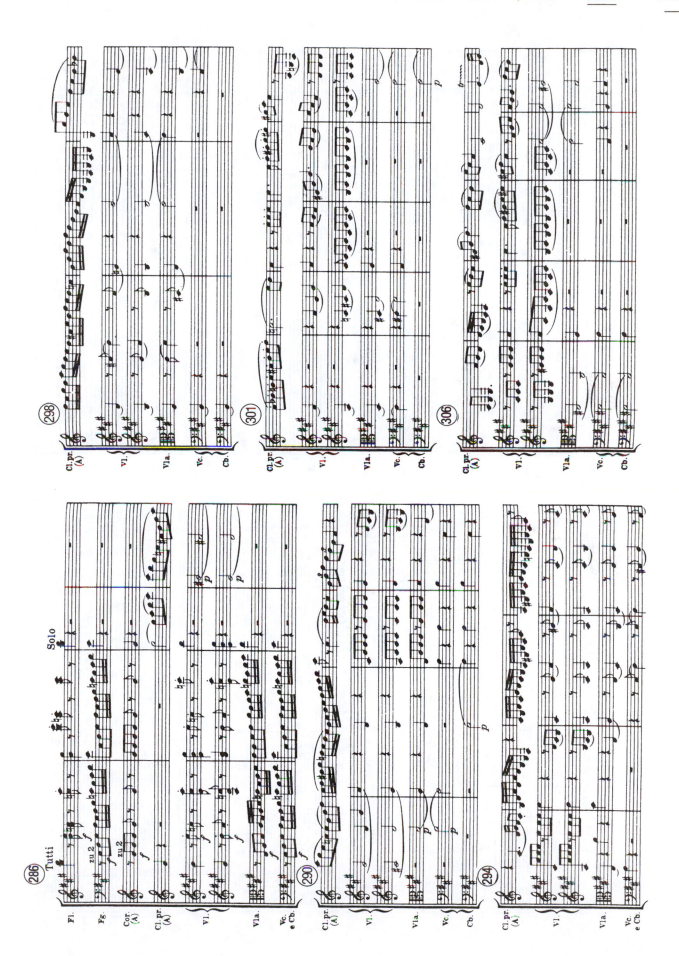

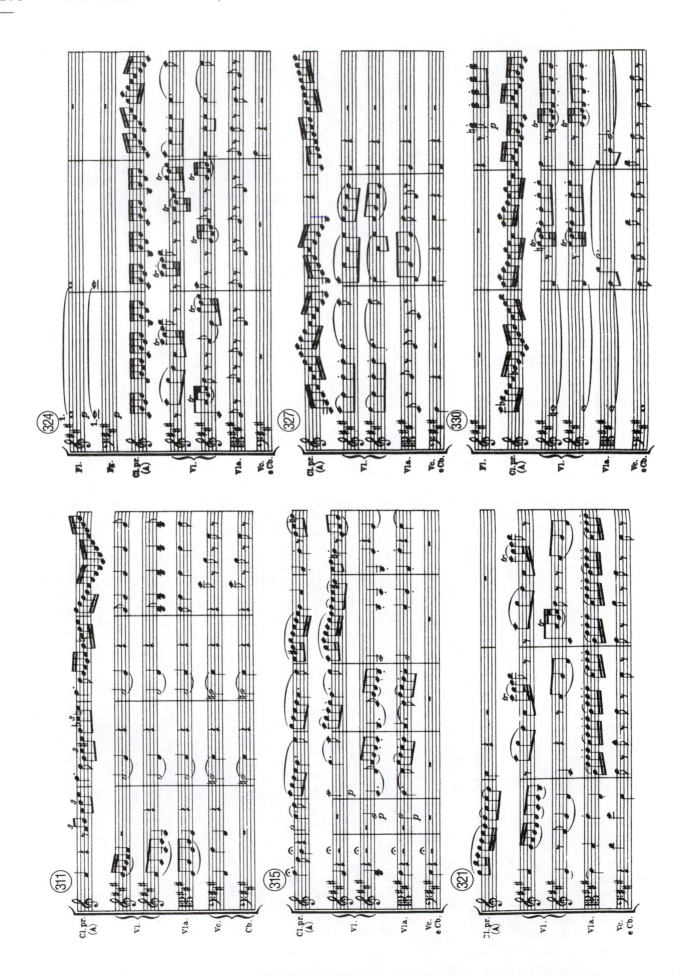

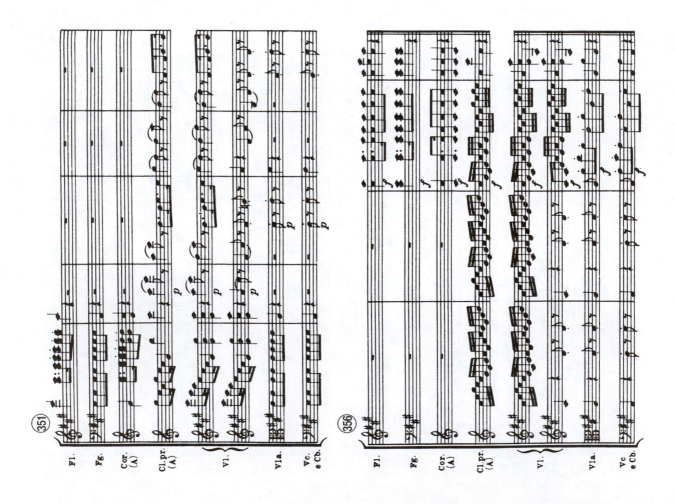

PIANO SONATA No. 1 in F MINOR

Op. 2, No. 1 (1795?), first and third movements

Ludwig van Beethoven (1770–1827)

■ FIRST MOVEMENT

Beethoven's thirty-two piano sonatas, a cornerstone of the Classical repertoire, illustrate each stage of the composer's creative life. Their study will greatly reward not only those who play them, but all who take interest in music and its structure. In examining the following movement, consider the thematic design, the sections of the form, and the broad tonal structure. At a later stage of study you might consider motivic relationships such as that between bar 2 and 140–142. The later bars describe an enlargement of the former. Similarly, the descent C-B♭-A♭-G-F-E♮, first appearing in bars 7–8, will be found in enlarged and elaborated form elsewhere in the movement.[9] What is the effect of these enlargements?

---

[9] Heinrich Schenker analyzes the entire sonata in the second volume of *Der Tonwille* (Vienna: A. J. Gutmann [= Universal Edition], 1921–24; repr. Georg Olms Verlag [Hildesheim, 1990]; Eng. trans. ed. Wm. Drabkin [New York: Oxford University Press, forthcoming]). See also Charles Burkhart, "Schenker's 'Motivic Parallelisms'" (Journal of Music Theory, 22/2 1978, p. 159ff.); also A. Cadwallader and D. Gagné, *Analysis of Tonal Music: A Schenkerian Approach* (Oxford University Press: 1998, p. 4ff). Each movement of all 32 sonatas receives detailed description in Donald Francis Tovey's *Companion to Beethoven's Pianoforte Sonatas* (London, 1931; repr. New York: A.M.S. Press, 1976).

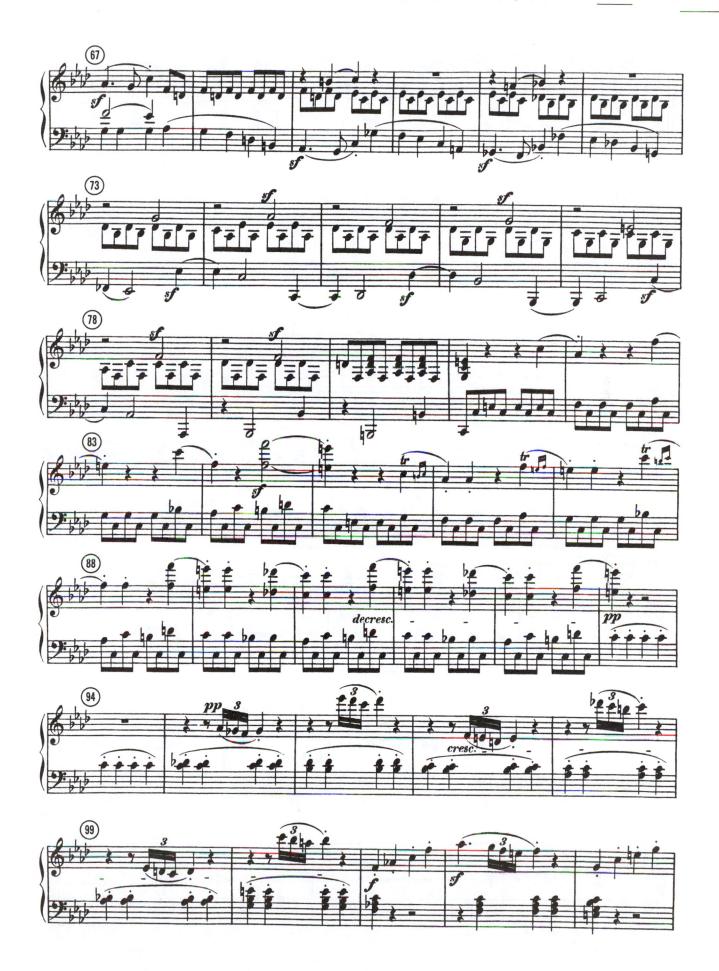

THIRD MOVEMENT

Compare the form of bars 1–40 with that of the trio. What is the harmony in bars 1–2? How do bars 13–14 fit into the phrase (and where is the small note to be placed)? Pianists will want to assess the fingering in bars 59–62 because it is Beethoven's own; apart from the question of playability, does it have *musical* advantages?[10] (For other pieces with trio, see "Trio" in the General Index.)

---

[10] Jeanne Bamberger treats this interesting question in her article, "The Musical Significance of Beethoven's Fingerings in the Piano Sonatas," *The Music Forum*, vol. IV (New York: Columbia University Press, 1976; see pp. 250f).

PIANO SONATA No. 4 in E FLAT MAJOR
Op. 7 (1796–1797?), second movement

Ludwig van Beethoven (1770–1827)

Study the form of this music of *"gran expressione."* How does it differ from that of the slow movement on page 228, which Beethoven composed at about the same time? A striking detail is the bass F♯–F♮ in measure 4. What becomes of this idea in the course of the movement?[11]

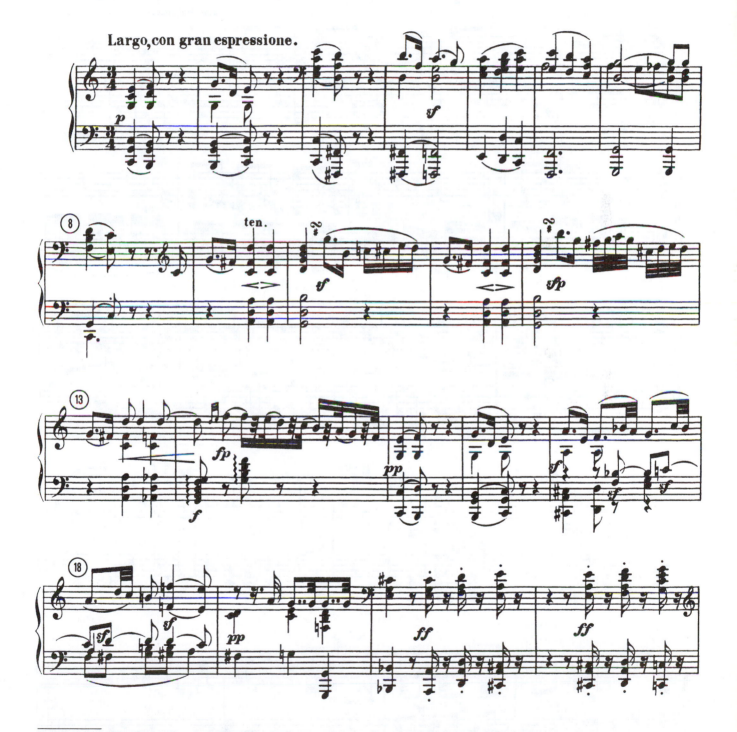

[11] Roger Kamien offers perceptive comment on this movement in "Chromatic Deatails in Beethoven's Op. 7" (*The Music Review*, August 1974, p. 149).

PIANO SONATA No. 5 in C MINOR
Op. 10, No. 1 (1796–1798), second movement

Ludwig van Beethoven (1770–1827)

Sonata No. 5 was the first of Beethoven's sonatas to have three, rather than four, movements. This movement reveals a form that he used more than once for slow movements. What is the relation of bars 24–27 to 28–31? After bar 31, where is the first full cadence? What is the significance of the chord in bar 45?

PIANO SONATA No. 8 in C MINOR ("SONATE PATHÉTIQUE")
Op. 13 (1797–1798)
Ludwig van Beethoven (1770–1827)

The adjective "Pathétique" in the title of this work seems to have come from Beethoven, or at least to have been approved by him, unlike *"Moonlight" Sonata,* which was a publisher's concoction. At any rate, the word is appropriate. It means full of pathos, or moving the feelings, particularly the feeling of sympathy for suffering. The quality of such feeling is noble, possibly tragic, not merely sentimental.

The first movement, both in its emotional depth and in its structure, far exceeds anything Beethoven had so far written. What is unusual about its form? And what is the form of the second and third movements?[12]

attacca subito il Allegro.

---

[12] Advanced analytic comment on the first movement is in Ernst Oster's article, "Register and the Large-Scale Connection" (*Journal of Music Theory*, April 1961, pp. 67–71).

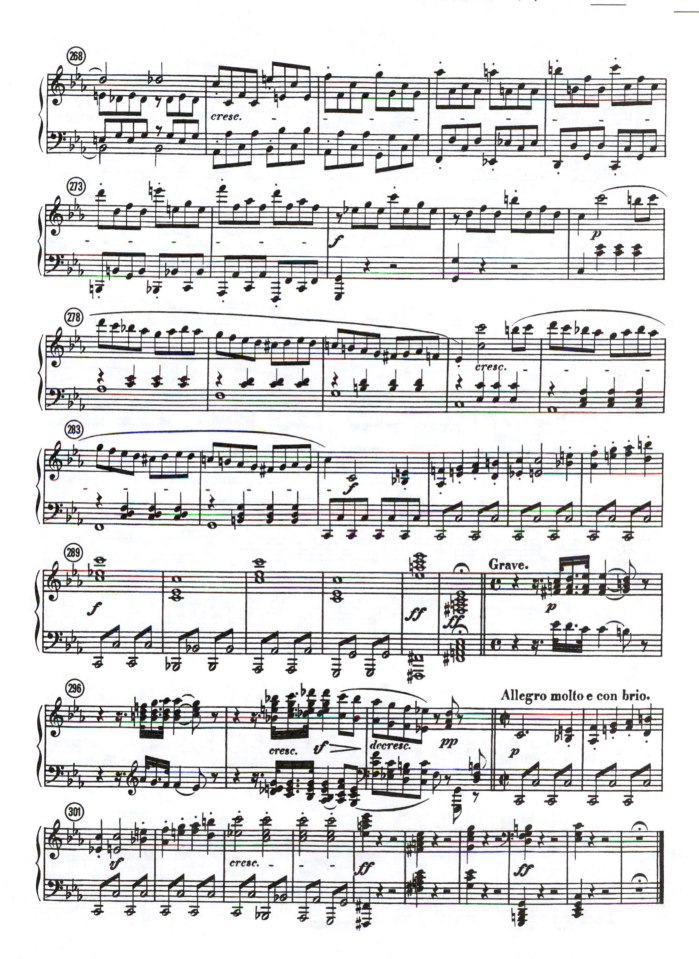

II

Adagio cantabile.

III

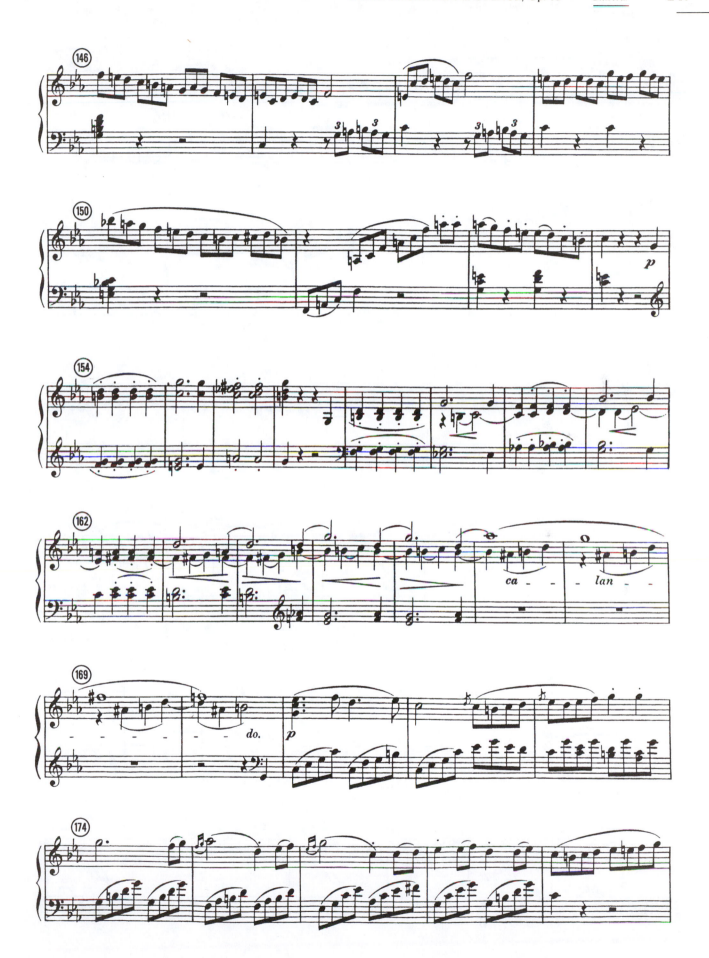

PIANO SONATA No. 9 in E MAJOR
Op. 14, No. 1 (1798–1799)

Ludwig van Beethoven (1770–1827)

This is the middle movement of a three-movement sonata. Beethoven gave it no name other than "Allegretto," which is to be taken here as a pulse of one to the bar. What characteristic type of middle movement does it most resemble? Consider the opening two bass notes: E–C. How does the rest of the movement expand upon this beginning? And why is there a bar at the end with no music in it?[13]

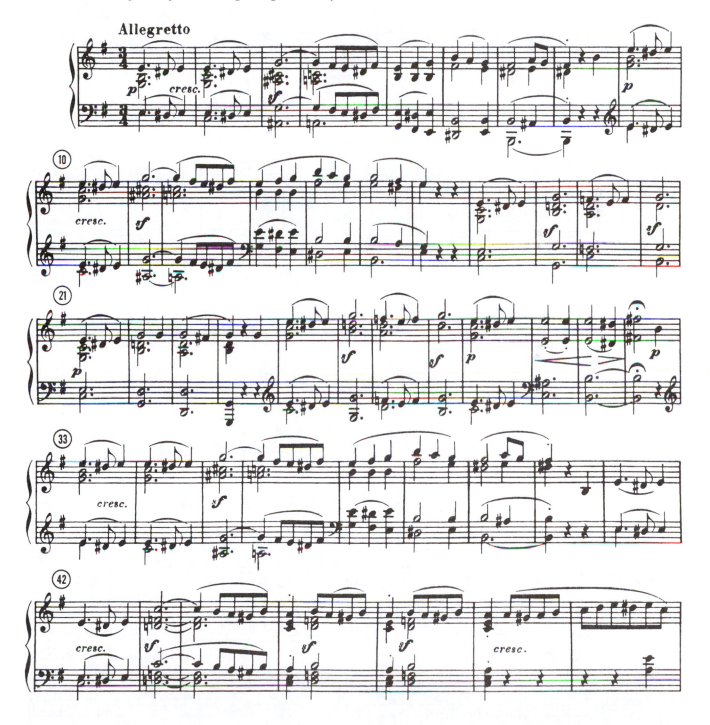

[13] In the first two editions of his biography of the composer, Beethoven's friend Anton Schindler gives a valuable and quite detailed description of how Beethoven performed this sonata. Carl Schachter discusses this movement in "Rhythm and Linear Analysis," *The Music Forum*, vol. 5, 1980).

SONATA FOR VIOLIN AND PIANO
Op. 24 (1800–1801), first movement

Ludwig van Beethoven (1770–1827)

Popularly called "The Spring" because of its sunny disposition, this work shows Classical sonata form worked out for *two* equal instruments—a genuine compositional problem. In this connection, compare this movement with that of the Brahms clarinet sonata (page 373), which solves the problem in another style.

This movement's harmonic structure also deserves investigation. At what point does it markedly differ from the more usual Classical practice?[14]

[14] See David Beach, "A Recurring Pattern in Mozart's Music" (*Journal of Music Theory* 27/I, 1983, p. 1); see also Carl Schachter, "The Sketches for the Sonata for Piano and Violin, Op. 24," *Beethoven Forum* 3, (Lincoln: University of Nebraska Press, 1991, p. 107), which includes much analytic comment on the first movement.

PIANO SONATA No. 15 in D MAJOR
Op. 28 (1801), third movement

Ludwig van Beethoven (1770–1827)

How would you describe the character of this short piece? Compare the form of the scherzo section with that of the trio. How does the D major harmony in, say, bar 78 or 79 differ in function from the one in bar 5? Why does Beethoven say to play the trio's last sixteen bars only one time— *una volta?*

Trio.

La seconda parte una volta.

Scherzo Da capo.

PIANO SONATA No. 21 in C MAJOR ("WALDSTEIN")
Op. 53 (1803–1804), first movement
Ludwig van Beethoven (1770–1827)

Dedicated to a patron, Count von Waldstein, and often identified by his name, this sonata opens with a tumultuous allegro of great scope. How has Beethoven here modified the traditional procedures of Classical sonata form? Where is the movement's chief climax?[15]

---

[15] Roger Kamien analyzes portions of this movement in "Aspects of the Recapitulation in Beethoven Piano Sonatas," *The Music Forum*, vol. IV (New York: Columbia University Press, 1976, p. 205ff). See also Charles Rosen, *Sonata Forms* (op. cit., pp. 79–80 and 289–290).

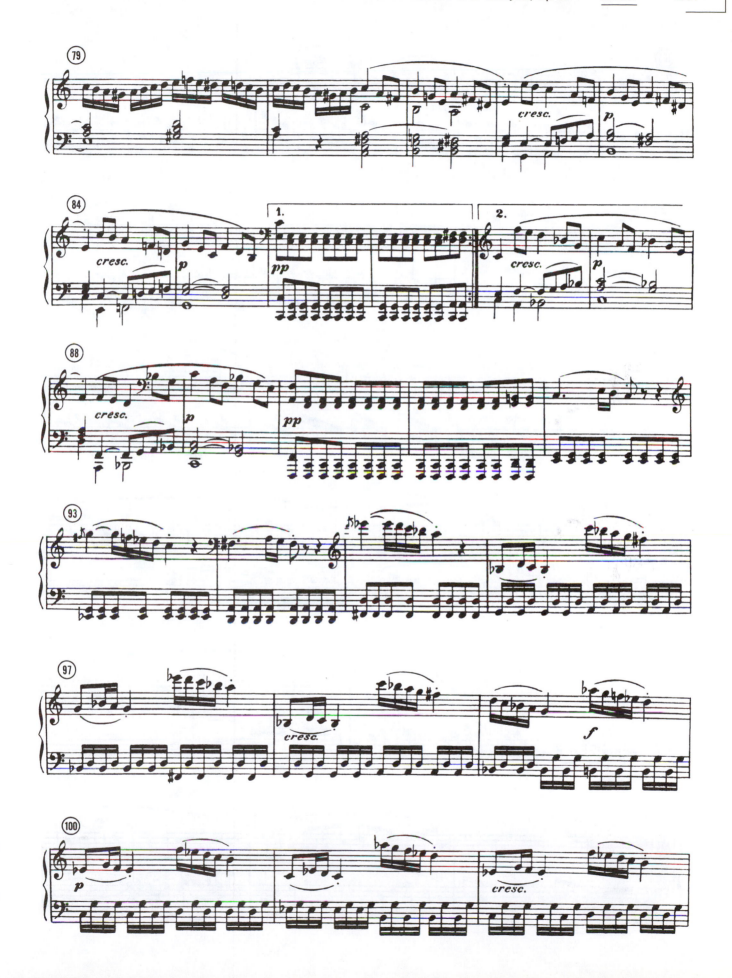

STRING QUARTET in E MINOR

Op. 59, No. 2 (1806), first movement

Ludwig van Beethoven (1770–1827)

The second of the three celebrated "Rasumovsky" quartets (all dedicated to and hence nicknamed for the chamber-music-loving Russian ambassador to Vienna) reveals Beethoven at full mastery, exploring new ways of composing for the most refined and flexible of media. The opening abrupt chords might at first be taken as mere introduction, but they will play a far deeper role in the course of the movement. How does the second theme begin? Bar 48 clearly seems to be headed for a full cadence which, in bar 49, is rudely cut off just before its expected tonic. Does that tonic ever arrive? And how does the recapitulation arrive? What is the significance of the key that starts to emerge at bar 171? How long does it endure? Notice that the movement ends *piano.* Overlooking the fact that many first movements appropriately end loudly, what advantage can a first movement's ending softly have for the entire quartet?

B.44.

STRING QUARTET No. 13 in B FLAT MAJOR

Op. 130 (1825–1826), second movement

Ludwig van Beethoven (1770–1827)

Though Beethoven in his late string quartets entered musical realms never explored before (and perhaps since), he still based these works on traditional forms and genres. What genre is represented by this terse *Presto* (from the composer's only six-movement work)? How have conventions been modified here? And how retained?

Part Four

Romantic Compositions

SMALL FORMS

Because one aspect of the Romantic sensibility was a predilection for miniatures, it is natural that Part Four include a large and varied selection of two- and three-part "song forms." Such forms occur in Part Three as well, but there they are usually embedded in larger forms; here they are more likely to be complete compositions. The seven pieces from Schumann's *Album for the Young*, chosen to progress from simple to elaborate, can serve to introduce elementary form categories. More advanced are the Mendelssohn *Song Without Words*, most of the Chopin preludes and mazurkas, and the Brahms A minor and C major intermezzos. To locate further examples and specific form categories, start with "Song form" in Index I.

CHROMATICISM

Part Four also provides many examples of nineteenth-century chromaticism useful for the study of harmony as well as analysis. Pieces that are quite chromatic all or most of the way through are Chopin's E minor and E major preludes and F minor mazurka, Franck's *Moderato* from his Chorale No. 1 for organ, Wolf's song "In der Frühe," and the Prelude to Act I of Wagner's *Tristan*. Numerous other pieces have significant chromatic details or passages, among them Schubert's *Waltz, Moment Musical*, and "Nähe des Geliebten"; Hensel's "O Herbst"; Schumann's "Er, der Herrlichste von allen"; Chopin's E flat major prelude, A minor and A flat major mazurkas, and D flat major nocturne; Brahms's C major intermezzo and the third of his *Variations*; and Amy Beach's song, "Dark is the Night."

Highly chromatic works in other parts of the book are Gesualdo's "Moro lasso," Purcell's *Lament*, the recitative from Handel's *Messiah*, Bach's *Crucifixus* from the B minor mass, the *Largo* from Joseph Haydn's string quartet, the seventh in Mozart's *Variations* as well as his C minor fantasia, and Debussy's *Afternoon of a Faun*. The appendices provide a very chromatic piece of jazz (page 553) and several chromatic chorales, notably *O Mensch, bewein' dein' Sünde gross*, and *So gehst du nun*. Additional chromatic phenomena are listed in Index I under entries beginning with the word "Chromatic," and many examples of individual chords, sequences, and modulations are cited in the chromatic section of Index II.

Vocal Music

The reason for using a vocal work in a harmony class will probably be because it contains a particular chord or voice-leading technique, not because it is vocal. Analysis classes, on the other hand, might well devote time to analytic issues that are peculiar to vocal music, particularly the union of music and words. It is all too easy for students to make the mistake of thinking of a vocal work in terms of music only, especially when its words are in a foreign tongue. It is important to remember that in most such works, particularly art songs, the text existed first, and that the composer, before composing a note, had to be deeply aware of its meaning. Likewise the analyst of a song, just like a singer, must understand the text thoroughly to make a valid interpretation of the song. The ideal is to discover how ideas in the text are represented in the music. Pointing to the music's general mood or to instances of "text painting" are at least modest first steps; deeper study will sometimes reveal more subtle relationships, as in, for example, the tonal metaphor in the two-bar introduction of Schubert's "Nähe des Geliebten."

In addition to the nine art songs in Part Four and the five more in Part Five, there are two short choral pieces—Hensel's *O Herbst* in this part and, in Appendix B, Wagner's *Wach' auf!* from *Die Meistersinger*. All German and French examples are provided with literal translations.

Large Forms

Study of the larger "homophonic forms" will likely draw mainly on examples in Part III, but can be continued here with Schubert's *Moment Musical*, Clara Schumann's *Andante espressivo*, and Brahms's A major intermezzo and clarinet sonata. Wagner's prelude to *Tristan* and Gustav Mahler's *Adagietto* present another side of the Romantic spirit—the predilection for hugeness.

DER KÖNIG IN THULE
Volkstümliches Lied (1812)
Text: Johann Wolfgang von Goethe (1749–1832)

Carl Friedrich Zelter (1758–1832)

The late eighteenth century saw a rise of interest in folklore and in preserving it. This interest impelled scholars (like the Grimm brothers, who collected fairy tales) and early Romantic poets, like Goethe here, who wrote folklike "ballads" inspired by ancient legends that often had an air of mystery or the supernatural. (Another example is Goethe's *Erlking* on page 296). Such poems were very attractive to composers like C. F. Zelter, among others, whose many settings of them figure notably in the development of the early, pre-Schubertian lied.

We give Zelter's *The King of Thule* in this anthology because of its unusual vocal part. What is unusual about it? What effect might the composer have wanted to achieve by using this procedure in this particular song? By the way, do not conclude that this feature is typical of the early lied; indeed, only very rarely is it found *all the way through* a composition. But it is often found at certain spots in, say, bass arias or cello sonatas. Can you think of any such example? Should a performer of such a composition be aware when this feature occurs? Might he or she perform that spot with greater understanding?

We can give here only two of the poem's six stanzas. At the end the old king hurls his beloved goblet into the sea and dies.

Translation from Wigmore, Richard, *Schubert: The Complete Song Texts*, page 188, New York: Schirmer, Inc. Copyright 1988. Used by permission.

THREE LIEDER
Franz Schubert (1797–1828)

Most poems that serve as texts for lieder are written in stanzas of equal length. The following lieder demonstrate three common ways in which such stanzas are set to music. How do the three settings differ in this broad respect?

◼ NÄHE DES GELIEBTEN, D. 162

(1815)

Text: Johann Wolfgang von Goethe (1749–1832)

Suppose that the successive stanzas of a poem "progress" in that they, say, tell a story, or build in intensity. Consider that if the musical setting of such a poem is strophic, such a progression cannot be reflected in the music. Is this a disadvantage? Does the poem of *Nähe des Geliebten* (The Nearness of the Beloved) so progress? That is, does it have a climactic stanza? If so, should this progression be expressed, and if so, how?[1]

What idea in the poem might Schubert have intended to portray in his unusual piano introduction?

I think of thee when the sun's light
Gleams on the sea;
I think of thee when the moon's glimmer
Is painted on the waters.

I see thee when, far down the road,
Dust rises,
And in dead of night, when on the narrow footpath,
The traveler quakes.

I hear thee when, with a dull roar,
The waves surge up,
And in the grove, where often I go to listen,
When all is still.

I am with thee; though thou be ever so distant,
Thou art beside me!
The sun sinks, the stars will soon be shining.
O wert thou here!

Nähe des Geliebten is reprinted from Peters Edition No. 20a. Reprint permission granted by the publisher, C.F. Peters Corporation, New York.

[1] Walter Frisch's essay, "Schubert's *Nähe des Geliebten:* Transformation of the *Volkston*," in *Schubert / Critical and Analytical Studies*, ed. Walter Frisch (Lincoln: University of Nebraska Press, 1986, p. 175), provides interesting background, analysis, and evaluation.

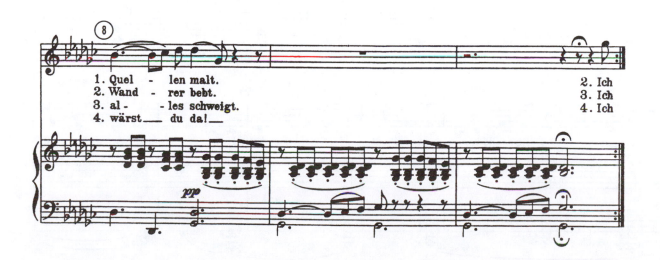

■ DER DOPPELGÄNGER

from *Schwanengesang*, D. 957 (1828)

Text: Heinrich Heine (1797–1856)

How are the three poetic stanzas treated in "The Double," one of Schubert's last, and most powerful, songs?

Still is the night, the streets are calm,
In this house lived my treasure;
She long ago left this town,
But the house still stands in the same place.

There stands also a man, and stares into the heavens
And wrings his hands for pain;
I shudder when his face I see,
[For] the moon shows me my own features.

Thou double, thou pale companion!
Why do you ape the love-sorrows
That tortured me in this place
So many nights in times gone by?

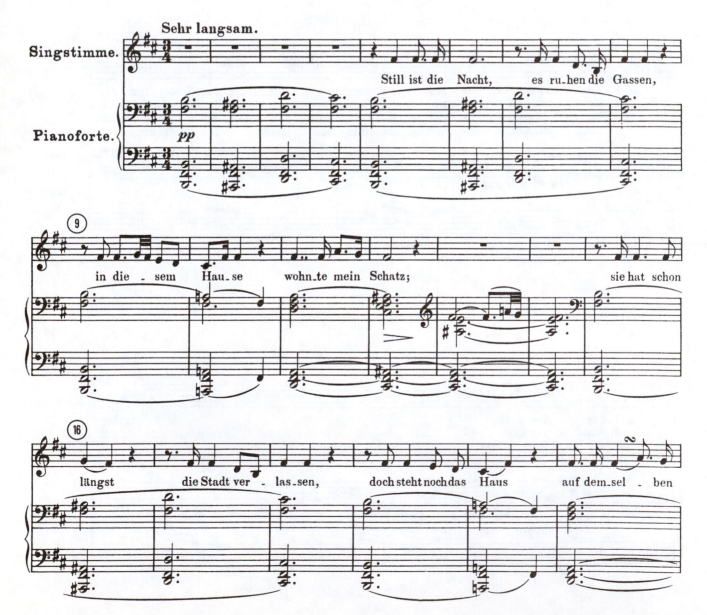

Platz.   Da steht auch ein Mensch,   und starrt in die Hö _ he,

cresc. poco a poco

und ringt die   Hände   vor Schmer _ zens _ ge _ walt;____   mir__ graust es,

fff   *ffz*   *decresc.*   *p*

wenn ich sein Ant _ litz se _ he,   der Mond zeigt mir   mei _ ne eig' _ ne Ge _ stalt.____

cresc.   *ffz*   *fff*

Du Dop _ pel _ gänger,   du bleicher Ge _ sel _ le!   was äffst du nach mein

decresc.   *p accelerando*   *cresc.*   *ff*

Lie _ besleid, das mich gequält auf die _ ser Stel _ le so man _ che

Nacht, in al _ ter Zeit?

ERLKÖNIG, D. 328

(1815)

Text: Johann Wolfgang von Goethe (1749–1832)

The close relation of the overall tonal scheme to the meaning of the text contributes much to the extraordinary effect of this famous song, composed when Schubert was eighteen.[2]

Who rides so late through night and wind?	*"Fair boy, wilt thou come with me?*
It is a father with his child;	*My lovely daughters shall wait on thee;*
He holds the boy in his arm,	*My daughters keep their nightly revels;*
He clasps him tight, he keeps him warm.	*They will rock thee, dance, and sing thee to sleep."*
"My son, why hidest thy face in fear?"	*"My father, my father, seest thou not*
"Seest thou not, Father, the Erlking?	*Erlking's daughters in that dark place?"*
The Erlking with crown and train?"	*"My son, my son, I see clearly;*
"My son, 'tis but a streak of mist."	*It is only the gleam of the old gray willows."*
"O dear child, come away with me!	*"I love thee, thy fair form ravishes me;*
Lovely games I'll play with thee!	*And if thou art not willing, I'll take thee by force."*
Many-colored flowers grow by the shore.	*"My father, my father, now he is seizing me!*
My mother has many golden robes."	*Erlking has done me harm!"*
"My father, my father, hearest thou not	*The father shudders, he rides fast,*
What Erlking softly promises me?"	*And holds in his arm the moaning child;*
"Be calm, be calm, my child;	*He reaches home with effort and toil:*
In the withered leaves rustles the wind."	*In his arms the child lay dead!*

---

[2] The resemblance of the left-hand piano motive to the overall tonal scheme is described in Charles Burkhart, "Schenker's 'Motivic Parallelisms'" *Journal of Music Theory* 22/2, Fall 1978, p. 157).

TWO PIANO PIECES
Franz Schubert (1797–1828)

These two pieces are grouped together not because they have any historical relation, but because both use a particular chromatic technique, the first simply, the second much more elaborately.

◼ WALTZ IN A FLAT MAJOR

Op. 9, No. 2 (D. 365) (1816)

In Schubert's day this piece was nickname *Trauerwalzer* (Mourning Waltz), but Schubert himself ridiculed the name. All the same, is there *some* sense to it?

◼ MOMENT MUSICAL NO. 6

from Sechs Moments Musicaux, Op. 94 (D. 780) (1824)

Schubert coined the French term *moments musicaux* for a set of character pieces of which the following one, rich in expressive chromaticism, is the last. Why are there two changes to the four-sharp signature? What is the form of the Allegretto? Of the entire piece? What are the historical antecedents of these forms?[3]

---

[3] A well-known article on this composition is Edward T. Cone's "Schubert's Promissory Note: An Exercise in Musical Hermeneutics" *19th-Century Music* 5/3 Spring 1982, pp. 233ff.; repr. and rev. in *Schubert, Critical and Analytical Studies*, Walter Frisch, ed. (Lincoln: University of Nebraska Press, 1986, pp. 13ff.).

Allegretto

O HERBST
A cappella chorus (1846)
Text: Joseph von Eichendorff (1788–1857)

Fanny Mendelssohn Hensel (1805–1847)

Though Fanny Mendelssohn rivaled her celebrated brother Felix as pianist, composer, and conductor, only a handful of her many works were published during her lifetime. She is known today chiefly for numerous songs and piano pieces, several chamber works, an orchestral overture, and several large choral works with orchestra. But because nearly 500 compositions still remain in manuscript (some in private possession), a complete assessment of her *oeuvre* has yet to be made.

In the year before her untimely death, she composed 17 short pieces for unaccompanied chorus. Written to texts by various German Romantic poets, they reveal great sensitivity to choral texture and poetic values. In bar 13 of the delicate *O Herbst,* how has she musically painted the word *öde,* meaning empty or desolate? Explain the augmented triad at bar 6, first beat, and the numerous secondary chords.[4]

O Autumn of gentle days,
all through your realm
how fantastic are your colors—
so fair, and yet so pale.

How bleak without companions
is my valley all across!
I hardly recognize you
in this solitude.

Such wondrous melody
comes from your pallid lips.
It is as though the ground
were gently opening beneath me

and I were resting, enfolded,
as you sing ever on—
as though the linden tree above
were shaking down her leaves and covering me.

O Herbst by Fanny Hensel-Mendelssohn from pages 4 and 5 of volume 5 of *Weltliche a-cappella-Choere von 1846* by Fanny Hensel-Mendelssohn, edited by Elke Mascha Blankenburg, Furore-Edition 514. Copyright 1988, used by permission.

[4] All of Hensel's secular choral works are recorded on CPO 999 012-2.

SONG WITHOUT WORDS
Op. 19b, No. 1 (1830)

Felix Mendelssohn (1809–1847)

Lieder ohne Worte (**Songs Without Words**) is the title of Mendelssohn's collection of forty-eight short piano pieces of markedly song-like character that he wrote at various periods of his life. Besides their artistic value, they are also well suited to the study of musical form. Explore the phrases and the form of this piece, the first in the collection. How do Mendelssohn's dynamics help express the form?

SEVEN PIECES
from *Album for the Young*, Op. 68 (1848)

Robert Schumann (1810–1856)

Like Bach and Bartók (see pages 63 and 447), and many other composers, Schumann wrote music for children. The following selection of pieces from his *Album for the Young* starts out easy and becomes increasingly challenging—both to play and to analyze. (For another short piece by Schumann see the *Theme* on page 356).

1—Melodie (Melody)

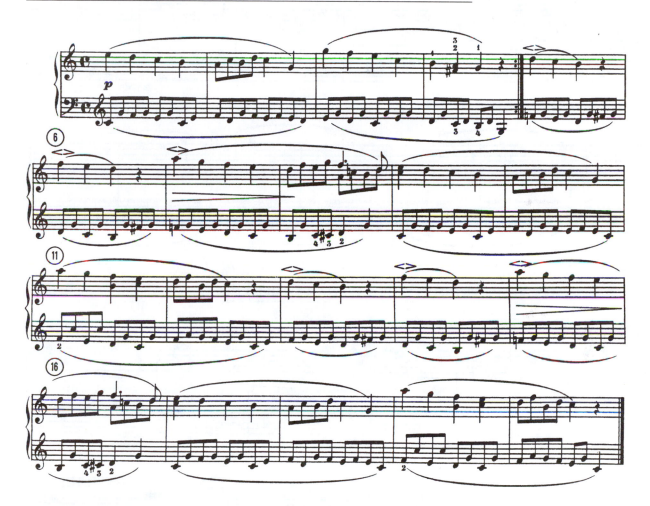

3—Trällerliedchen (Humming Song)

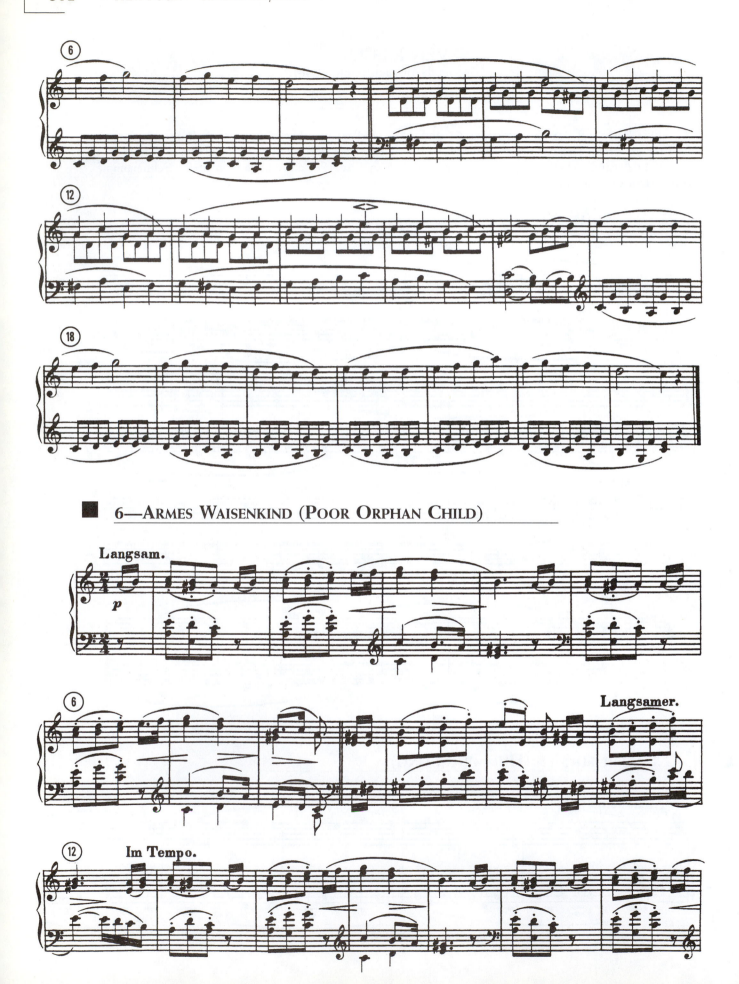

6—ARMES WAISENKIND (POOR ORPHAN CHILD)

8—WILDER REITER (WILD RIDER)

Explain all the $^6_4$ chords in this piece.

14—KLEINE STUDIE (LITTLE ETUDE)

Exactly how long is the first phrase of this little etude?

17—KLEINER MORGENWANDERER (LITTLE MORNING WANDERER)

Wanderer here means "hiker." This piece is a song for the trail. How does it manage to start with imitation? What happens to the phrases at bar 20, second ending?

31—KRIEGSLIED (WAR SONG)

VOGEL ALS PROPHET
from *Waldszenen*, Op. 82 (1848–1849)

Robert Schumann (*1810–1856*)

"The Prophetic Bird" from the character-piece cycle *Forest Scenes* is a typical Schumann study in biting dissonance. Explain the dissonances, especially the crunches in bars 11 and 13. Is the first note of the piece consonant or dissonant? What is the form of bars 1 through 18? Of the entire piece? Consider the use of the soft pedal (*Verschiebung*) in bars 23–24. Why did Schumann want it just here?

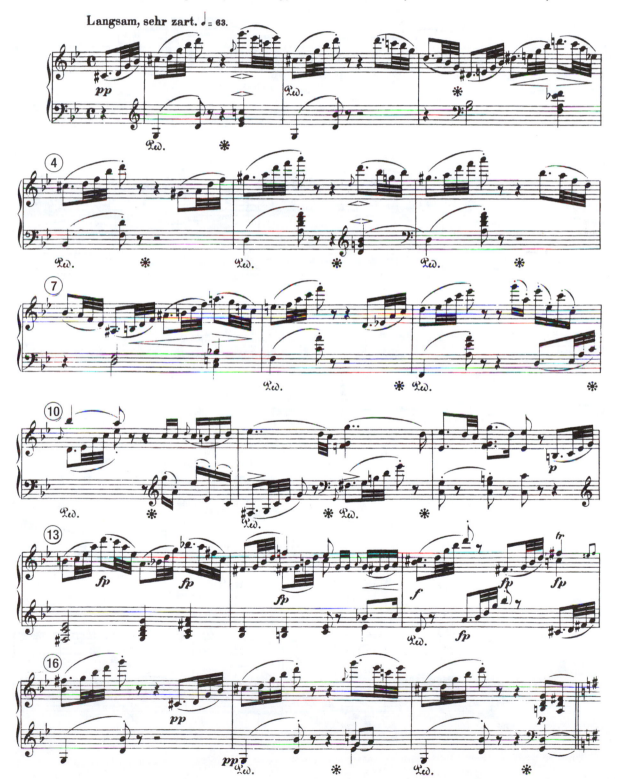

ER, DER HERRLICHSTE VON ALLEN
No. 2 from *Frauenliebe und -leben*, Op. 42 (1840)
Text: Adalbert von Chamisso (1781-1838)

Robert Schumann (1810—1856)

This selection from the song cycle *Woman's Life and Love* features expressive dissonance of a different sort from that on page 319. How does the dissonance arise in bars 4 and 5, and how should it be performed? At bar 54, the voice leading has strayed far afield; how does it get back on track? Why do all the beams cover *four* eighth notes? What is the musical form?

The complete cycle tells a familiar story in the voice of a young woman. By Song No. 2 he has not yet taken notice of her.

He, the most wonderful of all,	*Follow your course;*	*Only the worthiest of all*
how tender, how kind!	*I will merely gaze on your brightness,*	*may your choice make happy;*
Gentle lips, clear eyes,	*gaze on it humbly,*	*And I will bless that exalted one,*
high mind, and strong spirit.	*and be blessed and sad!*	*bless her a thousand times.*
As yonder, in the deep blue,	*Hear not the silent prayer*	*Then will I rejoice and weep;*
that star bright and glorious,	*I offer for your happiness.*	*blessed, blessed shall I be.*
so is he in my heaven—	*You must not know me, lowly maid,*	*Even should my heart break—*
bright and glorious, high, remote.	*O high and glorious star.*	*break, heart—what matters it?*

SIX PRELUDES
from Op. 28 (1836–1839)

Frédéric Chopin (1810–1849)

Inspired by the *Well-Tempered Clavier,* Chopin wrote a prelude for each of the twenty-four keys. In terms of both piano writing and musical structure, these aphoristic statements are among the most original creations in the Romantic literature.

■ PRELUDE 1 IN C MAJOR

In the right-hand part of this prelude, what effects are produced by the changes from two triplets to one quintuplet per bar? Where is the final cadence, and what is happening there?

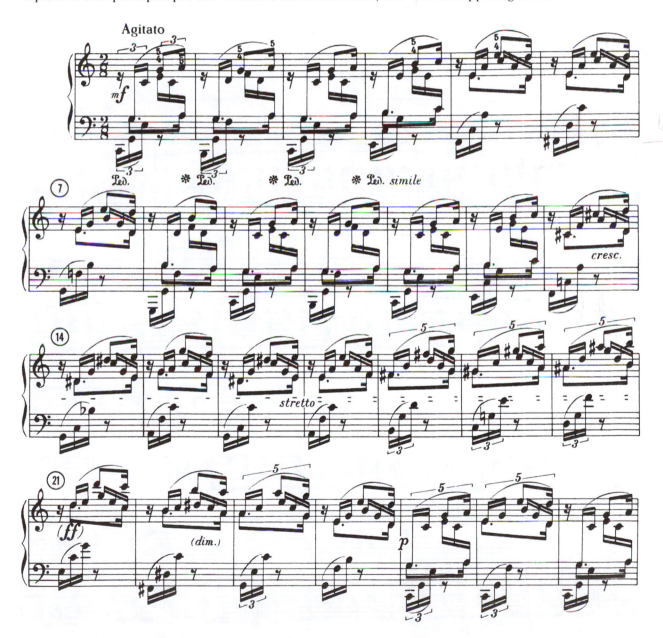

Prelude No. 1 is reprinted from Fryderyk Chopin/Complete Works, edited by I. J. Paderewski, L. Bronarski, and J. Turczynski, by permission of Polskie Wydawnictwo Muzyczne. Copyright 1949 by Instytut Fryderyka Chopina, Warsaw.

PRELUDE 4 IN E MINOR

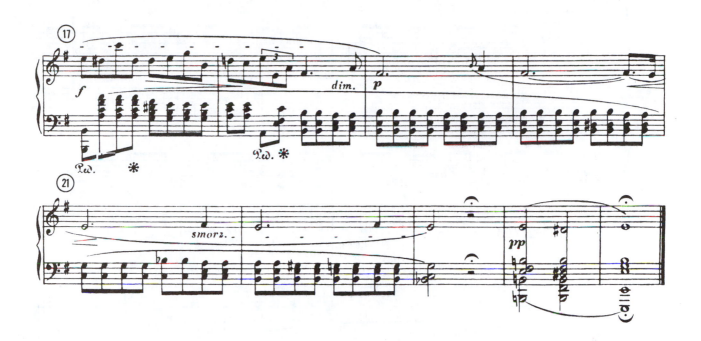

PRELUDE 6 IN B MINOR

How does the left-hand part serve simultaneously as principal melody and as foundation of the harmony? What happens at bars 7–8? Why did Chopin write a top-line slur there? Compare Schumann's *Wilder Reiter,* bars 9–16, on page 313.)[5]

[5] For an analysis, see Charles Burkhart, "The Polyphonic Melodic Line of Chopin's B-minor Prelude," in *Frederic Chopin / Preludes, Opus* 28, *Norton Critical Score* (New York: Norton, 1973, pp. 80ff., particularly Ex. 2, p. 83).

PRELUDE 9 IN E MAJOR

▣ PRELUDE 19 in E Flat Major[6]

---

[6] An analysis of the entire piece is given in Charles Burkhart, "The Two Curious Moments in Chopin's E Flat Major Prelude," in *Structure and Meaning in Tonal Music: Essays for Carl Schachter,* ed. Burstein and Gagné (Stuyvesant, NY: Pendragon Press: forthcoming).

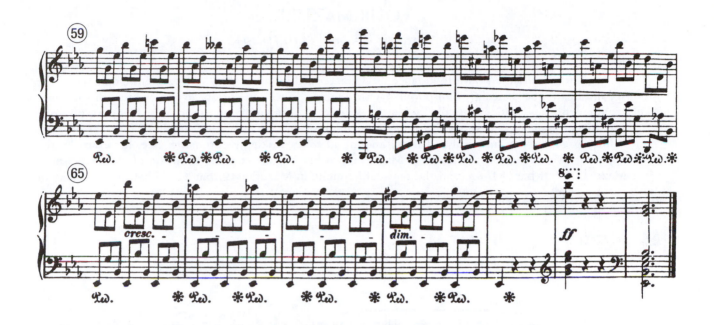

PRELUDE 20 IN C MINOR

FOUR MAZURKAS
Frédéric Chopin (1810–1849)

The mazurka, a Polish folk dance, is characterized by triple time and frequent emphasis on the second beat. The dance grew in popularity throughout European society in the eighteenth and nineteenth centuries, and eventually became a source for art music, most notably Chopin's fifty-one mazurkas for piano. These vivid, imaginative compositions, though built mainly of four-bar phrases, display great variety in mood and form, and are at times strikingly chromatic. See, for example, the apparent "wandering off the track" in Mazurka 6 at bar 17, the startling eruption of chromaticism in Mazurka 37 at bars 81–89, and the unusual harmony in Mazurka 49, bar 15. What do you make of these places?

■ Mazurka 5 in B Flat Major

Op. 7, No. 1 (1830–1831)

MAZURKA 6 IN A MINOR

Op. 7, No. 2 (1830–1831)

Reprinted from Peters Edition No. 1902. Reprint permission granted by the publisher, C.F. Peters Corporation, New York.

D.C. al Fine.

MAZURKA 37 IN A FLAT MAJOR

Op. 59, No. 2 (1845)

MAZURKA 49 IN F MINOR[7]

Op. posth. 68, No. 4 (ca. 1845–1846)

[7] For a discussion of the F-major middle section of this famous piece and a proposed earlier date, see Jeffrey Kallberg, "Chopin's Last Style" (JAMS 38, 1985, 264ff.). See also Felix Salzer, *Structural Hearing* (New York: Dover repr. 1962, vol. 1, p. 181).

NOCTURNE in D FLAT MAJOR
Op. 27, No. 2 (1835)

Frédéric Chopin (1810–1849)

The nocturne, a type of Romantic character piece featuring a lyrical melody over an arpeggiated accompaniment, was first developed by the Irish pianist John Field (1782–1837) and later brought to its highest form by Chopin. In this intensely expressive example, consider how the melodic design and broad harmonic scheme fuse to create an unusual form. By means of reduction, discover the essential harmony and voice leading of the remarkable passage at bars 40–46. What is particularly noteworthy about bars 58–59?[8]

---

[8] A few important corrections have been made in the edition reproduced here. Felix Salzer discusses this work in *Structural Hearing* (op. cit., vol. 1, p. 251).

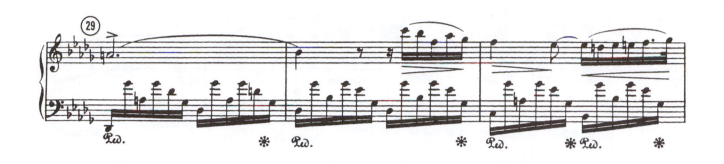

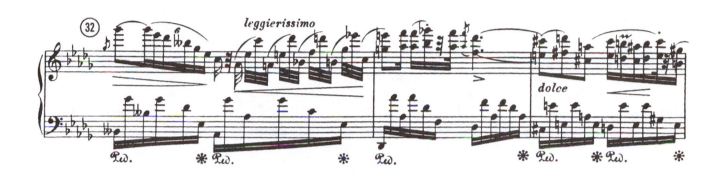

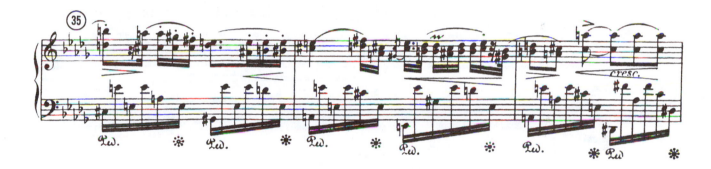

PRELUDE to ACT I

from *Tristan und Isolde* (1857–1859)
Arrangement for piano: Hans von Bülow

Richard Wagner (1813–1883)

An external problem posed by Wagner's great music drama, *Tristan und Isolde*—one that has fascinated musicians ever since its creation—is its relation to traditional tonality. Is this music tonal? Atonal? A mixture of both? These questions will never be answered to the satisfaction of all, but they inevitably arise in any serious study of the work. In the prelude, can a case be made for a "main" key despite the near absence of V-I cadences? In considering this question, remember that the prelude does not come to a formal conclusion but, rather, ends with a transition to Scene 1.[9]

Another aspect of the prelude, and somewhat less elusive than its tonality, is the role of the seven interrelated leitmotifs that recur throughout. The first appearances of these motives are as follows:

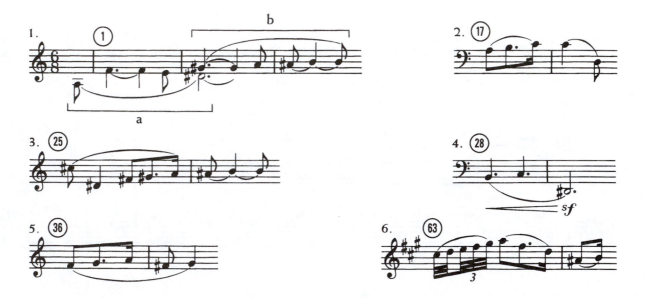

The matter of assigning specific programmatic meanings to the motives is particularly risky in *Tristan,* because this opera is concerned much more with psychological states than with identifiable objects of external reality. However, five of these motives have traditionally been assigned labels that perhaps can be applied without too much oversimplification: No. 1a is called the motive of Suffering, 1b Desire, No. 2 the Look or Glance, No. 3 the Love Potion, and No. 4 Death. Locate all the occurrences of the motives in the prelude. How do they contribute to the large, slowly emerging form?[10]

The piano arrangement here was made under the eyes of Wagner himself by Hans von Bülow, eminent pianist and conductor, who conducted the first performance of the opera in 1865. Although an arrangement can be of great help in analysis, it is of course a poor substitute for the full score, a sample of which has been appended.

---

[9] The Prelude is not a prelude to the entire opera, as commonly supposed, but an introduction to Act I, of which it is an integral part.
[10] Robert Bailey's *Wagner / Prelude and Transfiguration from Tristan and Isolde,* Norton Critical Score (New York: Norton, 1985) includes reprints of analytic essays by many well-known writers. Ernest Newman's *The Wagner Operas* (New York: Knopf, 2nd ed. 1963), an excellent introduction to its subject, contains insightful discussion of the *Tristan* leitmotifs on page 207ff. His discussion of the Prelude is reprinted in Bailey, pp. 153ff.

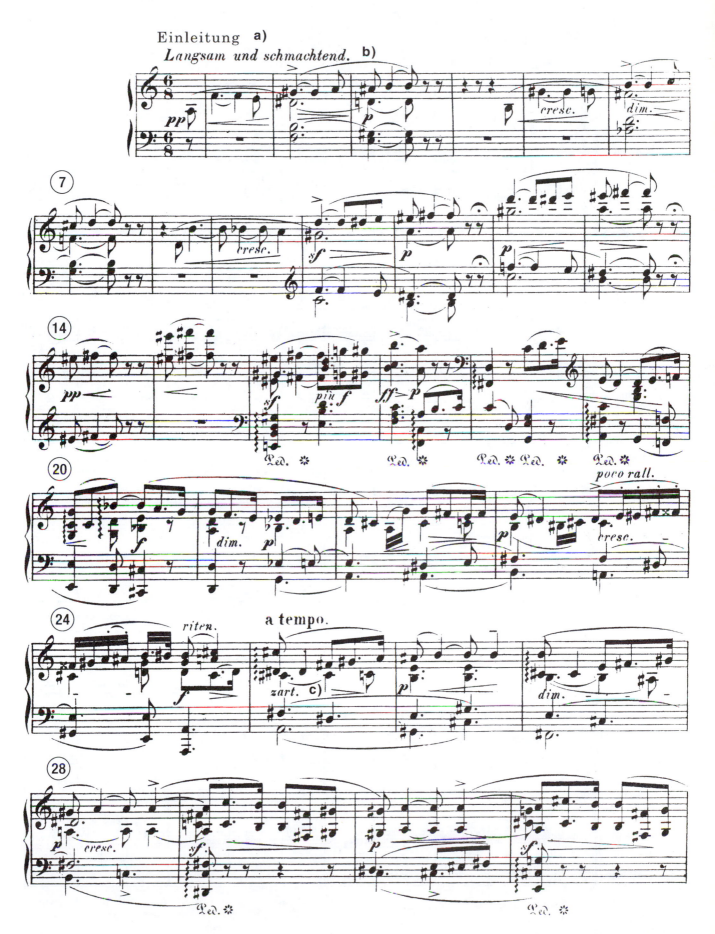

a) Introduction   b) Slowly and yearning   c) tenderly, gently

Piano arrangement continues on page 348.

Einleitung

Langsam und schmachtend

d) on the G string

e) animated   f) becoming animated

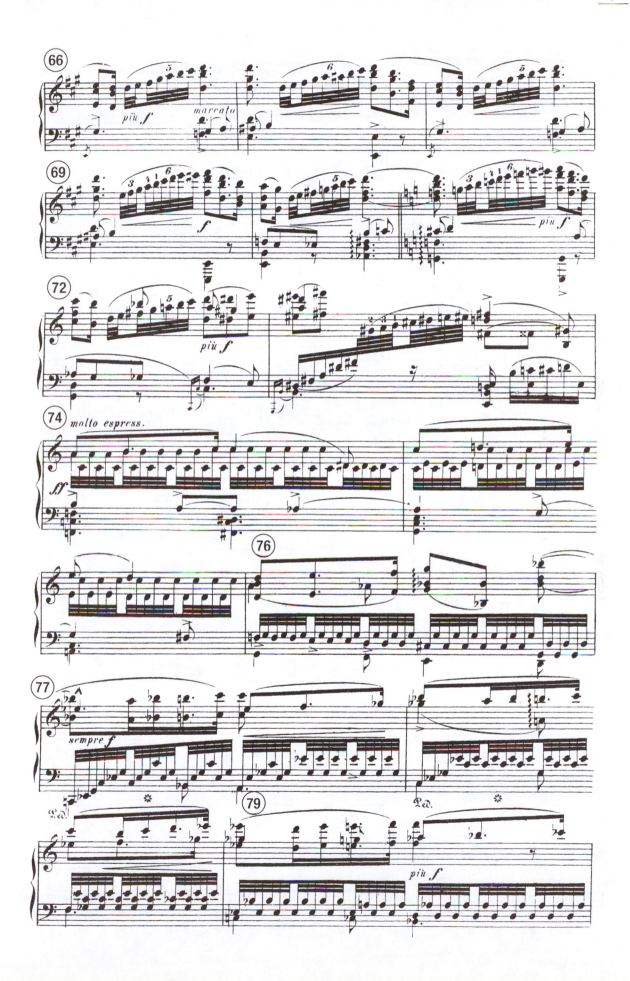

g) Gradually holding back somewhat the tempo   h) The curtain goes up

ANDANTE ESPRESSIVO

No. 3 of *Quatre pièces fugitives*, Op. 15 (publ. 1845)

Clara Schumann (1819–1896)

Clara Wieck, gifted daughter and also pupil of the famous piano teacher Friedrich Wieck, became an internationally known and widely admired concert pianist and composer by the age of 18. Two years later she married the poor and relatively unknown Robert Schumann and soon found that the demands of a growing family (the couple had eight children), together with ever-expanding concert and teaching careers, left her little time for composing. After Robert's untimely death in 1856, she abandoned composition entirely. Still, she managed to write, in addition to many piano pieces, some twenty-five songs, a masterful piano trio, and a strikingly original piano concerto. Her music, often harmonically bold, reflects the advanced tendencies of the day.[11]

The *Andante espressivo* comes from a group of four pieces Schumann originally published under the French title shown above, *"fugitive"* here meaning something like "fleeting"—a fleeting idea caught on the wings of inspiration, as it were. The overall form of this meditative piece is clear enough, but, as in many Romantic character pieces, the boundaries of the large sections are intentionally somewhat obscured, or "smoothed over." Consider just how this is done here. Also plot the main keys of the piece, noting how the changes of key are effected. In the middle of bar 14, will the *piano* dynamic be softer or louder than what immediately precedes? And why does Schumann place it exactly here?

Andante Espressivo from "Pianoforte-Werke zu zwei Händen" by Clara Schumann. Copyright by Breitkopf and Härtel. Used with permission.

---

[11] For an interesting account of the composer's life and work, see Nancy B. Reich, *Clara Schumann: The Artist and the Woman* (Ithaca, NY: Cornell University Press, 1985).

MODERATO
from *Chorale No. 1 in E major* for organ

César Franck (1822–1890)

During his long tenure as organist at the church of Sainte-Clotilde in Paris, the Belgian César Franck composed, among other works, a group of large organ pieces designed for concert rather than for liturgical use. They include the *Trois Chorals (Three Chorales),* each of which is based on an original, somewhat chorale-like melody. From the first of the three, *Chorale in E Major,* we give the opening section, marked *Moderato,* which presents the complete "chorale" in a simple homophonic setting. The organ pedals remain silent throughout this section but are used in the remainder of the work—an elaborate free variation of the chorale.

Discover the colorful display of *chromatic mediants* here, particularly the numerous real sequences lying a third apart, noting how each fits into the phrase. Also note the main keys of the piece and how they relate to each other. "GREAT" and "SWELL" are separate groups of pipes that are played from separate keyboards and that can be registrated differently. Franck was one of the first organ composers to indicate in detail the registrations he wanted, and those shown here are his. Listen to their effect on a recording of this work. What role do they play in the composition?

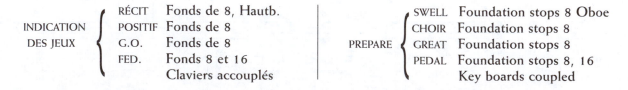

INDICATION DES JEUX	{	RÉCIT	Fonds de 8, Hautb.		PREPARE	{	SWELL	Foundation stops 8 Oboe
		POSITIF	Fonds de 8				CHOIR	Foundation stops 8
		G.O.	Fonds de 8				GREAT	Foundation stops 8
		FED.	Fonds 8 et 16				PEDAL	Foundation stops 8, 16
			Claviers accouplés					Key boards coupled

Otez Gambe et Hautbois –
Mettez Voix humaine et Tremblant
Gamba Oboe in –
Draw Vox humana, tremulant.

VARIATIONS ON A THEME
OF ROBERT SCHUMANN (Excerpt)
Op. 9 (1854)

Johannes Brahms (1833–1897)

In the summer of 1853, the young Johannes Brahms paid his first visit to the home of Robert and Clara Schumann—the beginning of a life-long friendship. That same year Clara had composed a set of piano variations on a short piece by Robert, the fourth piece in his *Bunte Blätter* (Colored Leaves), Op. 99. The next year, when Robert became ill, Brahms undertook to compose variations on the same theme. An expression of his respect and concern, this work, besides being based on Schumann's theme, contains various subtle references to other Schumann compositions as well, and also to one by Clara.

Discover the relation of each variation to the theme. How do they go beyond classical variation procedure (as illustrated in the Mozart variations on page 164)? Which variation adheres most closely to that procedure? Which is farthest from it, and how so? The complete work has sixteen variations. Several of the later ones, including No. 14, which we give here, show Brahms's skill as a contrapuntist. These may have been another expression of homage to Robert, who was deeply interested in the counterpoint of J. S. Bach.

Var. V.
Allegro capriccioso.

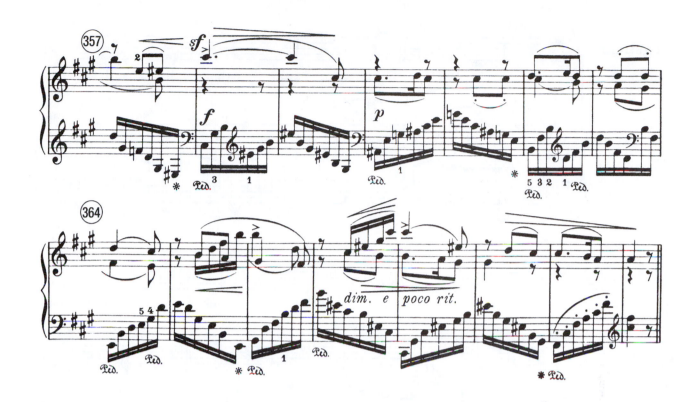

WIE MELODIEN ZIEHT ES MIR
Op. 105, No. 1 (1886)
Text: Klaus Groth

Johannes Brahms (1833–1897)

This well-known song by one of the greatest masters of the German lied is from a set of five expressly written for low voice. The poem that inspired it treats a most unusual (for a lied) subject—the nature of artistic creation, particularly the creation of a lyric poem.

Like melodies something steals	*If the Word comes and grasps it*	*Yet there dwells in verse*
gently through my mind,	*and brings it before the eye,*	*a hidden fragrance*
like spring flowers it blooms	*like gray mist it pales*	*which softly, from its silent core,*
and drifts away like fragrance.	*and vanishes like a breath.*	*calls forth a moistened eye.*

To paraphrase: The first vague feelings of inspiration, like melodies or fragrances, waft fleetingly through the poet's mind. They elude objectification in words; in the attempt to understand them, they vanish. Only in the form of a lyric poem—rhymed verse—can these inchoate feelings be communicated and move others to tears. In short, they succeed only when realized as art.[12]

How has Brahms set this text? How does his composition express the poem's meaning?

---

[12] This paraphrase has profited from the excellent articles by both Austin Clarkson and Edward Laufer published as "Analysis Symposium: Brahms Op. 105/1" in (*Journal of Music Theory*, vol. 15, 1971, pp. 6–57; repr. in Readings in *Schenkerian Analysis and Other Approaches*, Maury Yeston, ed. ([New Haven: Yale University Press, 1977], pp. 230–272).

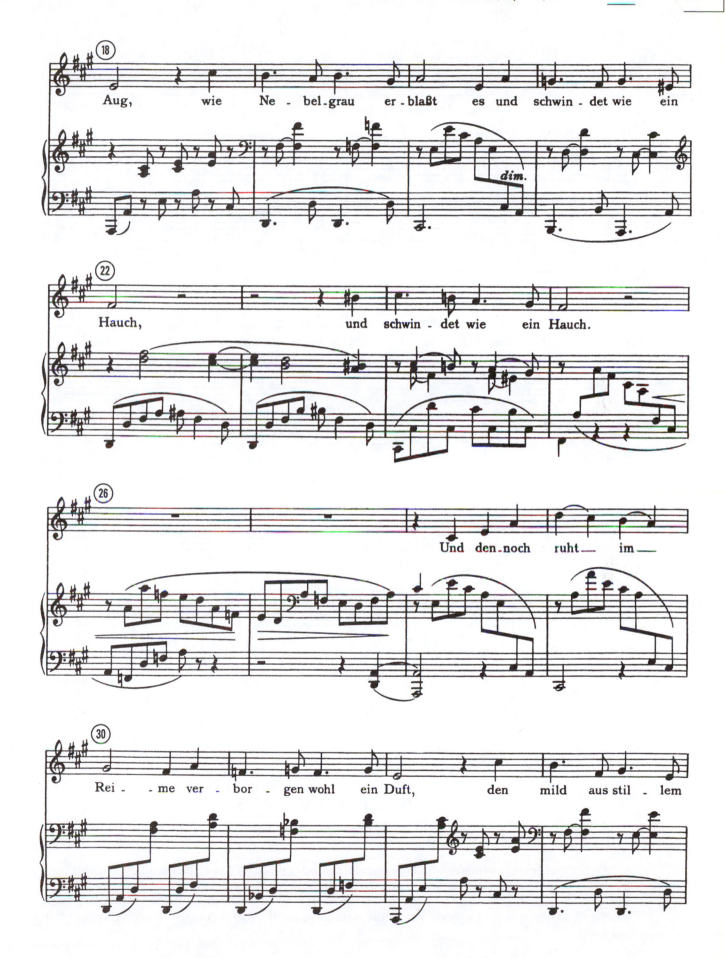

THREE INTERMEZZOS
Johannes Brahms (1833–1897)

Brahms contributed much to the Romantic character piece for piano, giving to many of his compositions in this genre the title "Intermezzo." An important consideration in studying each of the following intermezzos is the way a section or an entire piece will be unified by the repetition of a single motive. Another is how the pieces reflect the traditional small forms, yet realize them in highly original ways.

INTERMEZZO IN A MINOR

Op. 76, No. 7 (publ. 1879)

INTERMEZZO IN A MAJOR

Op. 118, No. 2 (1893)

INTERMEZZO IN C MAJOR

Op. 119, No. 3 (1893)

Grazioso e giocoso.

SONATA in F MINOR for CLARINET and PIANO

Op. 120, No. 1 (1894), first movement

Johannes Brahms (1833–1897)

Late in his career, his friendship with the clarinetist Richard Mühlfeld inspired Brahms to compose several important chamber works using that instrument. In the elegiac movement given here, compare the opening eight notes with their reappearance starting in bar 90. Such "motivic transformation," prevalent throughout this piece, is typical of much of Brahms's late work. How does this technique seem to point to future developments in the history of music?[13] This movement's form, though rooted in tradition, also reveals typically Brahmsian characteristics. What is happening beginning at bar 53? At the recapitulation, how is the opening key regained? Finally, a composer of an equal-partner duo must take care not to allow either instrument to assume a merely accompanimental role for too long. Go through the movement noting how Brahms distributes the material—both the main and the subordinate lines—between the two instruments. (And see page 251 for an earlier solution to this problem.)

---

[13] An interesting essay in this connection is Arnold Schoenberg's "Brahms the Progressive," in *Style and Idea* (New York: Philosophical Library, 1950; expanded edition, Leonard Stein, ed., New York: St. Martin's Press, 1975). See also Walter Frisch, *Brahms and the Principle of Developing Variation* (Berkeley: University of California Press, 1984, pp. 147–151).

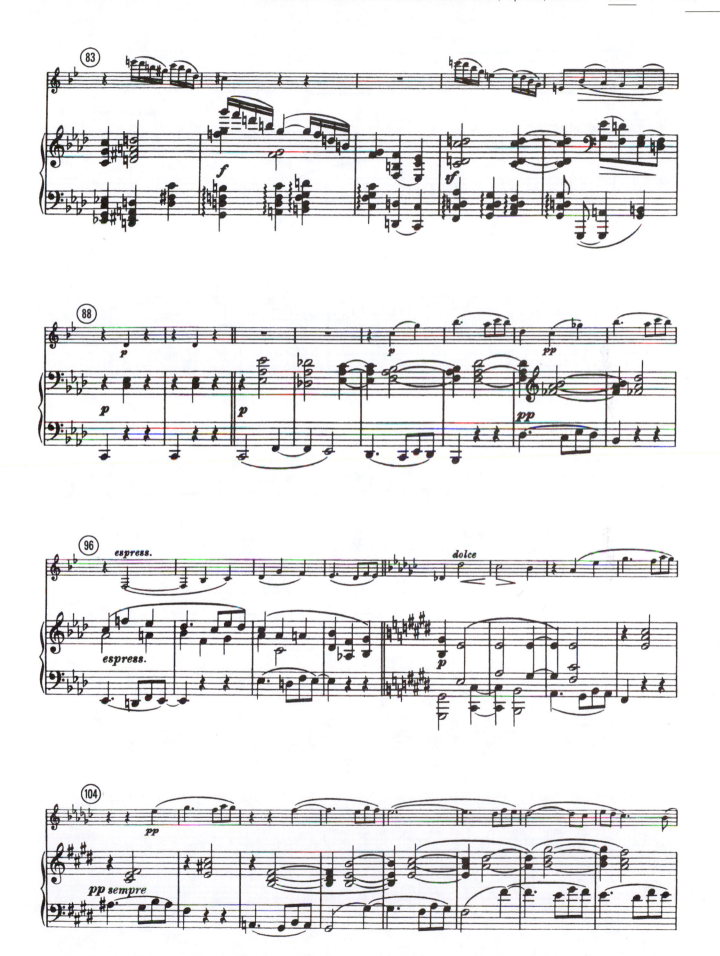

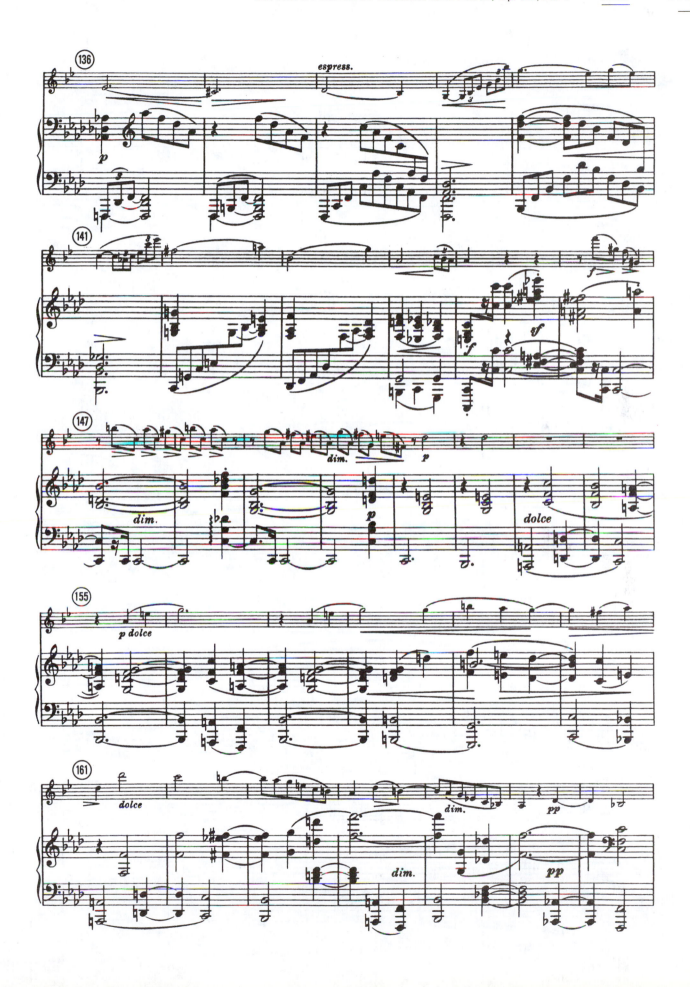

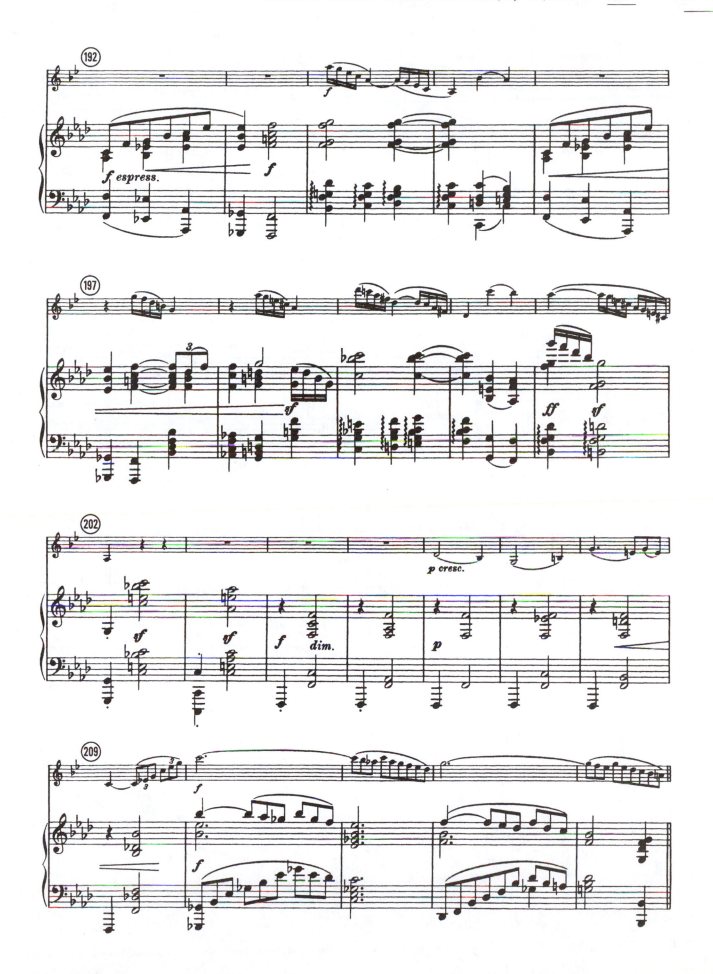

TWO SONGS
Hugo Wolf (1860–1903)

Hugo Wolf excelled in only one type of composition, the Romantic lied, and was its last great master. Though he was drawn to the Wagnerian idiom, he was far from dependent on Wagnerian models. Are any passages in the following song reminiscent of Wagner?

■ DAS VERLASSENE MÄGDLEIN

(1888)

Text: Eduard Mörike (1804–1875)

Early, when the cocks crow,	*Lovely is the flames' light*	*Suddenly I remember,*	*Tear on tear*
Before the stars fade out,	*With its flying sparks;*	*Faithless boy,*	*Tumbles down;*
I must stand at the hearth	*I gaze into it,*	*That I in the night*	*So begins the day—*
And light the fire.	*Deep in sorrow.*	*Of thee have dreamed.*	*O, would it were ended!*

The music of "The Forsaken Maiden" often hints rather than asserts. What is the harmonic background of the first five bars? Where is the first unequivocal statement of the tonic chord? How is the final cadence realized? How do the augmented triads at bars 20–26 express the words?

Both selections are reprinted from Peters Edition No. 3140a. Reprint permission granted by the publisher, C. F. Peters Corporation, New York.

so kommt der Tag her-an__

o ging' er wieder!

IN DER FRÜHE

(1888)

Text: Eduard Mörike (1804–1875)

No sleep has cooled my eyes,	*My troubled mind still tosses*	*Fear and fret no more, my soul!*
And already day appears	*To and fro among doubts*	*Be joyful! Already here and yonder*
At the window of my room.	*And creates dark phantoms.*	*Morning bells are waking.*

How are the three stanzas of the text of "In Early Morning" related to the form of the music? How is the meaning of the text expressed by the music? To what extent does the tonic-dominant relationship function in this song?[14]

---

[14] Felix Salzer analyzes this song in *Structural Hearing* (op. cit., Vol. 1, p. 238ff.). See also Gregory Michael Proctor, *Technical Bases of 19th-century Chromatic Tonality,* Ph.D. diss., Princeton, 1977, p. 220ff.).

ADAGIETTO
from *Symphony No. 5* (1901–1903)

Gustav Mahler (1860–1911)

The huge symphonies of Mahler at once draw on late Romantic traditions and express a distinctly modern sensibility. This example is the fourth movement of a five-movement work for large orchestra that lasts more than an hour. Despite its reduced instrumental forces, a sense of great breadth is produced by its very slow tempo and extreme expressiveness.

Study the long, slowly unfolding phrases of this intensely poignant music. Exactly where do they begin and end, and what large form do they gradually build? How does instrumental color help delineate the form? Why the slight speeding up at bar 10 and the return to tempo at 22? Also consider Mahler's personal way of treating diatonic dissonance—for example, in bars 2, 4, and 9–11. Does the $^6_4$ chord in bar 95 ever resolve?

a) Very slow   b) soulfully   c) Do not drag   d) somewhat more flowing than at the beginning

e) divided   f) broader bow strokes   g) Again extremely slow   h) with feeling   i) somewhat pressing on   j) flowing
k) many bow changes   l) holding back   m) (bow over) fingerboard

n) More flowing   o) with warmth   p) (on the) G string   q) bigger tone   r) not divided   s) D string

t) Hesitating   u) with the most intimate feeling   v) still slower

w) (with) much tone!   x) broad (strokes)   y) Pressing on   z) long

DARK IS THE NIGHT

No. 1 of *Three Songs,* Op. 11 (1889–1890)
Text: William Ernest Henley (1849–1903)

Amy Beach (1867–1944)

One of America's foremost composers of the Victorian era, Amy Beach, née Cheney (and also known as Mrs. H. H. A. Beach), started her musical life as an amazing prodigy who, at the age of one, could sing forty tunes accurately and always in the key in which she had first heard them. Growing up in the musical city of Boston, she early achieved success as both pianist and composer throughout the United States and later in Europe. She composed in all genres but is most remembered for her many songs. A milestone in her career was her Symphony in E minor ("Gaelic"), completed in 1896, which, it is interesting to note, employs themes from the song reproduced here.

In the accompaniment of the tempestuous "Dark Is the Night," Beach makes expressive use throughout of various chromatic chords, most notably augmented sixth chords and derivatives thereof. Often these are of short duration, like the "common-tone augmented sixth chord" in bar 1. In each such case, consider what "larger," or more basic, harmony the augmented-sixth chord is helping to extend.

Discounting the word repetitions in the text will reveal that Henley's poem consists of two simple stanzas of four lines each. Does the music likewise project a sense of *two*-part form? And how should bar 24 be rhythmically performed?[15]

---

[15] Adrienne Fried Block's *Amy Beach: Passionate Victorian* (New York: Oxford University Press, 1998) is an excellent account of the composer's life and work. "Dark is the Night" is recorded on the DELOS label, DE 3170, and on NORTHEASTERN, NR 9004-CD.

Part Five

Since Debussy

art Five illustrates some of the most important musical developments of the last 110-odd years—an eventful period characterized by the rise of many new approaches to the art of musical composition. The following survey groups all the pieces under several broad headings, following essentially a tonal to post-tonal path. Although any such list must be to some extent arbitrary and contain pieces that fall under more than one category, it may help teachers work out a sequence of study suitable to their needs.

TONALITY

Though common-practice tonality, strictly defined, ceased to be a viable option for most composers, tonality in a broader sense by no means disappeared as composers of very different points of view sought to extend or re-invent it.[1] At least three types of tonality, quite distinct historically and stylistically, are represented here—the lushly chromatic type of Debussy's *L'Après-midi d'un faune* and Ravel's *Le Martin-Pêcheur*; the more astringent, less triadic type of Bartók's *Bulgarian Rhythm* and the two Hindemith pieces; and that of the late twentieth-century "New Tonality" as shown in Terry Riley's *In C* and the aria from John Adams's *Nixon in China*. (Yet a fourth type is exemplified by the modal folk-song setting of Vaughan Williams given in Appendix B on page 563.)

CENTRICITY

This elastic term covers a wide spectrum of possibilities, embracing the many twentieth-century compositions that, without being strictly tonal, nevertheless give a kind of tonal impression. The reason they give such an impression is that a given tone or set of tones will be compositionally emphasized by some means such as loudness, register, repetition, or color, and will therefore stand out to the ear as the main, or "central," sonority, like the tonic in a tonal work. Centric compositions can even feature diatonic scales or triads, but because these seemingly tonal elements do not adhere to the principles of the tonal system—functional

---

[1] Traditional tonality continued to flourish and evolve in popular music and jazz, a development so distinct that it requires a section of its own (see page 543).

harmony, traditional voice leading—they are better understood in post-tonal terms. For example, Debussy's *La cathédrale engloutie,* though ostensibly in C major, is better understood as centric because of its many added tones, non-traditional voice leading, minimal functionality, and "static blocks" of sound. More radical examples built of diatonic materials are the movement from Stravinsky's *Octet* and his *Pas-de-Quatre* from *Agon.*

Many centric pieces (or passages) feature non-diatonic referential sonorities. The simpler members of this group are the movement from Schuman's *Three-Score Set,* and Bartók's *Syncopation.* Larger ones are the excerpt from Stravinsky's *Le sacre du printemps,* Ives' "General Booth," and Schoenberg's *Farben,* all of which will be studied for many other reasons as well. Other non-diatonic examples exploit *inversional symmetry.* Such pieces are much more distant from tonality because inversional symmetry does not exist in tonal harmony: In tonality, C-E-G may invert *melodically* to C-Ab-F, but harmonically this is just another *right-side-up* triad—a IVb—because tonal harmonies exist only from the root up, not from the middle out. Precisely the reverse is true in a post-tonal context, where real invertibility is axiomatic. Symmetry is exemplified in a group of pieces by Bartók: In *Bulgarian Rhythm* it occurs sporadically, the piece as a whole being enclosed within a G tonic. A more exclusive realization of it is *Diminished Fifth,* which is entirely based on the octatonic scale, an invertible construct. Symmetry on the structural level (not the note-to-note level) controls the structure of the great fugue from *Music for Strings, Percussion, and Celesta.* Here the single tone A is the axis of symmetry. An axis is not necessarily also a primary sonority, but in this case A is that as well. An additional example, also centered on A, is the Webern *Variations* movement, in which symmetry is employed on the structural level in a twelve-tone work.

It must be stressed that the mere use of a diatonic or octatonic collection, or of inversional symmetry, does not automatically produce centricity. It is how these materials are used—their context—that determines whether or not they create a centric effect. The relation of octatonic to tone "center" is particularly subtle in Toru Takemitsu's *Autumn.*

FREE ATONALITY

This term is often used to characterize the pre-dodecaphonic repertoire of Schoenberg and his school, but it is applicable to other music as well, such as Ives' "The Cage," the madrigal of George Crumb, and the wind piece of György Ligeti. These short works, together with the movement from Webern's work for string quartet, Op. 5, and Berg's song from his Op. 2, can prepare the student for two longer, more complex works by Schoenberg, the piano piece from Op. 11, and the orchestral *Farben.* Related to the latter is Ruth Crawford Seeger's string quartet movement, with its "contrapuntal dynamics."

SERIALISM

Three pieces of Stravinsky together comprise examples of both pre-dodecaphonic serialism and the combining of serial and tonal elements in a single movement. The first, though far from a serial work, is the variations movement from Stravinsky's *Octet* for winds, which treats the theme somewhat in the manner of a tone row. Of the other two, "Full Fadom Five" is based on a seven-tone row related to the E♭ minor scale, while the *Coda* from *Agon* presents a twelve-tone row (Stravinsky's first published one) in a fairly straightforward manner, surrounded by extensive non-serial elements.

Of the strictly twelve-tone works, the simplest is Krenek's movement for solo cello, which uses only one series-form. Webern's "Wie bin ich froh!" makes significant use of simultaneous inversionally complementary series-forms. A more complex demonstration of the same principle is embodied in the movement from Webern's piano *Variations*. In Dallapiccola's *Simbolo* the order of the individual pitches is obscured by a continuous texture of dyads and trichords, but because the succession of dyads and trichords *is* ordered, the various series-forms can be readily deduced. One might introduce combinatoriality through Babbitt's children's piece, "Play on Notes," before progressing to Schoenberg's well-known piano piece, Op. 33a, and Babbitt's *Semi-Simple Variations*, the latter of which serializes other parameters in addition to pitch.[2]

OTHER CONSIDERATIONS

Not all the choices in Part Five were made on the basis of pitch organization. Rhythm was a factor in some cases, notably Olivier Messiaen's *Liturgie de cristal*, the excerpt from Stravinsky's *Le sacre*, Bartók's *Syncopation*, Elliott Carter's brilliant study in metrical modulation for solo tympani, Ives' "The Cage," and Steve Reich's *Clapping Music*. Completely free rhythm occurs in Bruce Saylor's *Psalm*, and more radical indeterminacy is shown by Riley's In C and John Cage's piano piece.

A final criterion influenced a few of the choices—the persistence of certain classical forms and genres (sometimes just their wraiths) into modern times. Index I locates twentieth-century examples of small binary and ternary forms, sonata form, variations, fugue, canon, and rondo.

The following books on twentieth-century music are recommended:

THEORY AND ANALYSIS

Perle, George, *Serial Composition and Atonality* (Berkeley: University of California Press, 1962; 6th rev. ed., 1991).

Forte, Allen, *The Structure of Atonal Music* (New Haven, CT: Yale University Press, 1973).

Rahn, John, *Basic Atonal Theory* (New York: Longman, 1980; New York: Schirmer Books, 1987).

Lester, Joel, *Analytic Approaches to Twentieth-Century Music* (New York: Norton, 1989).

Straus, Joseph N., *Introduction to Post-Tonal Theory* (Upper Saddle River, NJ: Prentice-Hall, 1990; 2nd rev. ed., 2000).

HISTORY

(with much analytic comment)

Simms, Bryan, *Music of the Twentieth Century: Style and Structure* (New York: Schirmer Books, 1986; 2nd ed., 1996).

Watkins, Glenn, *Soundings: Music in the Twentieth Century* (Schirmer Books, 1987).

Morgan, Robert P., *Twentieth-Century Music* (New York: Norton, 1991).

Whittall, Arnold, *Twentieth-Century Music* (Oxford: Oxford University Press, 1999).

---

[2] There are two current methods of naming the series-forms in a twelve-tone analysis: (1) the series stated first in the composition is taken as the 0-transposition (the "movable-do" method); and (2) all series-forms, including the first, are calculated from 0 = C, 1 = C♯, etc. (the "fixed-do" method). This book uses the first method.

PRÉLUDE À "L'APRÈS-MIDI D'UN FAUNE"
(1892–1894)
Piano arrangement: Leonard Borwick (1868–1925)

Claude Debussy (1862–1918)

Debussy's *Prelude to "Afternoon of a Faun"* was his musical response to the poem of Stéphane Mallarmé (1842–1898), in which a faun playing his pan-pipes alone in the woods becomes aroused by passing nymphs and naiads, pursues them unsuccessfully, then wearily abandons himself to a sleep filled with visions. Though called a "prelude," the work is nevertheless complete—an evocation of the feelings of the poem as a whole. We give it in piano arrangement to facilitate analysis, but provide a brief sample, on page 414, of the score, a masterpiece of orchestration.

The opening strikes the listener as somehow ambiguous and incomplete. Where is the first hint of a tonic? the first unequivocal cadence? It is instructive to reduce a portion of the work to its essential voice leading. Do chords progress in traditional fashion? Does the tonic-dominant relation still exist? What is the nature of the whole-tone passages in bars 31–36, 50, 58, and 92?

Pierre Boulez has written that "modern music was awakened by *L'après-midi d'un faune.*" How so? In what ways was the work unprecedented?[3]

a) Very moderate   b) gentle and expressive   c) left hand   d) horn

[3]Pierre Boulez, *Notes of an Apprenticeship*, trans. Herbert Weinstock (New York: Knopf, 1968). Bars 1–30 are analyzed by Felix Salzer in *Structural Hearing* (New York: Dover repr., 1962, vol. 2, Graph 455). Aspects of bars 31–55 are discussed in Charles Burkhart, "Schenker's 'Motivic Parallelisms'" *Journal of Music Theory*, Fall 1978, p. 155f.). Analytic comment on the entire work is given on pp. 69–96 of *Debussy: Prelude to "The Afternoon of a Faun,"* edited by William W. Austin, in the *Norton Critical Scores* series (New York: Norton, 1970).

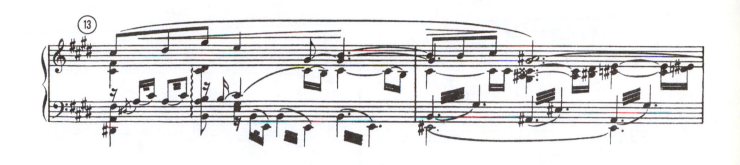

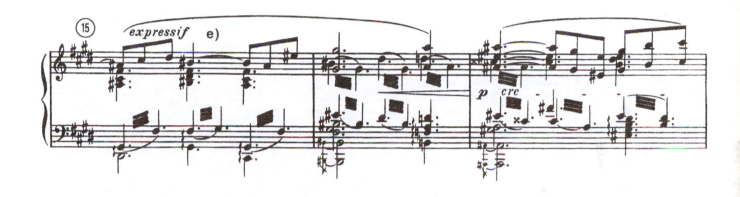

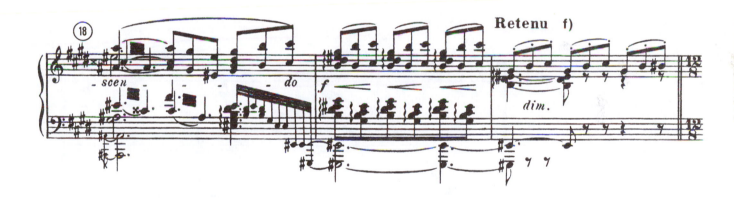

e) expressively   f) held back   g) *au Mouvement*, "a tempo"

h) right hand   i) Becoming animated

j) Ever more animated   k) English horn [and clarinets]   l) strings   m) *Premier Mouvement,* first tempo ("tempo primo")

n) Same tempo   o) expressive and very sustained   p) very expressive

q) violin solo   r) Tempo of the beginning

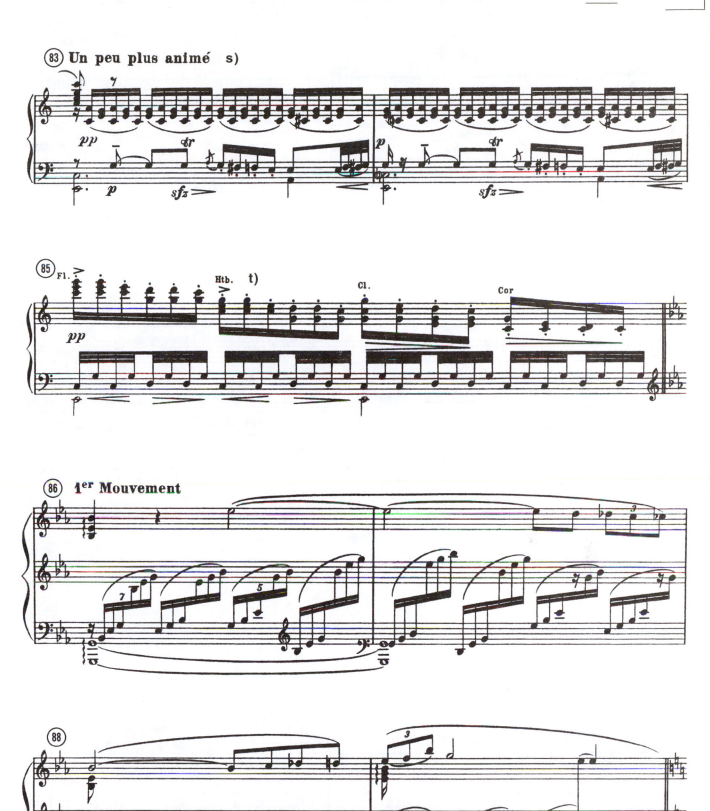

s) A little more animated   t) oboes [and English horn]

u) In a more animated tempo   v) In the first tempo, with more languor

w) Very held back   x) Very slow and very held back until the end

LA CATHÉDRALE ENGLOUTIE
from *Preludes*, Book I (1910)

Claude Debussy (1862–1918)

Much of Debussy's instrumental music is in one way or another pictorial. Is it necessary to know what the "picture" or "story" of such works is to enjoy them fully or perform them with understanding? Is study of such things "analysis"?

Apart from the medium, how does the style of *The Sunken Cathedral* differ from that of *Prelude to "Afternoon of a Faun"*? How do you explain the tones in bar 1? bar 17? bar 86? Are concepts such as voice leading and overall harmonic structure relevant to an understanding of this music?

Debussy chose to notate the meter of *The Sunken Cathedral* in a highly idiosyncratic manner that has confused many readers of the score. His time signature $\frac{6}{4} = \frac{3}{2}$ does not mean that a bar of ♩♩♩ ♩♩♩ is to equal in duration a bar of ♩♩♩, but rather that the quarter note in the sections notated chiefly in quarter notes is equal in duration to the half note in the sections notated chiefly in half notes. The following are the metrical proportions that Debussy intended: At the start of bar 7, the preceding ♩ equals the coming ♩; similarly, at bar 13, ♩ = ♩; at bar 22, ♩ = ♩; at bar 84, ♩ = ♩, and finally, at bar 86, ♩ = ♩. Thus there is a single basic pulse throughout the piece.[4]

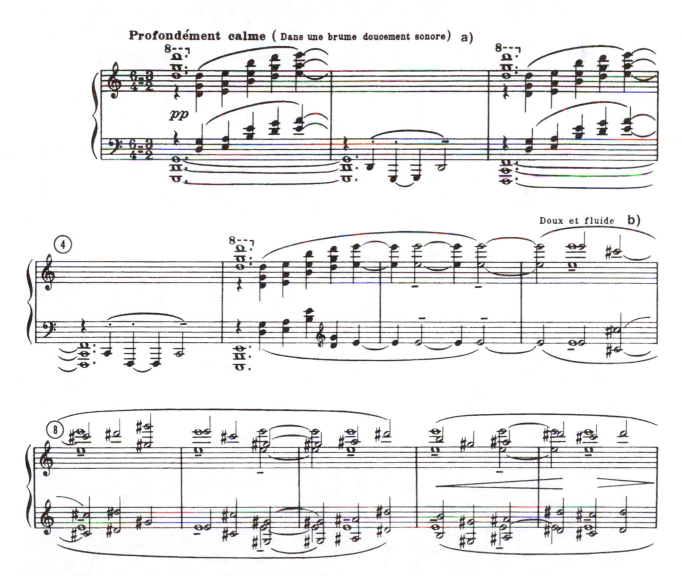

a) Profoundly calm (In a gently sonorous mist)   b) Gentle and flowing

[4] For support of these assertions, see Charles Burkhart, "Debussy Plays *La cathédrale engloutie* and Solves Metrical Mystery" (The Piano Quarterly, Fall 1968, pp. 14–16).

c) without nuances   d) Little by little emerging from the mist   e) marked, *marcato*
f) Increase progressively [in dynamics] (Without hurrying)

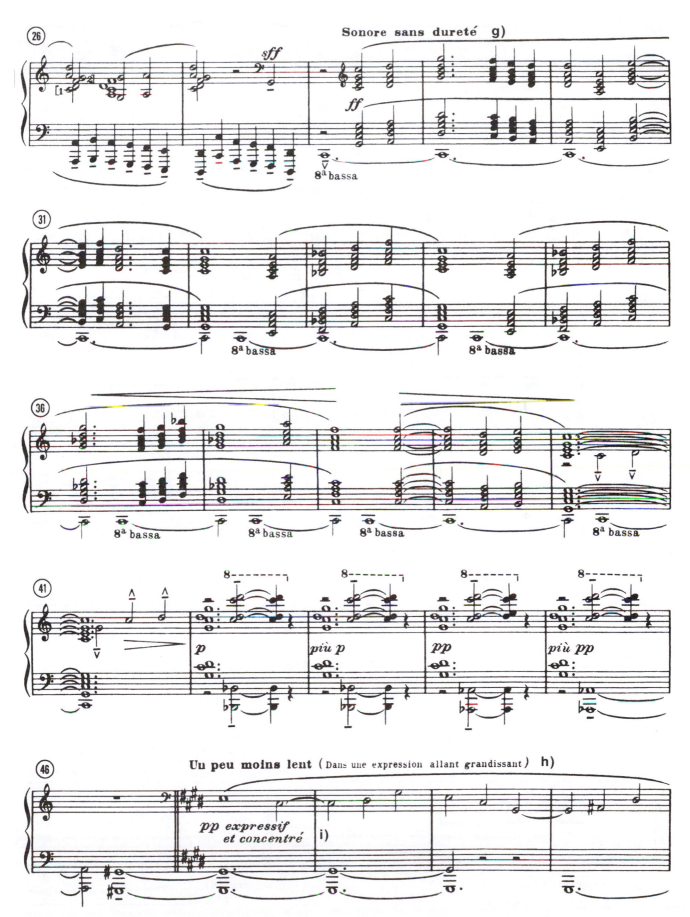

g) Sonorously without hardness   h) A little less slowly (With ever growing expression)   i) expressive and concentrated ("focused")

j) au Mouvement, "a tempo"   k) Floating and heavy   l) Like an echo of the phrase heard earlier

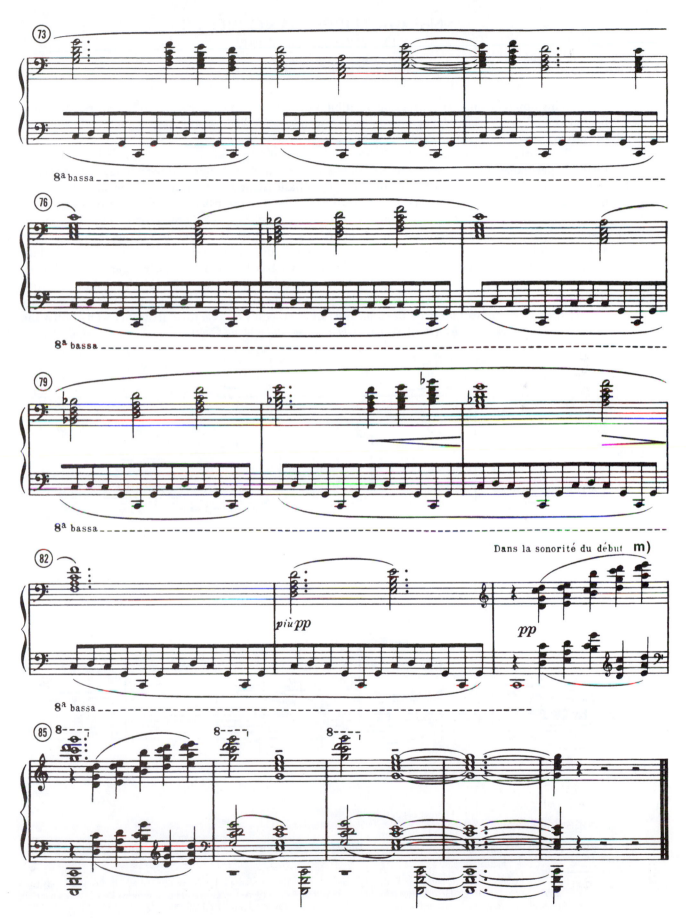

m) In the sonority of the beginning

No. 1 of THREE PIANO PIECES
Op. 11 (1909, revised 1942)

Arnold Schoenberg (1874–1951)

This powerful and expressive composition is one of Schoenberg's earliest atonal works. It should be performed with clear projection of the crescendo and diminuendo marks, and with a degree of rubato.

First, play or hear the piece repeatedly, and discover its motives, themes, and large sections. Listen in particular for recurrences of materials presented in the first thirteen bars. They are frequently somewhat modified in repetition, but still retain their basic shape and are quite recognizable. For example, what is being repeated in bars 34–36? (We have added the translation of German terms.)

Then listen for finer details of pitch organization. Notice especially the intervallic content of the first three notes b[1]-g♯[1]-g♮[1], and how this set of notes is subsequently treated to various operations such as transposition, change of register, verticalization, inversion, and retrograde. For example, see in bars 4 and 5 the G♯-b-g[1]; see also bar 10 (right hand only), bar 12's first four notes, bar 19—and many more places. (But do not look for a twelve-tone row; Schoenberg was still years from that concept.) Although this three-note set is important in the piece, other, related sets are also prominent. Not every note in the piece can be understood as a member of a set—only quite a few.[5] (Another well-known and shorter atonal work—the fourth of Webern's *Five Movements for String Quartet*, **Op.** 5—is on page 481.)

a) Moderate quarter-notes   b) slower

"3 piano pieces, op. 11/1" UE 9773. © 1929 by Universal Edition A.G., Wien © renewed 1956 by Gertrude Schönberg. Reprinted with permission.

---

[5] George Perle give extensive analytic comment on this movement in his *Serial Composition and Atonality*, 6th rev. ed. (Berkeley: University of California Press, 1991, pp. 10ff.). He discusses it further in *Twelve-Tone Tonality* (Berkeley: University of California Press, 1977, pp. 162 ff.). See also Joseph N. Straus, *Introduction to Post-Tonal Theory* (Upper Saddle River, NJ: Prentice Hall, 2000).

c) much faster   d) with muting (soft pedal) until the sign   e) Press the keys down without sound   f) *Flageolett-Töne*, harmonics
g) without pedal   h) very slow   i) *Moderato*   j) quicker   k) slow

1) more flowing

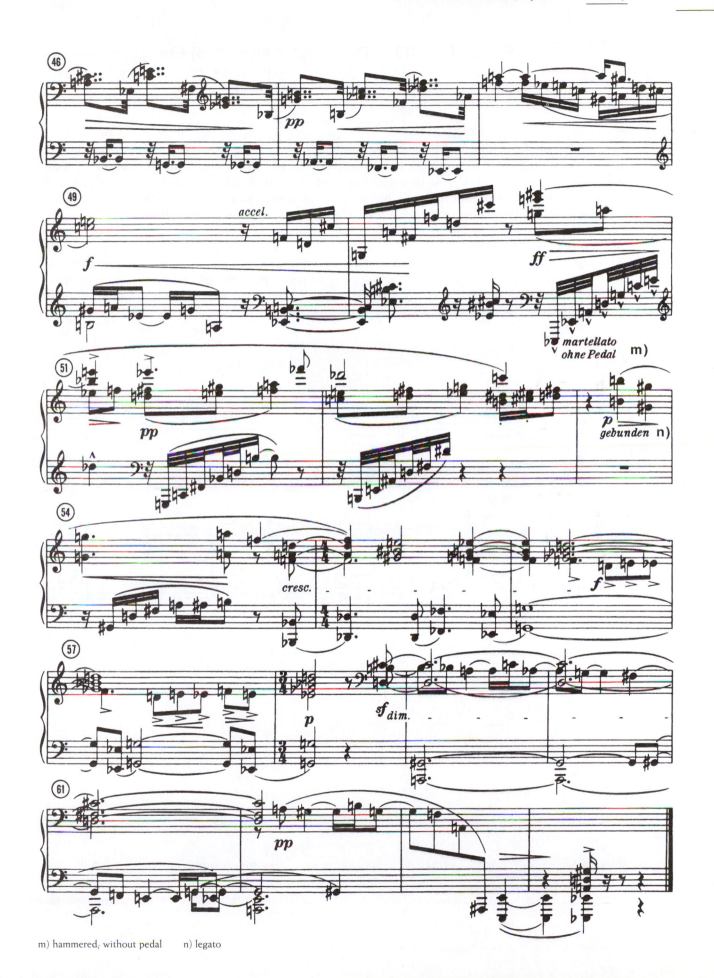

m) hammered; without pedal   n) legato

SUMMER MORNING BY A LAKE (COLORS)

No. 3 of *Five Pieces for Orchestra*, Op. 16 (1909)
Arrangement for two pianos: Anton Webern (1913)

Arnold Schoenberg (1874–1951)

The idea for this composition, Schoenberg's famous experiment in "tone color melody" (*Klangfarbenmelodie*), came to him from an impression of the colors of the sunrise reflected in the waters of a lake. Because the work must be understood first in terms of color, we show the beginning of the orchestral score (in the 1949 revision), but we give the entire piece in a piano arrangement (made by a noted student of Schoenberg) because it facilitates enormously the study of this fascinating work.

The piece was long the victim of a popular misconception, namely, that it consisted of but a single chord, sustained from start to end, that changed only in its color, that is, in its instrumentation. Although it is true that the instrumentation does so change, there is much more to the pitch organization than just one chord. Perceptive listening will also reveal that, though this piece has no tonic *triad*, the chord that both opens and closes it is obviously of highest priority. What happens to this chord *besides* the changes in instrumentation as the work progresses?[6]

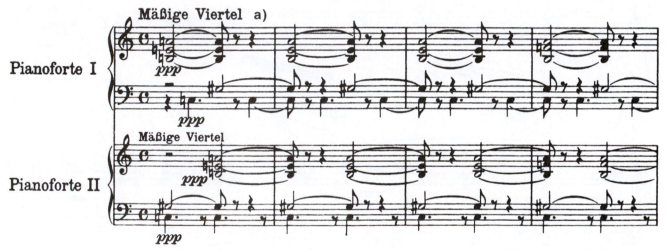

Piano arrangement continues on page 426.

a) Moderate quarters

---

[6] The instructions at the bottom of the sample page of score are Schoenberg's. His famous statement on "tone-color melody" occurs on the last pages of his *Harmonielehre* (first ed. 1911), published in English as *Theory of Harmony*, trans. Roy E. Carter (Berkeley: University of California Press, 1978). Three of the many published analyses of Opus 16, No. 3 are: Charles Burkhart, "Schoenberg's Farben" (Perspectives of New Music, Fall–Winter 1973, pp. 141ff.); Allen Forte, *The Structure of Atonal Music* (New Haven, CT: Yale University Press, 1973, pp. 166ff.); and John Rahn, *Basic Atonal Theory* (New York: Thomson/Schirmer, 1980, pp. 59ff.).

Sommermorgen an einem See—Summer Morning by a Lake
(Farben)   (Colors)

ARNOLD SCHOENBERG

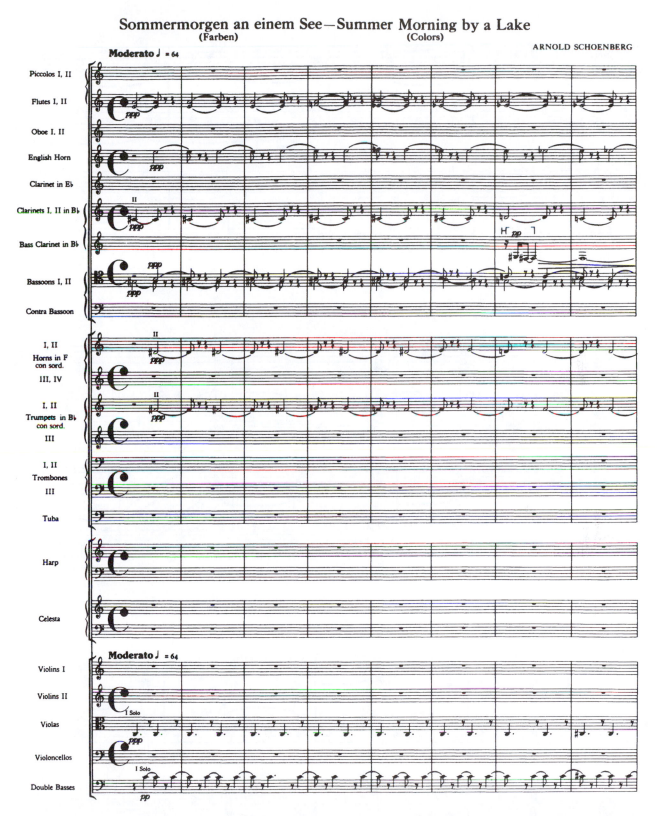

The change of chords in this piece has to be executed with the greatest subtlety, avoiding accentuation of entering instruments, so that only the difference in color becomes noticeable. The conductor need not try to polish sounds that seem unbalanced, but watch that every instrumentalist plays accurately the prescribed dynamic, according to the nature of his instrument. There are no motivs in this piece that have to be brought to the fore.—Arnold Schoenberg

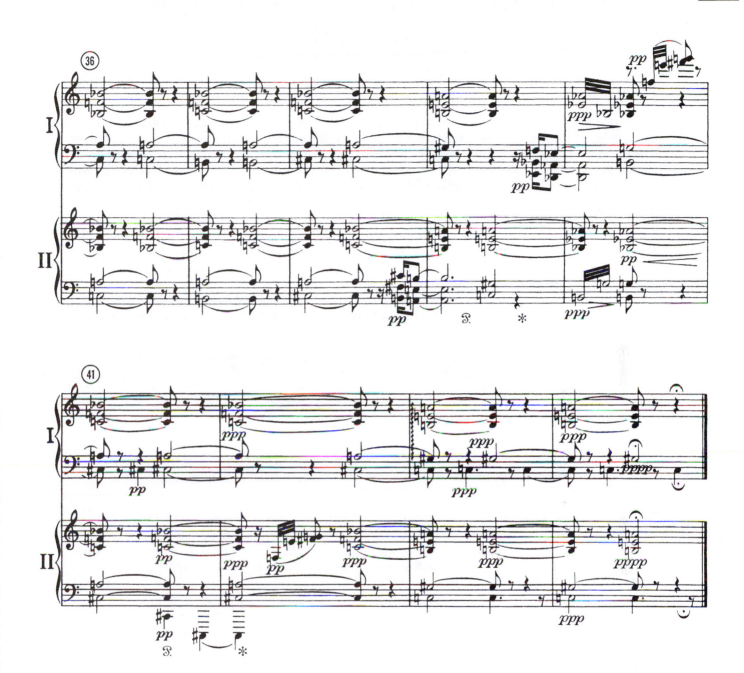

PIANO PIECE
Op. 33a (1928)

Arnold Schoenberg (1874–1951)

In a series of works composed in the early 1920s, Schoenberg gradually developed the basic principles of the twelve-tone system. However, he was dissatisfied with the early form of his theory in one respect, namely, that it provided no systematic basis for *simultaneity* in twelve-tone composition. He felt that the solution would lie in the stating of two different forms of a series simultaneously. But which forms? The problem was how to choose them in an *organic* rather than a merely haphazard or fortuitous way.

The following diagram (which, take note, does *not* show the series-forms of *Piano Piece,* Op. 33a) is an illustration of Schoenberg's eventual solution to his problem—a solution that was to be of far-reaching significance for his later work (others found different solutions). It shows that a twelve-tone series can be constructed in such a way that its first hexachord (A) consists of pitches entirely different from those of the first hexachord (A) of the series' inversion transposed five semitones upward. Thus P0's A does not duplicate the pitch content of I5's A, but is necessarily identical in pitch content (though not pitch *order*) with I5's second hexachord (B). Conversely, P0's B excludes I5's B and duplicates I5's A.[7]

Although Schoenberg nearly always worked with a series-pair relating as P0 to I5, it is possible to design a series in such a way that *other* transpositions of its inversion will combine with it in the manner shown. Not all twelve-tone series will yield an inversion that will so combine. The special property of those that do (can you discover that property?) has been termed *combinatoriality* by Milton Babbitt, who has extensively developed Schoenberg's idea in his own theory and composition (see pages 515 and 516).

Schoenberg's famous Op. 33a, an independent piano piece, is a brilliant demonstration of composition with combinatorially related series-pairs. Clearly, its primary series cannot be completely deduced from the work's first two bars, but bars 3–5 compared with 1–2 will soon yield it. Remember that bar 1 decides which series-form is to be called P0 (see footnote 2, page 401).

Make a complete twelve-tone analysis of this piece. You need not place an order-number beside every note; simply encircle and number each of the four- or six-note subsets that, taken together, form a twelve-tone series, and identify each series-form. (In two bars, there are apparently small inconsistencies or misprints.) Do not forget that you are analyzing a piece of music. Locate first the different themes and sections. What is the role of the fluctuations in tempo? What is the form? After your twelve-tone analysis, consider how the various series-forms used help create the form? And for what *musical* reason may Schoenberg have omitted four pitches in bar 20? (We have added the translations of German terms.)

---

[7] See Schoenberg's classic essay, "Composition with Twelve Tones," in his *Style and Idea* (New York: St. Martin's, 1975, p. 225; repr. California, 1984, p. 214).

a) Moderato

b) more vehemently   c) hammered   d) calmer

e) energetically   f) increasing, intensifying

g) Calm

TWO SONGS
Charles Ives (1874–1951)

Charles Ives, the first great American composer, produced a body of works remarkable for their striking modernity, all the more so considering their often strikingly early dates.[8] The first of the two songs below shows Ives limiting himself to very uniform material. More typical of his style is the heterogeneity of the second song. How are its disparate elements fused into an esthetically successful unity?

■ THE CAGE

(1906)

Text: Charles Ives

This song is from a collection called *114 Songs* that Ives, whose work went long unrecognized, printed privately in 1922 and sent gratis to many musicians, critics, and libraries. Think about the meaning of its text. Study the piano and voice parts alone, then how they mesh, and then consider how the music expresses the text. Because the work has so few bar lines, one wonders why Ives placed one before "wonder." (Note that accidentals apply only to the notes they immediately precede.)[9]

[8] For an interesting comment on the debated issue of the Ives chronology, see Philip Lambert, *The Music of Charles Ives* (New Haven, CT: Yale University Press, 1997, p. 207). Lambert analyzes "The Cage" on p. 150f.

[9] This version of "The Cage" is essentially that given in *114 Songs*. Two other versions were published as part of *A Set of Pieces for Theatre or Chamber Orchestra* in *New Music* (San Francisco: Pacific Music Press, January, 1932, v. 5/2). Because these are notated with more precision, a few rhythmic details therefrom have been incorporated here.

A boy who had been there three hours be-gan to won-der, "Is life an-y-thing like that?"

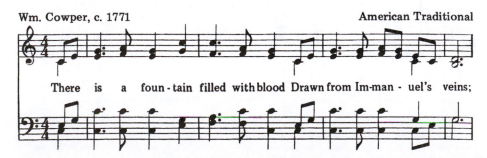

◼ GENERAL WILLIAM BOOTH ENTERS INTO HEAVEN

(1914; publ. 1935)

Text: Lines 1–23 and 30–37 of Vachel Lindsay's poem of the same name.

Growing up in a small New England town, the young Charles Ives, son of the local bandmaster, soaked up the many and varied popular songs that were part of the common culture: patriotic songs, marches, minstrel songs, hymns, gospel songs, folk songs. Throughout his creative life, their tunes remained an important part of the experience on which he drew, and he frequently quoted snatches from them in his compositions.

The musical quotations in "General William Booth Enters in Heaven" are chiefly from the gospel song *Cleansing Fountain,* given here in the form it has taken since the mid-nineteenth century. Ives very likely heard it at the camp meetings of his boyhood. (William Cowper [1731–1800] is a noted English poet, some of whose poems became very well known as hymn texts. We give here the first of four stanzas.)

CLEANSING FOUNTAIN

Wm. Cowper, c. 1771   American Traditional

There is a foun-tain filled with blood Drawn from Im-man - uel's veins;

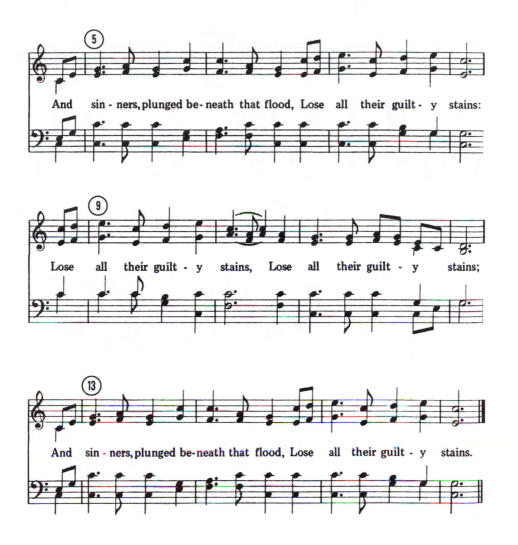

The words of *Cleansing Fountain* were not used in Ives' song, which uses only the poem of Vachel Lindsay (1879–1931). (Lindsay quotes a line from *another* gospel song, "Are You Washed in the Blood of the Lamb?", but Ives did not use the tune of that song.) Readers of Lindsay's poem sometimes wrongly take it to be satiric. On the contrary, it is a tribute to William Booth, founder of the Salvation Army, whose uninhibited "soldiers" waged their battles in squalid slums and prisons to save society's outcasts. In the poem Booth marches his motley band through the gates of heaven. Ives was especially proud of this song, calling it "a Glory trance." His music not only matches the color and high spirits of the poem, but also captures its underlying seriousness.

"General Booth" also quotes from two other popular melodies: the first, quoted at bars 52–55 (piano part), is the minstrel song "Golden Slippers" by James A. Bland (1854–1911); the other is too well known to need identification here. Study the role of the quotations in the structure of the composition. How does each one fit in?[10]

---

[10] "General Booth" was also arranged for solo voice, chorus, and orchestra. The small notes in the score given here refer to the chorus part of that arrangement.

(1914)

LE MARTIN-PÊCHEUR
No. 4 from *Histoires Naturelles* (Scenes from Animal Life)(1906)
Text: Jules Renard (1864–1910)

Maurice Ravel (1875–1937)

From a cycle of five songs, each devoted to a different bird or insect, the atmospheric *Kingfisher* requires the utmost rhythmic precision of the performers, who also must avoid the slightest hint of sentimentality.[11]

> *Not a bite this evening, but I report a rare experience.*
> *As I was holding out my fishing-rod, a kingfisher came and perched on it.*
> *We have no bird more splendid.*
> *He seemed like a big blue flower at the end of a long stem.*
> *The rod bent under his weight.*
> *I held my breath, quite proud to be taken for a tree by a kingfisher.*
> *And I am sure he did not fly off out of fear,*
> > *but thought he was merely passing from one branch to another.*

What is the key and the nature of the tonic chord? Analyze the colorful "high-number" chords in the opening progression and how they move from one to the next. See the repetitions of this progression and discover the relation of each to the opening. Where is the last repetition? How does the voice leading arrive on the final G sharp? (We have added the translation of the French terms.)

[11] The great baritone Pierre Bernac gives very helpful comment on this song in his *The Interpretation of French Song* (New York: Norton: 1978, p. 256).

a) As slowly as possible   b) Very calm

c) Hurry   d) a tempo   e) suddenly

THREE PIECES
from *Mikrokosmos* (1926–1937)
Béla Bartók (1881–1945)

Mikrokosmos ("the universe in small"), a series of 153 short piano pieces that grow progressively more difficult, is, in addition to its great value to the student of piano playing, a rich compendium of materials and techniques that displays the many facets of the composer's work. This selection emphasizes some of the most typical and basic of these facets.[12]

■ BULGARIAN RHYTHM
_____

No. 115, Vol. IV

What relates bar 2 to bar 1? What holds the whole piece together?

---

[12] *The Music of Béla Bartók* by Elliott Antokoletz (Berkeley: University of California Press, 1984) examines many individual works and views the composer's *oeuvre* in terms of a single comprehensive system. A monograph on Bartók's use of the "Golden Section" is Erno Lendvai's *Béla Bartók: An Analysis of His Music* (London: Kahn and Averill, 1971).

[23 sec.]

SYNCOPATION

No. 133, Vol. V

How is the effect of syncopation created in this piece? Would a listener who had never seen the score hear the rhythm as syncopated? In bar 1, could you just as readily hear the eighth notes as 123, 1234, 123? What should the player do to make sure the effect of syncopation is felt by the listener? (See also the question on rhythm in the comments on page 452.) Aside from questions of rhythm, what gives overall coherence and direction to the pitches?[13]

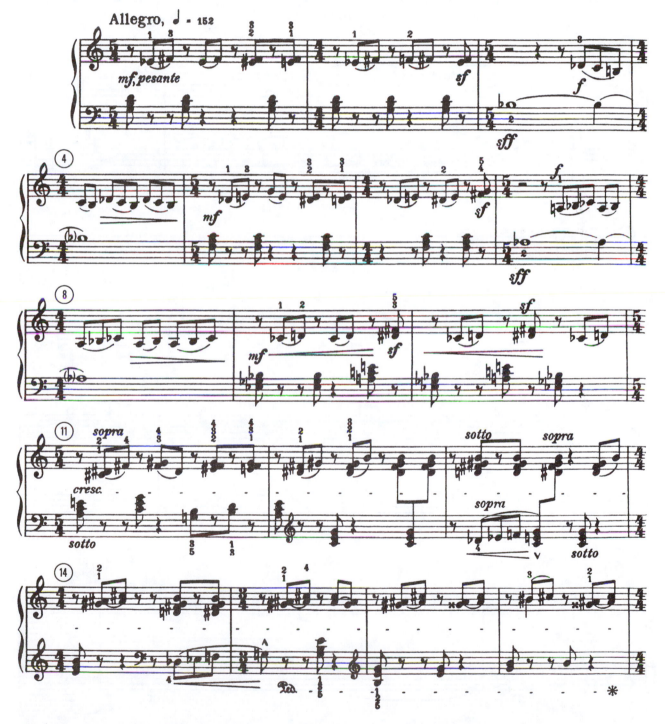

[13] Roy Travis gives a tonal analysis in "Towards a New Concept of Tonality?" (*Journal of Music Theory* 3/2, 1959, pp. 257ff.), and David Lewin a transformational one in *Generalized Musical Intervals and Transformations* (New Haven, CT: Yale University Press, 1987, p. 225ff.).

[1 min. 5 sec.]

◼ DIMINISHED FIFTH

No. 101, Vol. IV

What scale is used in this composition? Exactly where do phrases begin and end? How are larger units created? To what does the title refer?[14]

[14] Joseph N. Straus, (op. cit., pp. 121–122), discusses this piece.

MUSIC FOR STRING INSTRUMENTS, PERCUSSION, AND CELESTA, (1936)
First Movement
Béla Bartók (1881–1945)

The fugue is an ancient musical form that received a new lease on life in the mid-twentieth century. In this famous example (which opens a four-movement work), subject and episode are readily located. But a more interesting aspect of this fugue is its overall "tonal" plan, which is a unique fusion of old and new. One way to begin exploring it is to make a diagram showing the pitch level of each statement of the subject. How does the powerful climax fit into the overall plan?

The rhythm of this fugue suggests another kind of question. Notice that many of its bars are divided into unequal parts (shown by dotted lines). See, for example, bar 19, which has a 3 + 3 + 2 grouping. Now turn to the Bartók piece starting on page 449 and see its second bar, which is likewise 3 + 3 + 2. Apart from the difference in tempo, how do these passages differ in their basic rhythmic effect?

Another twentieth-century fugue is given on page 490.

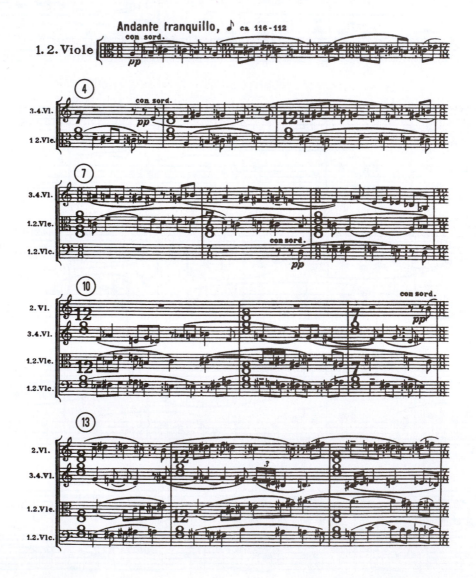

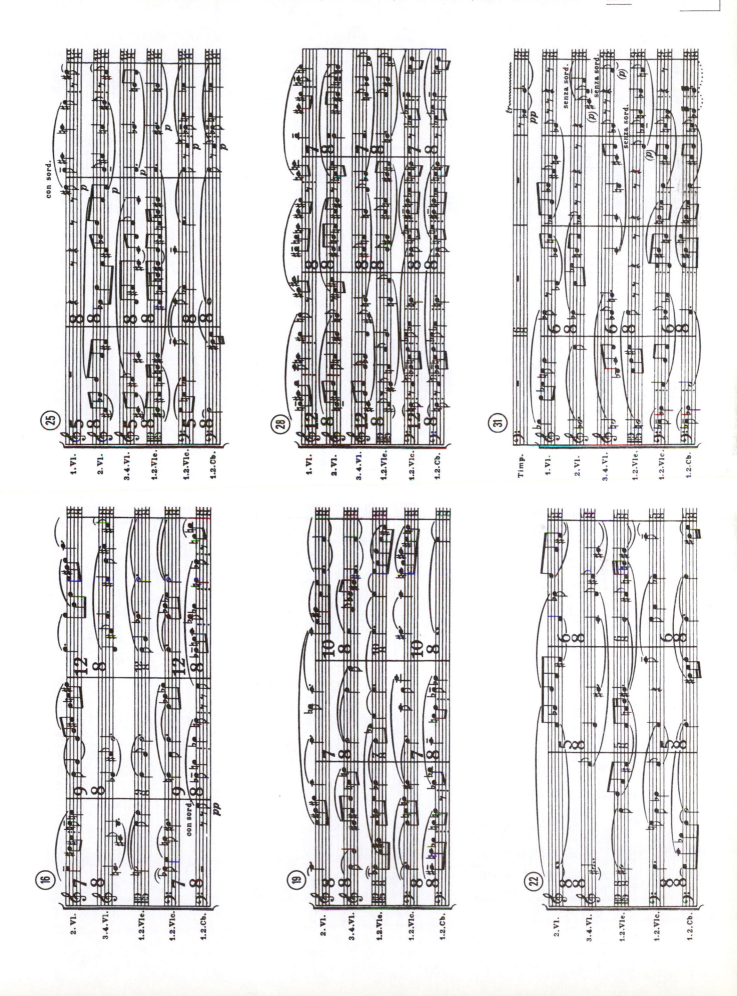

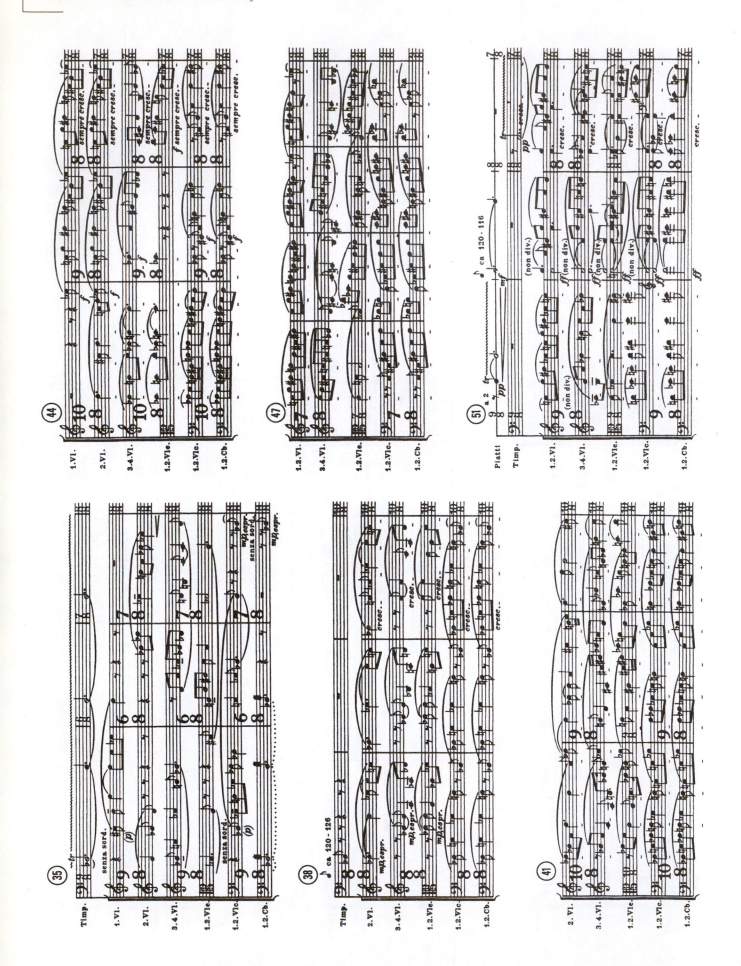

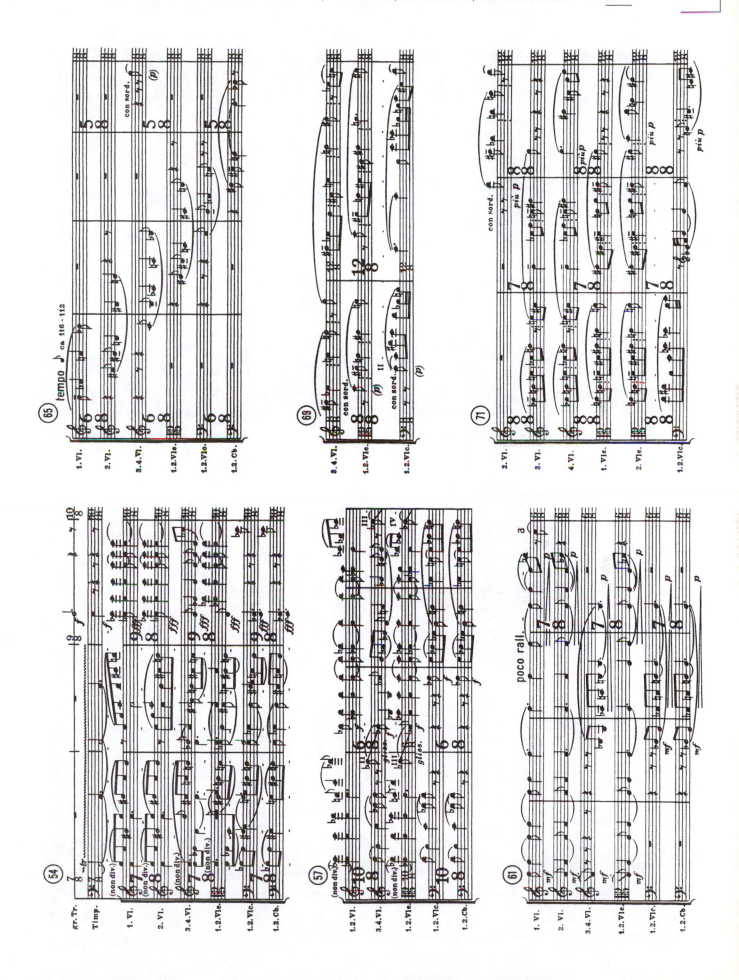

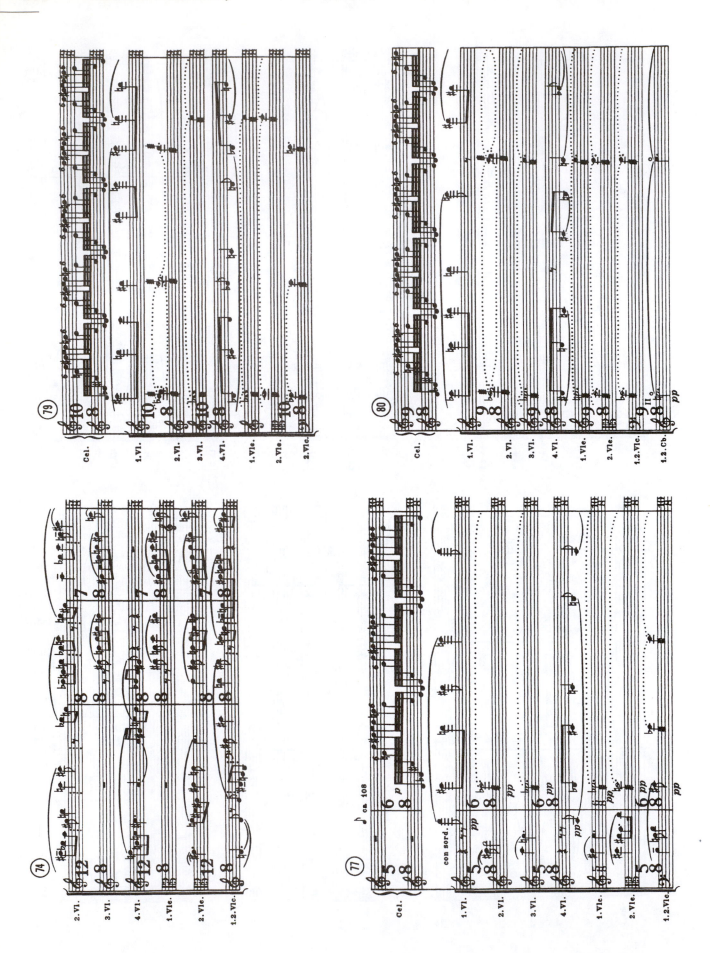

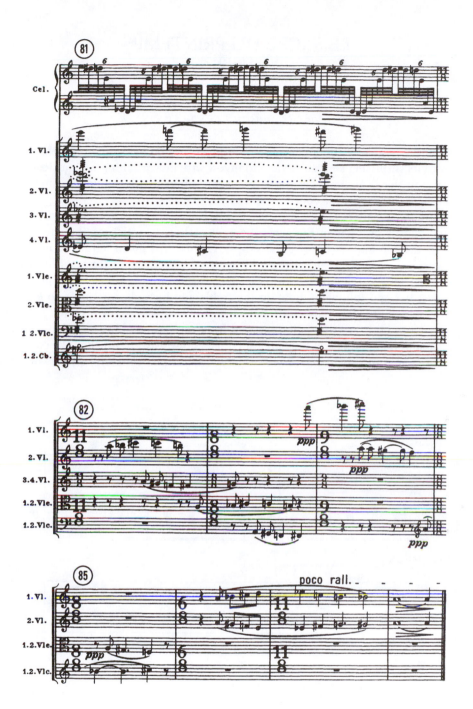

LE SACRE DU PRINTEMPS
(1911–1912)
Introduction to Part II
Arrangement for piano, four hands, by the composer

Igor Stravinsky (1882–1971)

Igor Stravinsky, arguably the greatest twentieth-century composer, sought throughout his long creative life—with its surprising shifts in style—to invest with new meaning the musical materials inherited from the past. At the same time, his music represents a break with the past of such magnitude that it has forced scholars to devise new concepts to explain it.[15]

The revolutionary ballet, *The Rite of Spring*, is a defining work in the history of modern music. It depicts the ritual dances of a pagan Russian tribe as it gathers to welcome the spring and sacrifice a chosen maiden to the sun and earth for good crops. The excerpt given here, the introduction to the second of the work's two parts, depicts the night before the sacrifice. It leads without pause into the next section, "Mysterious Circles of the Adolescents," the beginning of which is also included (bars 56–63). In the first bar and following, how do the treble and bass chords relate to each other? Trace the evolution of the melodic idea that emerges in bar 9, treble. Analyze the conduct of the several ostinatos that appear later. How are they differentiated from each other? How are they related?

Useful as piano reductions are, they are, of course, no substitute for the full score. Space forbids giving both, but a sample showing bars 38–40 of the score (original version) appears on page 463.[16]

[15] Edward T. Cone's "The Progress of a Method" *Perspectives of New Music* 1/1, 1962, pp. 18–26), introduced the now-familiar concept of *stratification*. Arthur Berger's "Problems of Pitch Organization in Stravinsky" (*PNM* 2/1, 1963, pp. 11–42), was a seminal study that alerted scholars to the octatonic element in Stravinsky, an idea subsequently expanded by Pieter C. van den Toorn in *The Music of Igor Stravinsky* (New Haven, CT: Yale University Press, 1983) and later by Richard Taruskin in his monumental *Stravinsky and the Russian Traditions: A Biography of the Works to Mavra* (Berkeley: University of California Press, 1996). Taruskin also adduces such concepts as *stasis, discontinuity, block juxtaposition, moment,* and *structural simplification* as aspects of Stravinsky's "Russianness." Joseph Straus's *Remaking the Past* (Cambridge, MA: Harvard University Press, 1990) discusses Stravinsky's reinterpretation of tonal materials; and Jonathan Cross, in *The Stravinsky Legacy* (Cambridge: Cambridge University Press, 1998) sees Stravinsky's work and its influence in terms of the notion of non-development.

[16] Detailed analytic comment on *Le sacre du printemps*, especially its rhythmic organization, is given by Pierre Boulez in his *Notes of an Apprenticeship*, trans. by Herbert Weinstock (New York: Knopf, 1968). The opening of Part II is discussed on pages 75–79 and 99–105. See also Allen Forte, *The Harmonic Organization of The Rite of Spring* (New Haven, CT: Yale University Press, 1978), and Pieter C. van den Toorn's *Stravinsky and The Rite of Spring / The Beginnings of a Musical Language* (Berkeley: University of California Press, 1987).

Piano reduction continues on page 464.

CERCLES MYSTERIEUX DES ADOLESCENTES

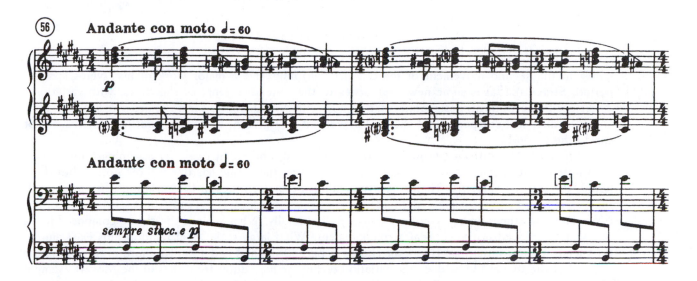

THEME and VARIATIONS A, B, and C
from *Octet for Wind Instruments*, second movement
(1923; revised 1952)

Igor Stravinsky (1882–1971)

In the second movement of the *Octet for Wind Instruments*, a major work of his "Neo-Classical" period, Stravinsky takes some new approaches to the venerable genre of the theme with variations. There are five variations, designated A through E, with A recurring to form the order A B A C D A E, and E leading without pause into the final movement. We give A, B, and C, omitting (for reasons of space) the second A.

As an aid to discovering how the theme is varied, one might begin by assigning a number to each note of the theme. (Discounting bar 2's turn figure, the theme has thirty-three notes—but don't ignore the turn completely!) Then similarly number the theme notes in the variations. In Variation B, the theme becomes increasingly attenuated, even briefly disappears, but most of it (perhaps all of it?) is present, sometimes embellished, sometimes quite literally. What scale is the theme composed in? Is this scale employed in the chordal accompaniment? What large-scale tonal relationships exist among the theme and the variations? (Note the chords in bars 53–54 and find a similar chord progression near the end of the theme.) How does the variation technique here differ from that in the Mozart example on page 164? (Other themes with variations are given on pages 76 and 356.)

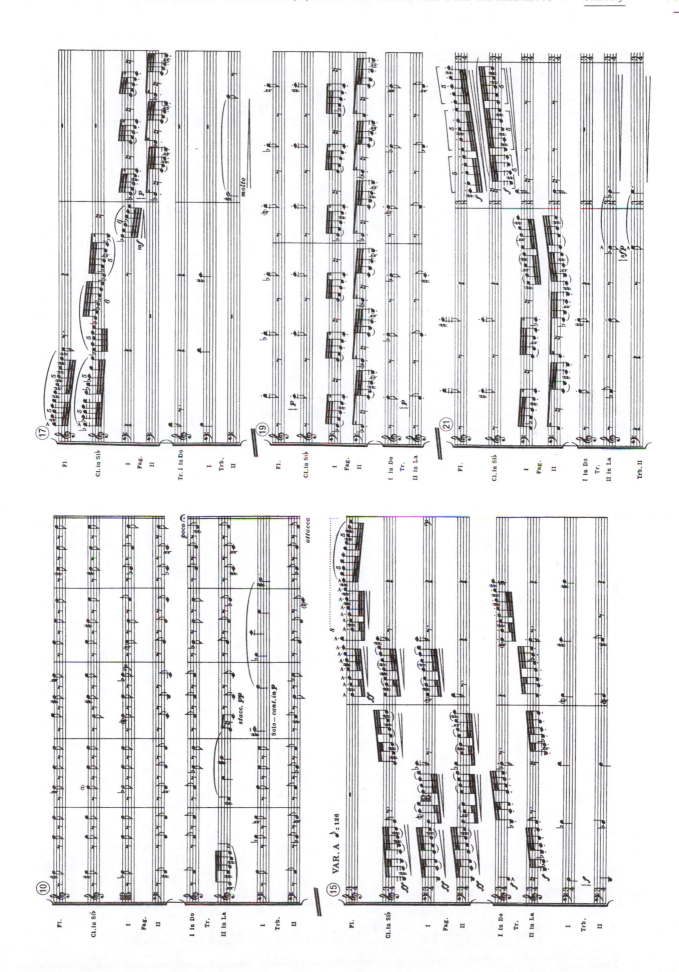

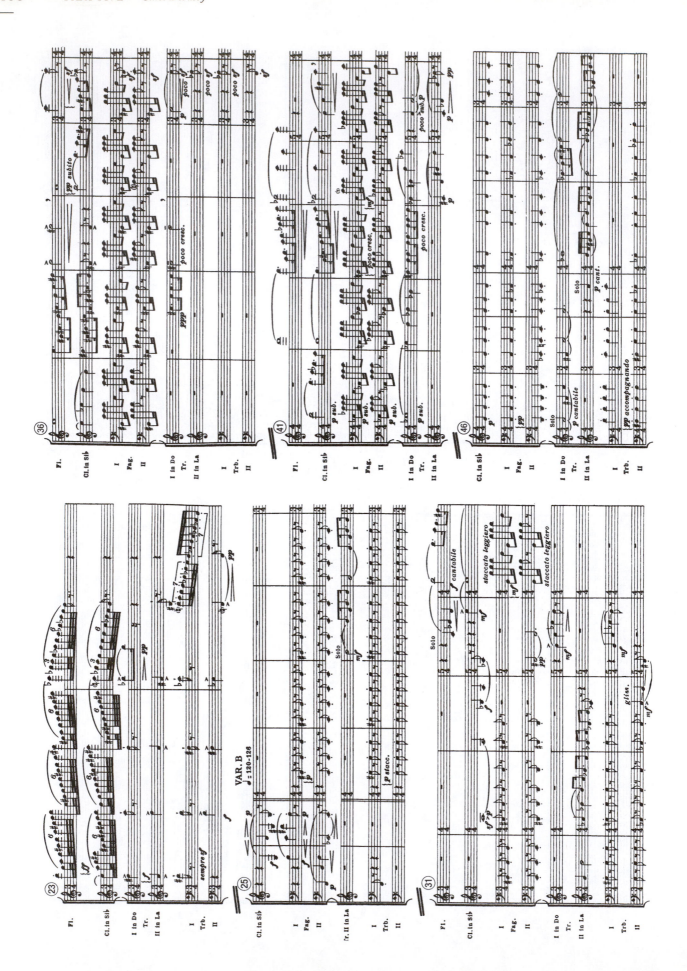

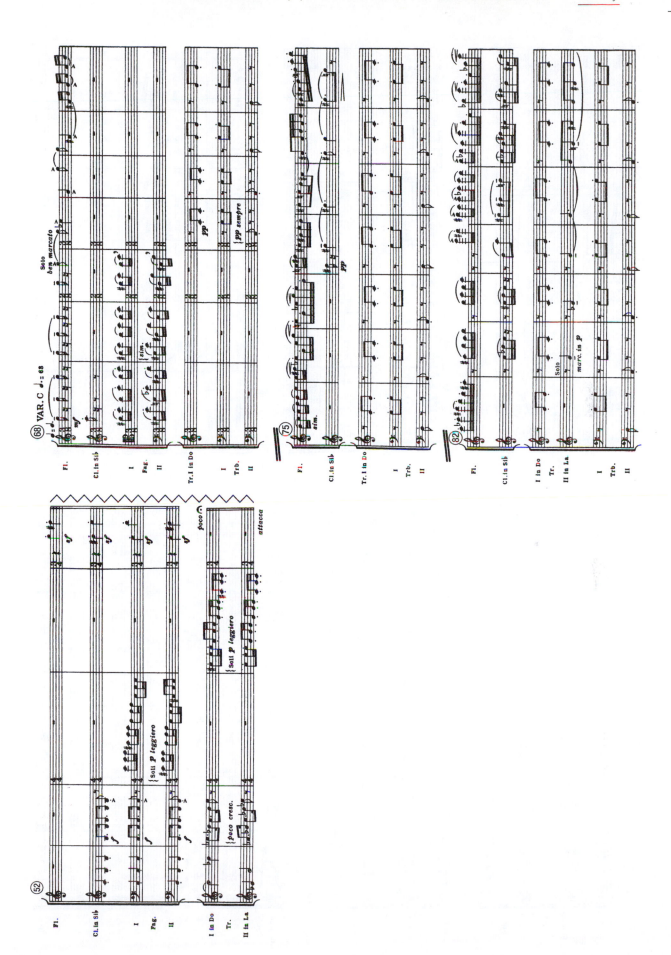

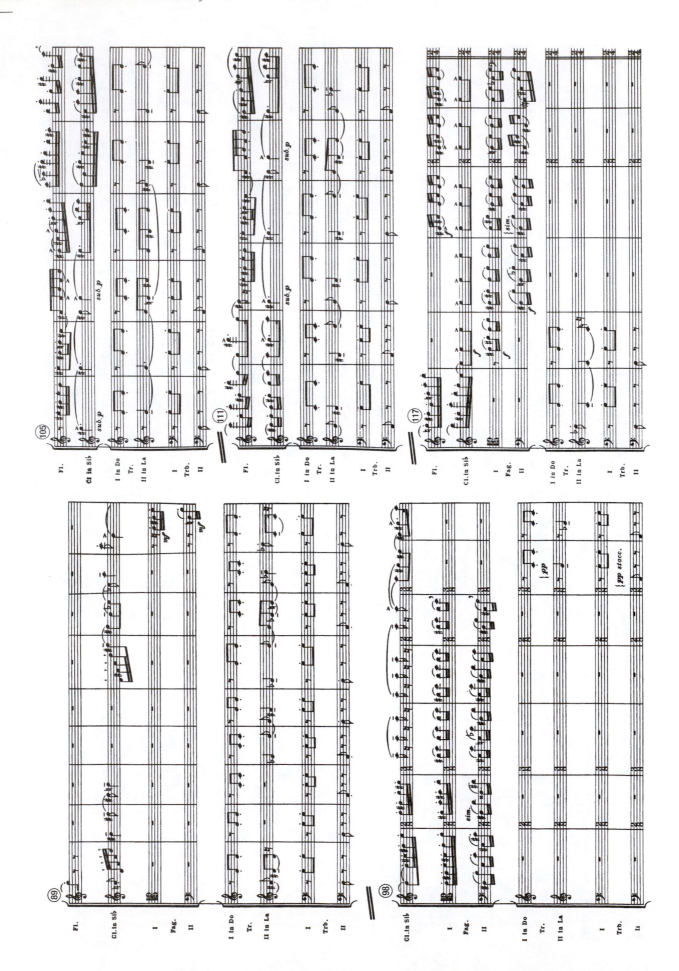

FULL FADOM FIVE
No. 2 of *Three Songs from William Shakespeare* (1953)
Igor Stravinsky (1882–1971)

From 1951 to the end of his compositional life, Stravinsky's method of composing gradually evolved in the direction of an ever more comprehensive serialism, but in a style quite his own, distinct from that of either Schoenberg or Webern. At first he worked with series of less than twelve pitches. The present work employs a series of just seven pitches that is first presented in the voice part, bars 2–3. We will call this series P0, but before examining it in detail, read the song's text. This is the well-known "Full fathom five" (but in Elizabethan spelling), one of Ariel's songs from Shakespeare's *The Tempest.* Someone's father has drowned and his body, instead of decaying, is strangely transformed while mermaids sound his funeral bell. Why did Stravinsky form his series of just *seven* tones?

Now consider the pitches of P0 (bars 2–3, voice). Write out the collection of seven pitches as a scale. What are its properties? Then identify all the series-forms used through bar 15. (You will find in the instruments a few places where Stravinsky chose to depart from the series briefly. Still, what gives these spots musical coherence and relates them to the series?) How do all the series-forms relate to each other in terms of pitch content?

Finally, turn to bar 1 and notice the many ways in which it is different. Clearly P0 is not present, but consider how bar 1 is related to it in terms of unordered pitch content. Then what happens in bars 16 to the end? Why does the piece end the way it does?[17]

---

[17] George Perle discusses *Three Songs from William Shakespeare* in his *Serial Composition and Atonality* (Berkeley: University of California Press, 6th ed., 1991, p. 10–15), and in all previous editions. See also Joseph N. Straus, *Stravinsky's Late Music* (Cambridge: Cambridge University Press, 2001, 224 et passim).

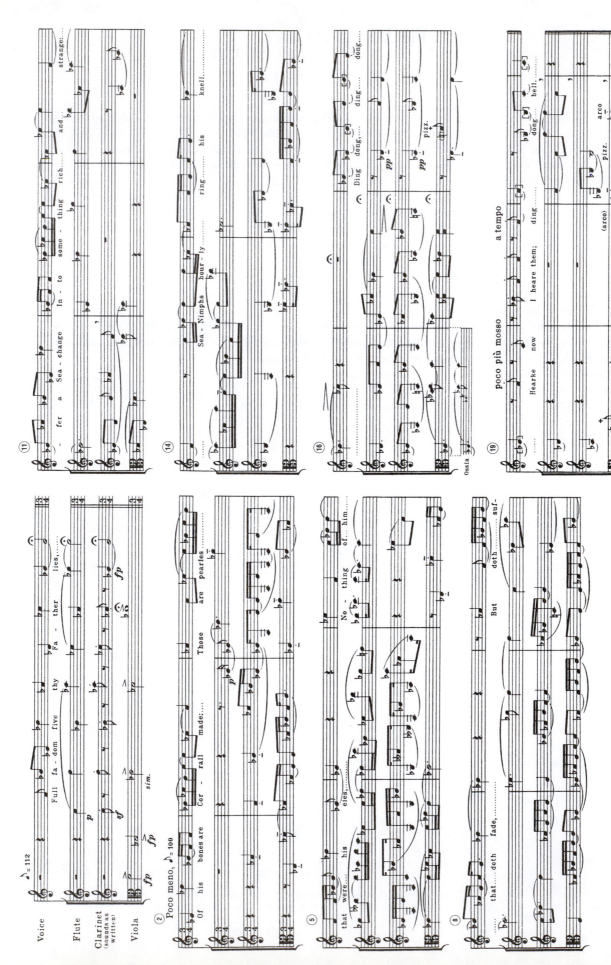

Three Songs from William Shakespeare (Stravinsky). © Copyright 1954 by Hawkes and Son (London) Ltd. Copyright Renewed. Reprinted by permission of Boosey and Hawkes, Inc.

PAS-DE-QUATRE and CODA
from *Agon* (1953–57)

Igor Stravinsky (1882–1971)

Stravinsky's life-long interest in composing for the dance led to numerous collaborations with the brilliant choreographer, George Balanchine, another Russian émigré. Among their joint creations is the ballet *Agon* (the Greek word for contest), premiered in 1957 by Balanchine's company, the New York City Ballet, which still performs it regularly. It is a plotless, abstract work consisting of a series of short dances, some of which are based on French court dances of the seventeenth century. The orchestra is large, but much of the work is scored for small groups. Written during the period when Stravinsky was gradually adopting a serial way of writing, *Agon* employs serial procedures in several of the dances, but not in all. One might think this would produce an effect of inconsistency in the work, but it all sounds like Stravinsky and is recognized as a masterpiece.

■ PAS-DE-QUATRE

Opening the work is the *Pas-de-Quatre*, with its annunciatory fanfares. (The same music will return at the end, with telling effect.) It is not serially organized. A good way to get into the piece is to discover its sections and what defines them. Then locate the sonorities that stand out as focal points, or "pitch-centers." Do these build a kind of basic progression roughly comparable to a "key plan" in a tonal work? Moving to a more detailed level, notice that the pure C-major scale (or F-Lydian) used at the outset is mixed with the G-major scale in bars 5–6 (see horns). Then explore the rest of the piece for the mixing of two or more diatonic scales or scale-segments, not overlooking how Stravinsky orchestrates these elements.

■ CODA (starts on page 478)

The term "Coda" is used several times in the score of *Agon* to denote the climactic third dance in a set of three. The antic *Coda* given here is preceded by a more stately *Saraband* and *Galliarde*. It contains the first twelve-tone series in Stravinsky's published work. However, several elements in the piece are non-serial: the opening C-G, the long violin melody in sixths (bar 9ff.), and a couple of other short, not-hard-to-find spots. At the outset harp and cello clearly state the first run-through of the twelve-note series. When you have found the remaining statements (except perhaps for those in the last six bars—a special problem[18]), consider how the series-forms combine, especially at bar 51ff. You can get a broad view of the piece by drawing a kind of map of it in terms of the series-forms, noting in which instruments and registers they occur. What form emerges? How do the non-serial elements contribute to it?

---

[18] Stravinsky here combines parallel segments of two different series-forms to produce chords. One of the series-forms is that introduced by Flute I in bar 51. The other, which has not yet been used, is scarcely deducible from the score. Stravinsky's sketches show it to be the form beginning Bb-E-B♮. See Joseph N. Straus, *Stravinsky's Late Music* (op. cit., 175–179), and the additional comments on pp. 93–94 and 117–118. It is also clear from the sketches that Stravinsky thought of the opening series-form of this movement as I0, even though P0 had not yet been used anywhere in the work. Straus follows Stravinsky's way of naming the series-forms.

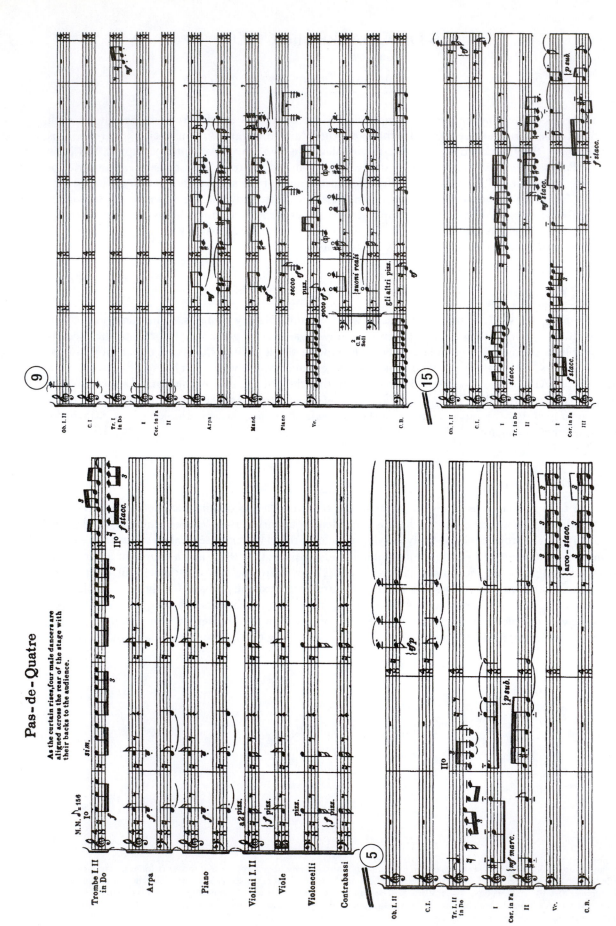

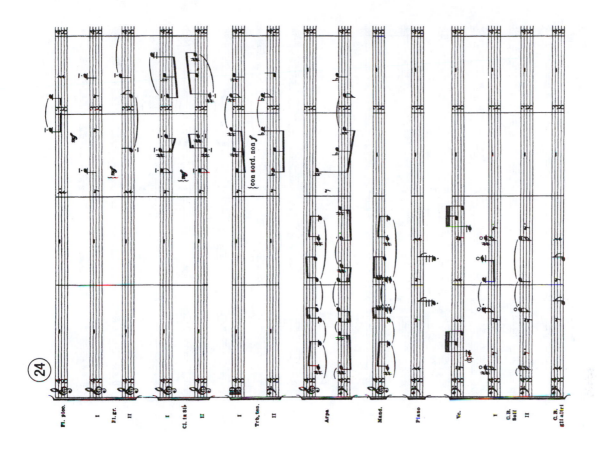

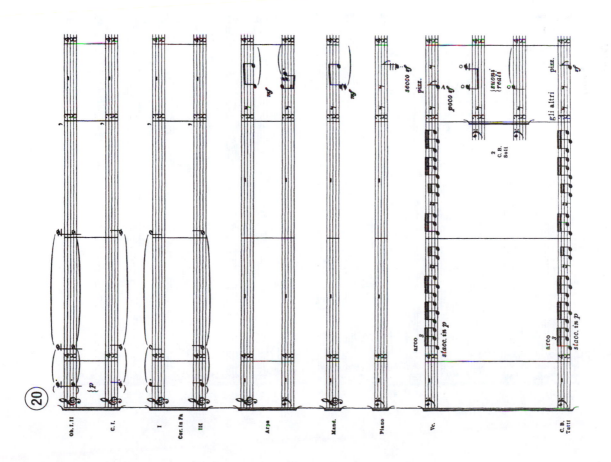

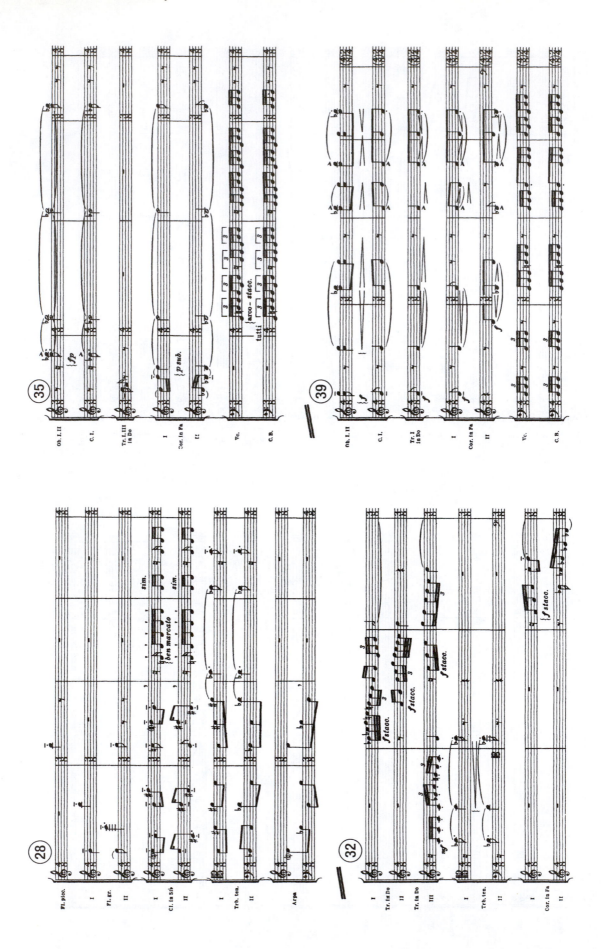

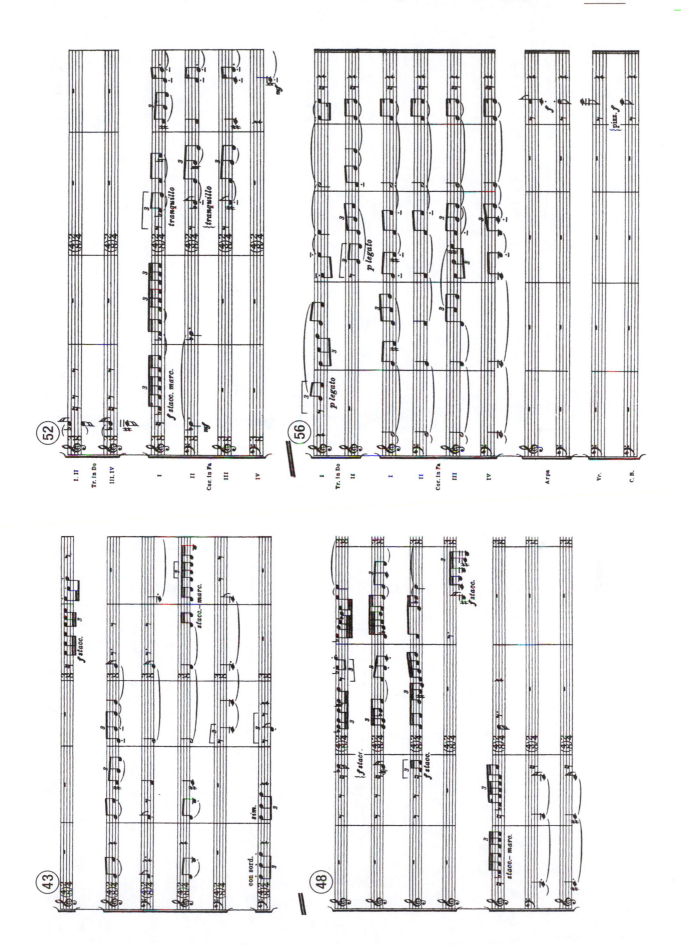

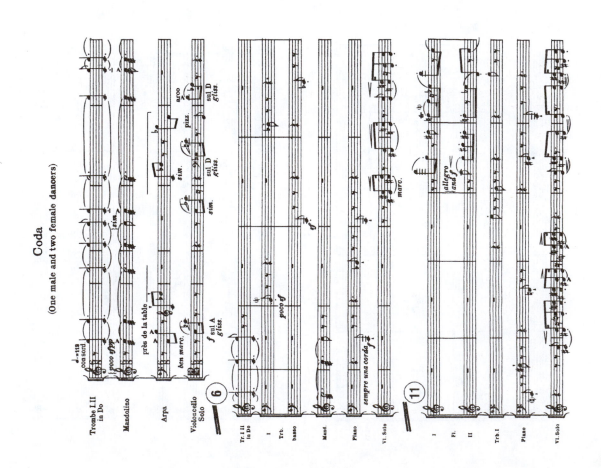

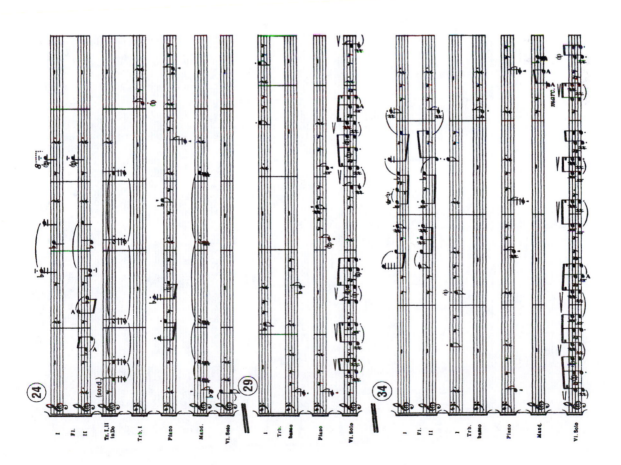

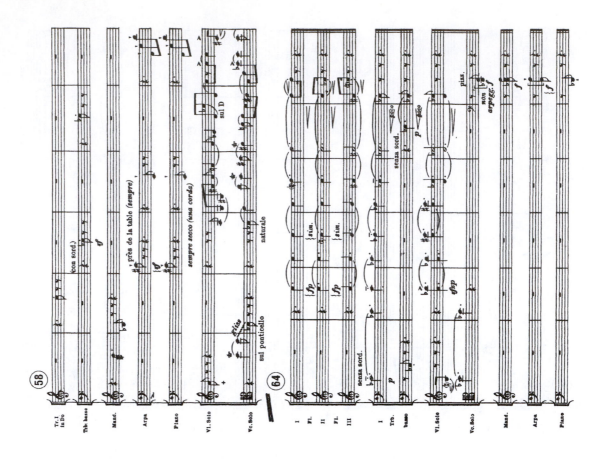

FIVE MOVEMENTS FOR STRING QUARTET

Op. 5 (1909), fourth movement

Anton Webern (1883–1945)

In his small output, which consists of mostly quite short compositions, Webern treated atonal and (later) serial materials with the utmost economy and rigor. This movement is unified to a high degree by means of repetitions of particular pitches, intervals, and motives. How do special instrumental timbres also contribute to its coherence? A longer "free" atonal work, Schoenberg's Opus 11, No. 1, is on page 420.[19]

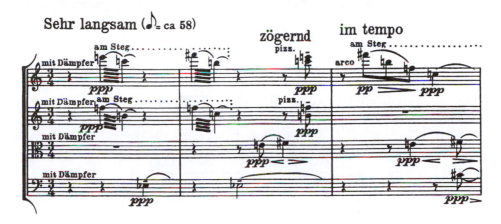

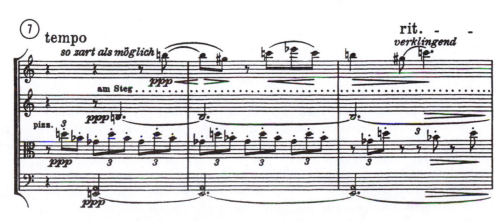

[19] Joseph N. Straus, in his *Introduction to Post-Tonal Theory* (op. cit.), discusses all three Webern works given here.

WIE BIN ICH FROH!
No. 1 of *Drei Lieder*, Op. 25 (1935)
Text: Hildegarde Jone (1891–1963)

Anton Webern (1883–1945)

How glad I am!
Once more all's turning green about me and shining so!
And overflowing with flowers is my world!
Once more I'm at the center of Becoming and yet on earth.

Notice first the phrases and the larger sections of this delicate song. By what several means are they articulated? Do opening or closing pitches or any phrases or sections reveal audible structural connections? On a smaller level, notice how often the piano simultaneously (or nearly so) duplicates the exact pitch of the voice, producing a quite audible relation between the two.

Rarely is it immediately obvious that a work is written in the twelve-tone system. If it is so written, one will presumably find intervallic correspondences that eventually account for every note in terms of an ordered twelve-tone set. In "Wie bin ich froh!," the first twelve notes happen all to be different pitch classes, but this fact alone does not prove that they constitute a series that will be systematically exploited throughout the work. If they are such a series, the order of the sixth to ninth tones cannot be determined from the opening because these tones are stated simultaneously. Perhaps the voice part, which cannot state tones simultaneously, will corroborate the twelve opening piano tones. Does it? Consider the relation between the piano's opening and the voice's. The discovery of their exact relation will not only make it possible to establish the order of the piano's sixth to ninth tones, but will leave little doubt that the song is a twelve-tone work.

All the series-forms used in the piece can now be found, and an order-number placed beside every note. These steps are necessary, but they do not constitute a complete twelve-tone analysis. They only make it possible to consider the more interesting questions about a twelve-tone composition. How are the characteristics of P-0 alone exploited in the composition? How do the various series-forms used in the piece relate to each other? How are these relationships compositionally exploited? How are the simultaneous occurrences of the same pitch in both voice and piano parts accounted for in twelve-tone terms? How is the dispersal of the various series-forms related to the form of the entire song? Answers to these questions will not only promote understanding of this song, but will also demonstrate that an early step in composing a twelve-tone piece is to devise a series whose properties will make possible the kind of piece one wants to write.

VARIATIONS FOR PIANO
Op. 27 (1936), second movement

Anton Webern (1883–1945)

Throughout this piece, the upper staff is to be played exclusively by the right hand, and the lower by the left, notwithstanding changes of clef. What is the relation of each hand's part to the other?

What is the twelve-tone series on which the piece is based? Study the progression from each pair of series-forms to the next. By what means are the opening two pitch classes, B♭ and G♯, arrived at in bars 11 and 22? Consider the way in which all the series-forms used are dispersed over the entire work, as well as the register in which each pitch class of each form lies. How much of the work was determined by precompositional decisions? What elements in the composition are "free"?[20]

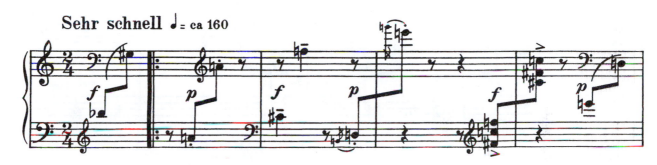

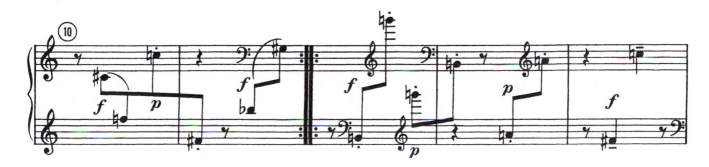

[20] Peter Westergaard analyzes this famous movement in his article, "Webern and Tonal Organization'" *Perspectives in New Music*, vol. 1, no. 2, 1963, pp. 107ff.). He cites four of the many other writings that deal with it.

SCHLAFEND TRÄGT MAN MICH
No. 2 from *Vier Lieder,* Op. 2 (1908–1909)
Text: Alfred Mombert (1872–1942)

Alban Berg (1885–1935)

In sleep I am borne unto my homeland.
From afar I come, over peaks, over abysses,
Over a darkened sea unto my homeland.

Although Berg's earliest compositions were rooted in tonality, the four songs of Opus 2 show him embarking on new paths. In this song, all the basic material is presented within the first four bars. Notice the melodic ideas there and trace them through the rest of the song. More far-reaching (and more significant for Berg's later work) is the way in which the harmony is controlled. Instead of the triad, another "chord," or better, collection of intervals, regulates the harmony throughout. Study the interval content of the opening seven piano chords and the progression from each chord to the next. How do they relate to the harmonies in the rest of the song? (Might the last chord in bar 15 contain a misprint?)

It is possible to see Berg's use of a key signature here as totally anachronistic. Is any vestige of tonality still present in this music?[21]

[21] Aspects of this song are discussed by George Perle in "Berg's Master Array of the Interval Cycles" (*Musical Quarterly*, 63/1, January 1977), reprinted in *The Right Notes* (Stuyvesant, NY: Pendragon Press, 1995, pp. 207ff.). See also Joseph N. Straus, *Introduction to Post-Tonal Theory* (op. cit., pp. 107–111).

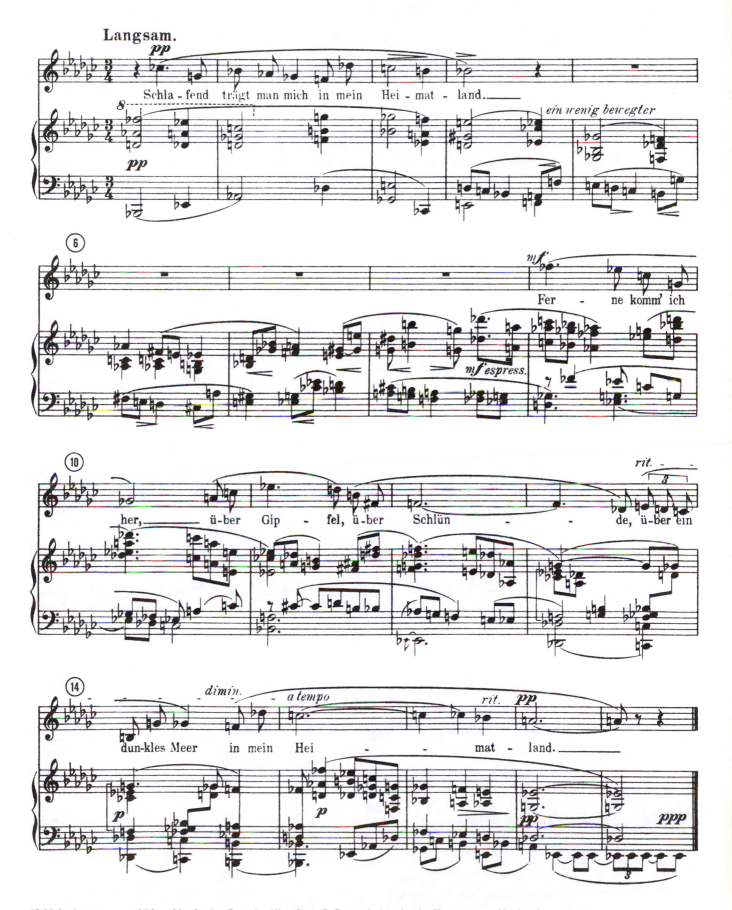

A SWAN
from *Six Chansons* (1939)
Text: Rainer Maria Rilke (1875–1926)

Paul Hindemith (1895–1963)

A foe of atonality and serialism, Hindemith sought to create a musical language that was both contemporary and founded on tonal centers. How does this chanson differ from a work in traditional E minor or E major? By what means is E projected as the tonic? Is the harmony triadic? How is dissonance treated? What tonal functions are preferred at cadences? (Hindemith's theory of tonality is briefly discussed on page 490).

"A Swan" is the second of a set of six chansons for four-part unaccompanied chorus.

A swan advances on the water,	*It draws near, doubled,*
Quite surrounded by himself,	*Like this swimming swan,*
Like a gliding picture.	*To our troubled soul,*
Thus, at certain moments,	*Which adds to that being*
A being that one loves	*The trembling image*
Is [seen as] a moving space.	*Of happiness and doubt.*

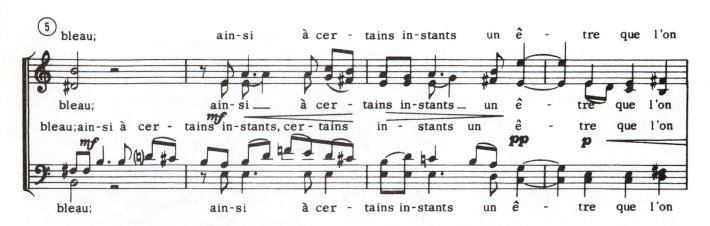

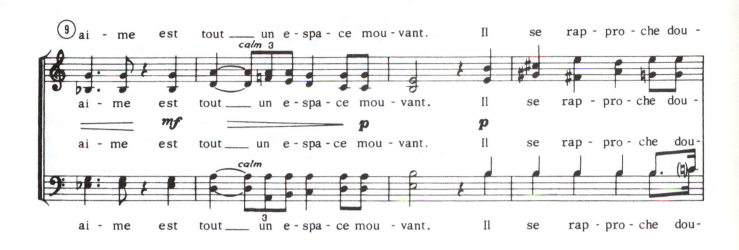

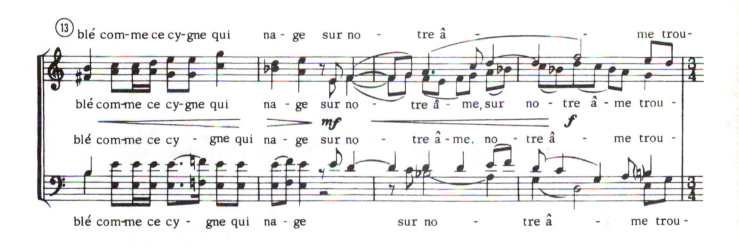

FUGA PRIMA in C
from *Ludus Tonalis* (1942)

Paul Hindemith (1895–1963)

In Hindemith's theory, a "key" is a set of relationships among any group of tones in which one tone emerges as supreme. This tone is called the tonic. (More recent theory would incorporate Hindemith's "tonic" under the term *center.*) Its supremacy can be established by various means. These do not necessarily include triadic harmony or diatonic scales (though both often occur in Hindemith's music). Because "major" and "minor" do not denote separate tonics, only twelve keys exist—one for each pitch of the chromatic scale. Hindemith used no key signatures in his notation because of their traditional implications.

Ludus Tonalis (The Play of the Tones) is a series of twelve fugues (one for each key) interspersed with interludes, the whole framed by a prelude and postlude. Although the work clearly owes a debt to Bach's *Well-Tempered Clavier* (see page 104), it is also a demonstration of another of Hindemith's theories in that the keys of the fugues are arranged in an order—C, G, F, A, E, Eb, Ab, D, Bb, Db, B, F#— that indicates their diminishing tonal relatedness to C.[22]

What species of fugue is this, the opening fugue? What is the function of measures 30–34? How, in spite of its high degree of chromaticism, does the piece project C as its tonal center? (Another twentieth-century fugue is on page 452.)

[22] Hindemith's major theoretical statement is volume 1 of *The Craft of Musical Composition* (New York: Associated Music Publishers, 1942; paper repr., Miami: European American Music Distributors Corporation, 2001). See also David Neumeyer, *The Music of Paul Hindemith* (New Haven, CT: Yale University Press, 1986).

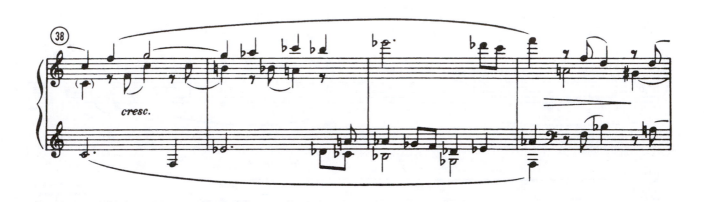

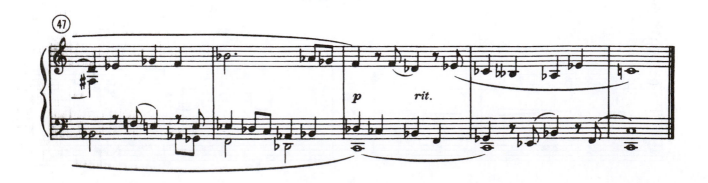

SUITE FOR VIOLONCELLO SOLO

Op. 84 (1939), first movement

Ernst Krenek (1900–1991)

Krenek's five-movement suite is based on a single twelve-tone series. In the first movement, the series is used in only one of its forty-eight possible forms. After placing an order-number beside every note of the piece, consider how the composer has made music of his twelve-tone material. Identify the various melodic ideas and analyze the form.

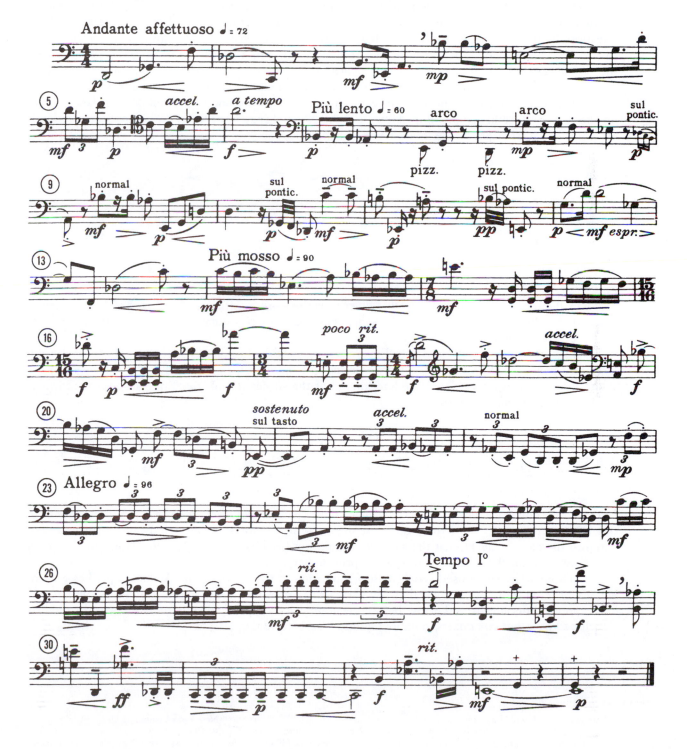

STRING QUARTET
(1931)
third movement

Ruth Crawford Seeger (1901–1953)

Ruth Crawford is identified with the American "experimental" group of composers active in the 1920s and 1930s that included Charles Ives, Henry Cowell, and Carl Ruggles. Her compositions include works for piano, chorus, voice with instruments, and numerous pieces for various instrumental combinations, among which is the remarkable string quartet completed in 1931. The third movement (Andante) of this four-movement work was described by Cowell in a 1933 letter to Ives as "without question the best movement for quartet that any American has written." Though this movement seems to be related to the sound-world of Schoenberg's Op. 16, No. 3, given above on page 424 (how are the two works similar?), its four instrumental parts are differentiated by means of a highly original technique of "contrapuntal dynamics." In bars 1–4, notice the rhythmic placement of the "hairpin" $\lessgtr$ in the viola part. How does this hairpin relate rhythmically to the one in the cello? What larger effect do the two produce in combination? How does the effect change in bars 5–7? Working from the loudest point of each hairpin to the loudest point of the next, thus,

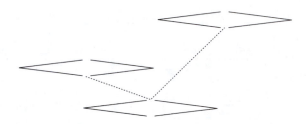

discover the repetitive large patterns that emerge as the work progresses. What is the large pattern in bars 19–23? In the work as a whole, how are these patterns coordinated with other parameters, for example, with change of meter?

In a letter of May 29, 1948, to Edgard Varèse (who had requested information on her music), Crawford commented on this movement, pointing out, among other things, that she conceived of the entire movement as a single melodic line formed of the succession of "new" pitches and passed from instrument to instrument, thus:

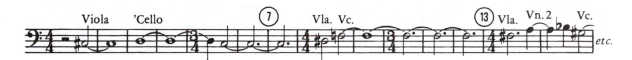

In the score, how has Crawford marked each of these "melody notes" from bar 5 on? Where does each one occur within $\lessgtr$? Writing on the score, circle all the notes of this melody and follow it as you listen to the movement. How is the melody brought out from bar 77 on? (Crawford's personal copy of the score confirms that there is a serious misprint in bar 35.)

Though Crawford used serial pitch organization in some works, the Andante's pitches are not serially ordered. But consider whether any particular pitches play a large-scale structural role.

Several decades would elapse before the approach to texture taken here by Crawford would be developed by other composers, notably György Ligeti (see page 520).[23]

[23] I am grateful to Joseph Straus for this information. See his *The Music of Ruth Crawford Seeger* (New York: Cambridge University Press, 1995, pp. 158ff.). See also Judith Tick, *Ruth Crawford Seeger* (New York: Oxford University Press, 1997), which gives Crawford's own analysis of the quartet's third and fourth movements on pp. 357ff., and Ellie Hisama, *Gendering Musical Modernism* (New York: Cambridge University Press, 2001), which gives an analysis of the third movement on pp. 12ff.

The dotted ties (•‥……••) indicate that the first tone of each new bow is *not* to be attacked; the bowing should be as little audible as possible throughtout.
The decrescendi should be as the crescendi.
The movement must not drag.

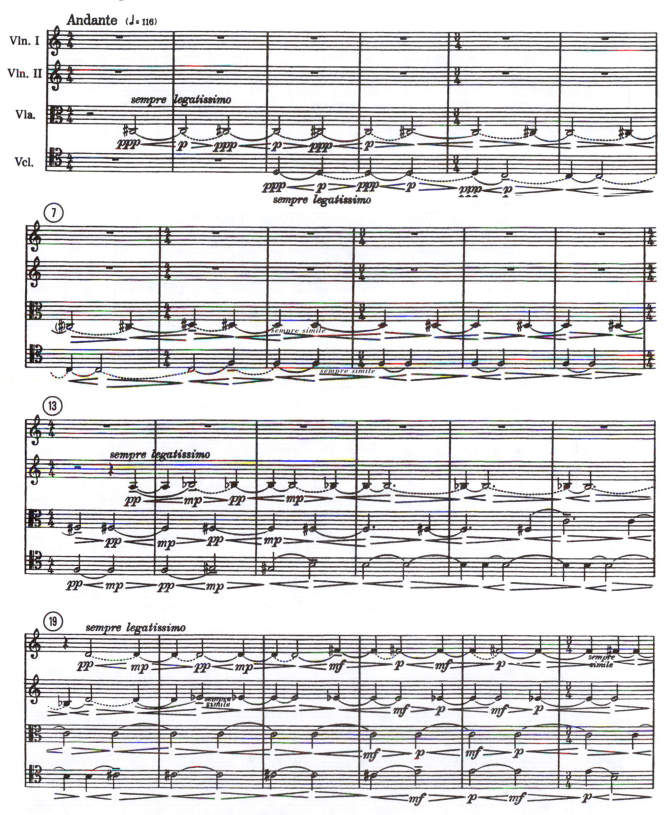

Accidentals affect only those individual notes before which they occur.

String Quartet, third movement by Ruth Crawford Seeger. © 1941 Merion Music, Inc., used by permission of the publisher.

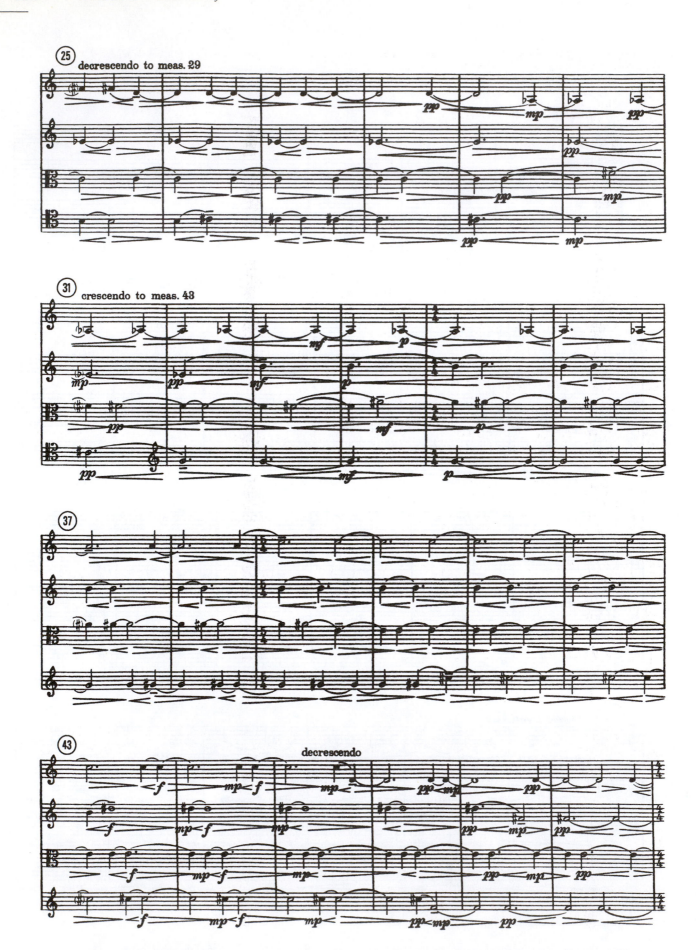

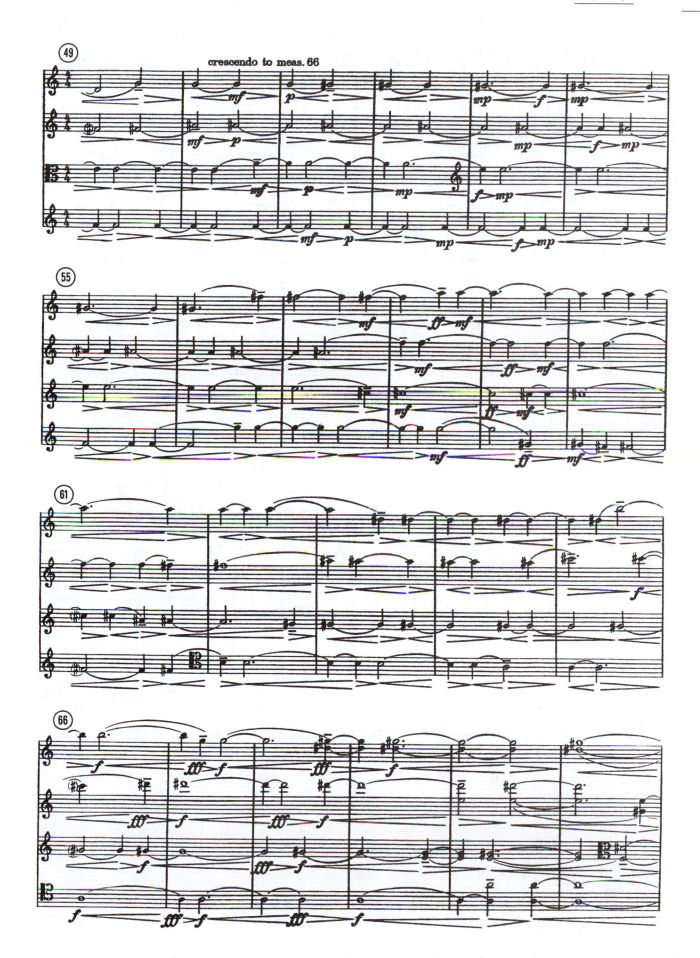

*) The half-notes in measures 85-88 should be faster than the quarter-notes in measure 77.

SIMBOLO
No. 1 of *Quaderno Musicale di Annalibera* (1952–1953)
Luigi Dallapiccola (1904–1975)

This is the opening piece in a "musical notebook" dedicated to the composer's daughter, Annalibera. The eleven pieces in the book, all founded on the same twelve-tone series, are conceived as a single work and are not to be performed individually. The work also exists in orchestrated form.

The title recalls the Notebook for Anna Magdalena Bach (see page 63). Also, the name of Bach is quite explicitly referred to in "Simbolo's" bar 7 by the highest notes, B♭-A-C-B♮, which are called B-A-C-H in German. This tetrachord, in various forms, dominates the piece. Could it have some relation to the piece's title? If so, what is possibly being symbolized?

The delicate textures of "Simbolo" require the utmost sensitivity of the performer. Its carefully notated rhythms should be carefully realized, but without stiffness. (In bar 40, exactly how do the two hands synchronize their parts?) In exploring the piece, examine first, as always, the phrases and sections. Where do formal divisions occur, and how are they produced? What pitches play a structural role thanks to registral emphasis?

As to the serial organization, we may assume from the first twelve pitch classes that the twelve-tone series begins A♯-B, but beyond that the order of the *individual pitches* in the dyads and trichords cannot be determined. This remains true throughout the piece. Nevertheless, because the order of the dyads and trichords remains constant, it is quite possible to determine the various series-forms. How do they connect one with the next? How do they *relate* with each other to form "networks?"[24]

---

[24] These and other interesting issues are discussed by David Lewin in "Serial Transformation Networks in Dallapiccola's 'Simbolo,'" the first chapter of his *Musical Form and Transformation* (New Haven, CT: Yale University Press, 1993).

Simbolo, No. 1 of Quaderno Musicale di Annalibera by Luigi Dallapiccola. © Sugar Music. Used with permission.

2 min. 45 secondi

LITURGIE DE CRISTAL
First movement of *Quatuor pour la fin du temps* (1940–1941)

Olivier Messiaen (1908–1992)

Olivier Messiaen was the most outstanding French composer of the mid-twentieth century, and also a very influential teacher, whose many distinguished students included Pierre Boulez and Karlheinz Stockhausen. A deeply religious Roman Catholic, Messiaen wrote many works illustrative of Christian doctrine, such as the early *Le banquet celeste* for organ (Messiaen was organist at the Church of La Trinité for sixty years), the well-known piano work *Vingt regards sur l'Enfant Jésus* (*Twenty Contemplations on the Infant Jesus*) of 1944, and his opera on St. Francis of Assisi (1975–1983). Another rich source of inspiration for Messiaen was the music of birds, whose songs he transcribed and incorporated into many colorful works, for example, the *Oiseaux Exotiques* (*Exotic Birds*) of 1955–1956 for piano, winds, and percussion. But birds were more than just singers; they were spirits from another world—messengers of God.

Messiaen composed and first performed the eight-movement *Quartet for the End of Time* while a prisoner in a German prisoner-of-war camp. Inspired by a visionary passage from *The Apocalypse* (or *Revelation*) of St. John, the Bible's last book, in which the angel of God announces that "there will be no more time," the work begins with a movement entitled *Liturgie de cristal* (*Crystal Liturgy*), which Messiaen himself described as portraying the awakening of birds at dawn, whose singing, "transposed to the religious plane," becomes "the harmonious silence of heaven." The movement reveals Messiaen's predilection for what he called *rhythmic pedal*, that is, a series of durations that constantly repeats, like an ostinato. Here the piano part exhibits such a "pedal," which starts with the following durations:

How does it continue? Where does the series of durations start to repeat? How many durations does the complete series consist of?

Now see the piano's *chords*. They too occur in a fixed series, but one that is *longer* than the durational series. Find it. How many repetitions of each series—the durational and the chordal—would have to occur before their beginnings again coincide? Messiaen constructs the cello part in a similar way, but here the two series are shorter and independent of the piano's. And piano and cello are both rhythmically independent of the flute and clarinet parts, which are rhythmically much freer. What might the composer have intended to suggest by the total rhythmic "picture"?[25] (We have added translations of the French terms.)

Comparison with the Machaut work on page 9 will reveal an early example of the type of scheme used here in the piano and cello parts.

---

[25] In the score of the *Quatuor*, Messiaen comments briefly on the entire work and also on his rhythmic theories. He gives a full exposition of his theories of rhythm and pitch in his book, *Technique de mon langage musical* (Paris: Leduc, 1942 [Eng. trans., *The Technique of my Musical Language*, 1956]). Paul Griffiths discusses the *Quatuor* in Chapter Six of his *Olivier Messiaen and the Music of Time* (Ithaca: Cornell University Press, 1985).

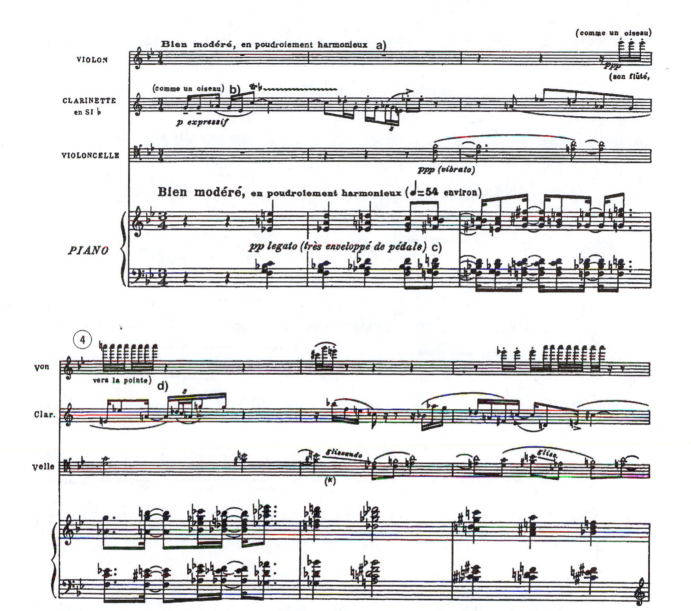

a) Quite moderately, in a harmonious dusty haze (quarter equals about 54)   b) like a bird   c) very enveloped by the pedal
d) flute-like sound, toward the tip (of the bow)

(∗) Glissando bref; id. aux passages similaires. (Brief glissando; likewise in similar passages)

CANARIES
No. 7 from *Eight Pieces for Four Timpani (One Player)*
(1950–1966)

Elliott Carter (b. 1908)

This humorous virtuosic take-off on a seventeenth-century French dance is offered here as an analysis problem in rhythm. It abounds in proportional changes of tempo, a device sometimes called "metrical modulation." Merely figuring out the arithmetic is not enough. Non-timpanists should practice tapping out at least the first 25 bars on a table top.[26]

Canaries is also a study in what can be done with just four pitches. What is the form of the piece?[27]

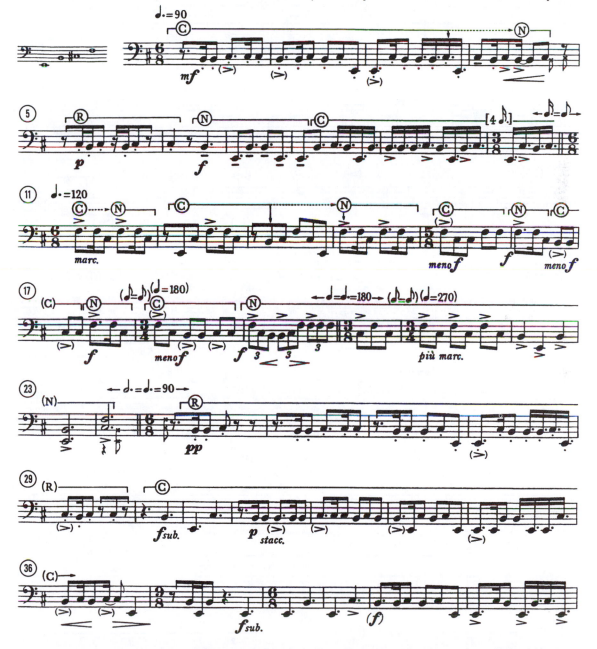

[26] Non-timpanists will have enough to do without considering the elaborate performance directions (C, N, R, DS, NS), which refer to ways of striking the drum to produce different timbres. An indispensable part of the composition, these directions are fully explained in the published set of eight pieces. Pitches notated as an x indicate hand damping.

[27] David Schiff discusses all eight pieces in his *The Music of Elliott Carter* (Ithaca: Cornell University Press, 2nd ed., 1998, pp. 132–135).

FOR PAUL TAYLOR AND ANITA DENCKS
(1957)
John Cage (1912–1992)

The decades immediately following the Second World War saw the rise of two quite contrasting approaches to the creation of music. One favored increased predetermination via an ever more comprehensive application of serial methods (see the piece on page 516 by Milton Babbitt); the other favored the removal of control over the processes of composition and performance via methods involving chance, or "indeterminacy." The most influential exponent of indeterminacy (and inventor of the term) was the American John Cage, who, beginning in the early 1950s, and motivated in part by his interest in Zen Buddhism, sought to create a "purposeless" music in which sounds did not express or symbolize any ideas, feelings, or formal schemes, but were simply allowed to exist for themselves—in short, merely to be. His stated aim was "to imitate nature in her manner of operation." Even silence—"what we hear if we are just quiet," such as some noise in the street, the wind blowing, our own breathing—became for Cage a "compositional" element. His scores of this period are written in various types of "graphic" notation that allow the performer varying degrees of freedom in their realization.

In 1957–1958 Cage composed his *Concert for Piano and Orchestra*, which not only made great technical demands on the pianist, but employed eighty-four distinct compositional techniques, each pictured by a more or less distinct type of graphic notation. At about the same time, Cage wrote several small occasional pieces using techniques used in the *Concert*. One of these is given here in Cage's manuscript. Though composed for a recital given by the dancers Paul Taylor and Anita Dencks, it is also intended as an independent piece of music. Study the score of this piece and realize it.

The entire three-minute piece stretches across the lower half of the page on an imaginary time line beginning with "12 seconds" on the left and ending at "3" (minutes) on the right. Four explicit points within this duration are given: 36", 60", 1'24", and 1'36". The four black dots each represent a single "sound event." There are only four in the piece. Sound No. 1, judging by the position of its dot on the time line, occurs at about 41", and Sound 2 at about 53". Where will you place Sounds 3 and 4?

Now see Cage's legend in the upper left corner. Note that Sounds 3 and 4 occur within "I," that is, "Interior Piano Construction," which would seem to mean that some point inside the piano, either the body or the strings, is to be struck. Sounds 1 and 2 are "A," that is, "Auxiliary" to the piano—anything but the piano.

The remaining symbols on the page refer to various parameters of each sound, as follows: The solid lines embracing A (and likewise I) represent the boundaries of a dynamic spectrum ranging from soft to loud. The closer a dot is to the dotted line (F), the lower in frequency it will be; the farther the higher. (Note that the rather isolated F in the lower center of the score belongs to A, not to I.) Likewise, the closer a dot to the dashed line (D), the shorter its duration, and vice versa. And the closer to the dash-and-dot line (T), the fewer overtones, and vice versa.

You are now ready to complete your realization. Sound 1, because it is represented as closer to the soft end of the spectrum than to the loud, might be realized as, say, *mezzo piano*. Because it is nearly touching the dashed line it will be quite short (but Sound 4 will be even shorter); because it's quite far from F-for-low-frequency, it will be quite high. (Sound 2 is somewhat lower. About how much so?) And because it's fairly far from the T-line, it will be rich in overtones. Such are the general characteristics of the sound, but the actual sound itself is undesignated. That choice is yours. What about a soft tap on a little bell, or on a metal bar, quickly dampened? Or a short, soft blowing of air—something like "white noise?" Within the given limits, any sound-producing medium, of either determinate or indeterminate pitch, is allowed, including other instruments (for A). In choosing the precise sound, imagination and taste are assumed. Humor and perhaps even occasional irreverence are not ruled out, but remember that Cage always insisted on a disciplined performance. He aimed to make the performer free, but never foolish.

Work up your realization and perform it. Remember that its four sounds are little islands in a sea of silence (as someone has said of Webern's music), and that the silence is part of the piece.

Cage might well be considered more of a musical philosopher than a composer in the usual sense, and he has written much about his ideas. Donald Jay Grout has suggested that Cage's music is based on assumptions fundamentally different from those of traditional Western art—assumptions so "ingrained in our thinking that most of us never imagine it possible to question them."[28] What might such assumptions be?[29]

Two further examples of indeterminacy, quite different from this one, are on pages 531 and 534.

[28] Grout, D. J., *A History of Western Music*, 4th edition, with Claude V. Palisca (New York: Norton, 1988, p. 750).

[29] Cage's major literary statement is *Silence* (Middletown: Wesleyan University Press, 1961). For an excellent summary of the evolution of Cage's career with its quite different yet related periods, see Paul Griffith's *Cage* in the *Oxford Studies of Composers* series (New York: Oxford University Press, 1981). Parts of my account are indebted to this book. Also, for their generous assistance, I am very grateful to John Holzaepfel and David Tudor.

For Paul Taylor and
Anita Dencks : Stony Point, N.Y. Ic. 9/57

F .... LOWEST FREQ.
D ------- SHORTEST DUR.
T ——— LEAST OVERTONE STRUCT.
INTERIOR PIANO CONSTRUCTION
AUXILIARY SOUNDS

123 SECONDS

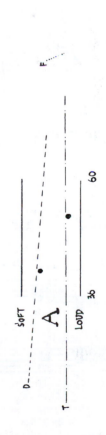

SOFT
F
D
T
LOUD
1:24   1:36

SOFT
D
A
T
LOUD
30   60
F

THREE-SCORE SET
(1943)
second movement

William Schuman (1910–1992)

The effect of polytriads—two or more different triads sounding simultaneously—has attracted many composers. Are polytriads heard as separate entities or as a single sonority? What factors make some sound better than others? In the following piece, how are they constructed? Does any tone or set of tones have overall priority?

For a more complex example of polytriads, see the excerpt from Stravinsky's *Le sacre du printemps*, page 458.

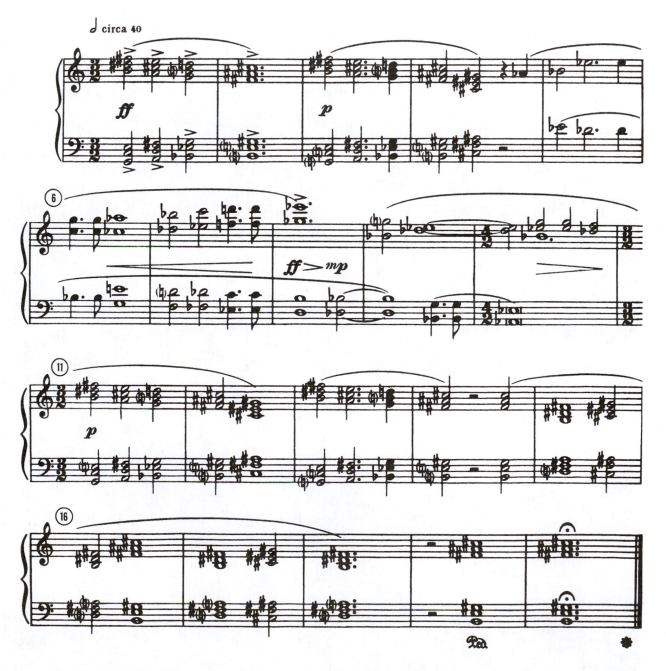

PLAY ON NOTES
for children's voices and bells
(publ. 1966)
Text: Milton Babbitt

Milton Babbitt (b. 1916)

In addition to creating a large body of compositions, Milton Babbitt has made a major contribution to twelve-tone theory. The following two pieces both demonstrate his extensions of Schoenberg's conception of combining different forms of a twelve-tone series (see page 430).

"Play on Notes" was written for performance by children.[30] It is clear that bars 1–2 form a twelve-tone aggregate expressed as two hexachords. What is the relation of these hexachords to each other? Rearrange the pitches of each hexachord to produce two stepwise scales. What is the nature of each scale, and what is the relation between them? Examine the rest of the piece. Would it be adequate to view its pitch material entirely in terms of a *six*-tone set? Notice the nature of the vertical dyads formed by the bell and voice parts. What produces such remarkable consistency? Finally, do not overlook the song's words.[31]

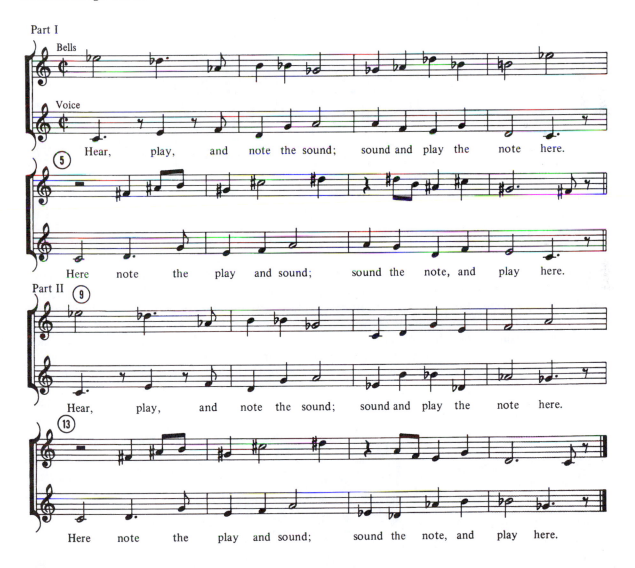

Play on Notes by Milton Babbitt from Exploring Music Book 6. Copyright © 1975 Holt, Rinehart, and Winston.

[30] When the bell part must be played on the piano, double it in the higher octaves. Do not double the voice part. Use treble voices only!
[31] See Robert Gauldin's analysis in "A Pedagogical Approach to Set Theory," *Theory and Practice* (Ithaca: Music Theory Society of New York State, September 1978, p. 3).

SEMI-SIMPLE VARIATIONS
for piano (1956)

Milton Babbitt (b. 1916)

Though this piece appears to be a theme followed by five variations, it is actually six variations on a twelve-tone series. The opening bars begin at once to "vary," or elaborate upon, the basic pitch materials.

The basic series (P0) is clearly set forth as the topmost pitches of bars 1–12. Write it out in one register. What is the relation of its two hexachords? What is the basic pitch content of each hexachord? Which series-form duplicates P0 exactly? How many actually different series-forms can P0 yield? With which series-forms is P0 combinatorial?

On the most fundamental level, the pitch of the piece is structured throughout in four continuous horizontal "lines." Each of the four lines is kept registrally distinct, but the registers change at formally important points. Figure 1 is a schematic diagram of bars 1–12. Each line is composed of a different series-form (the topmost being, as stated above, P0). These series-forms are so constituted that twelve-tone aggregates are subsequently formed by vertically adjacent (1) hexachords (see ovals) and (2) trichords (see rectangles). This scheme continually repeats (with series-forms peculiar to each repetition) throughout the piece.

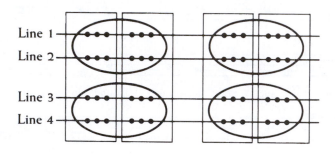

Figure 1

Figure 2 gives the first trichord of each line in its actual register. Comparison with the composition will show that these fundamental pitches are not expressed as four-note "chords," as pictured in Figure 2, but subjected to considerable rhythmic displacement and some repetition. The lines, for the most part, do not form "voices" in the conventional sense; instead, members of *different* lines are associated to form a pointillistic fabric of short sixteenth-note motives. Figure 2, then, represents a "background" that receives rhythmic elaboration in the "foreground." Following the start given in Figure 2, write out and identify each of the three remaining series-forms (lines 2, 3, and 4) of bars 1–12.

Figure 2

In bars 13–18, "variation" of a deeper sort occurs. The basic series P0 is itself now subjected to change, its members being permuted so that the ordering of the first hexachords reads: B♭-A-F♯-B-A♭-C. What is the nature of this derived hexachord? Compare it with the first hexachord of P0. What elements have remained the same? If the composer now follows a procedure consistent with that in P0 (he does), what *must* the second hexachord of this derived twelve-tone series be? Now this derived series governs only the *top two* lines of Variation II. The bottom two are formed of another derived series. This series can readily be deduced from Figure 3, which begins to set out the linear background of Variation II. Can you complete it? What is the relation of the top dyads to the bottom ones? How does the foreground procedure in Variation II compare with that of bars 1–12?

Figure 3

Again following precedents in the music of the Second Viennese School, notably Webern, Babbitt has also serialized the domain of rhythm in this piece. The first sixteen beats constitute a series of all sixteen different partitions of the quarter note possible with a sixteenth-note unit. This is the basic rhythmic series. It begins thus: Finish it. (Notice that only *attack points* are considered.) Variation I has a fixed rhythmic relation to the theme: What is it? Babbitt's method of "inverting" a rhythm in this piece is to replace an attack with a rest, and vice versa. For example, inverts as . What form of the rhythmic series occurs in Variation II? In addition to serialization on the quarter-note level, what larger, more obvious instances of rhythmic serialization occur in the piece?

There is even a dynamics series in *Semi-Simple Variations.* How is it distributed? From a more general point of view, how do dynamics and register help articulate each variation?[32]

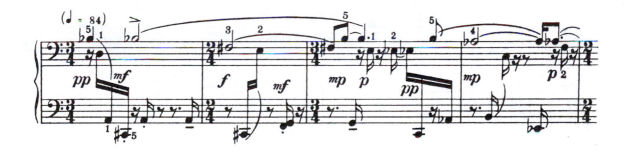

Semi-Simple Variations by Milton Babbitt. © 1957 Theodore Presser Company. Used by permission of the Publisher.

[32] The foregoing owes much to Elaine Barkin's "A Simple Approach to Milton Babbitt's *Semi-Simple Variations*" in "*The Music Review,* 1967, vol. 28, p. 316), and to Christopher Wintle's "Milton Babbitt's Semi-Simple Variations" in (*Perspectives of New Music,* 1976, vols. 14:1/15:2, p. 111). Wintle's very thorough article includes an instructive introduction to Babbitt's theory. This volume of *Perspectives* also contains a bibliography of Babbitt's own writing. *Semi-Simple Variations* is recorded on LP (*Opus One* 67) and CD (*Complete Piano Music of Milton Babbitt,* Harmonia Mundi 905 160). The composer has approved a somewhat faster tempo than the one given in the score.

VAR. IV

VAR. V

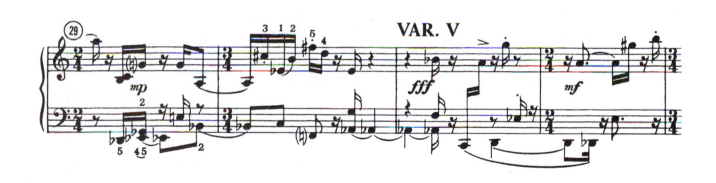

No. 1 of TEN PIECES FOR WIND QUINTET
(1968)
György Ligeti (b. 1923)

After leaving his native Hungary following the 1956 revolution and subsequent Soviet suppression, György Ligeti emerged into international prominence with his "cluster" compositions for huge orchestra, *Apparitions* (1958–1959) and *Atmosphères* (1961), works in which his primary concern was to produce a slowly changing texture by means of many simultaneously sounding voices that cannot be (and are not intended to be) individually perceived. A later very successful work was his opera, *Le Grand Macabre* (1974–1977, revised 1996). Since 1985, he has written a series of remarkable piano etudes that, while building on the tradition of Chopin and, especially, Debussy, explores new pianistic and compositional ground.

The *Ten Pieces for Wind Quintet* of 1968 alternates ensemble pieces (the odd-numbered movements) with highly virtuosic mini-concertinos for each of the five instruments (even-numbered movements). Piece No. 1 (and several others) reveals Ligeti's focus on texture typical of his work of the 1960s. To discover just what he is doing here, it may be helpful—in addition to examining individual lines—to write out a rhythmless "reduction" in concert pitch showing exactly how the sonorities change from one to the next. What are the governing principles? What motivates the C♯ in bar 16? How is this piece related to the Crawford movement on page 494 and to Schoenberg's *Farben*, page 424?[33]

33 The standard English work on Ligeti's music is Paul Griffiths *György Ligeti* (London: Robson Books, 1983, 2nd ed. 1996). See also C. D. Morrison, "Stepwise Continuity as a Structural Determinate in György Ligeti's *Ten Pieces for Wind Quintet*" (*Perspectives of New Music*, 24/1, 1985–1986, 158–182).

Molto sostenuto e calmo
($\downarrow$ = 40)

*) Flauto contralto in Sol

**) Corno Inglese

Clarinetto in Si♭

***) Corno in Fa

Fagotto

NB. Die Partitur ist transponierend notiert.

NB. *The score is written in the relevant transpositions.*

*) Altflöte wechselt − in den später folgenden Stücken − zur Flöte und Piccoloflöte.

*) *Alto Flute later changes to Flute and Piccolo.*

**) Englischhorn wechselt − in den später folgenden Stücken − zu Oboe d'amore und Oboe.

**) *English Horn later changes to Oboe d'amore and Oboe.*

***) Horn: Es wird ein Doppelhorn (Fa - Si♭) verlangt. Die in B - Stimmung gespielten Stellen sind auch in F notiert.

***) *A double horn (F - B flat) is required. The passages played in B flat tuning are also notated in F.*

****) Dynamische Balance= Das **pp** aller Instrumente richtet sich nach dem **pp** des Englischhorns. Falls das Englischhorn auffällt, spielen die übrigen Instrumente (besonders die Altflöte) statt **pp** stets **p** oder **mp**, statt **mf** stets **f** (gilt für die Takte 1 - 14).

****) *Balance of dynamics:* **pp** *in all instruments matches the English Horn's* **pp**. *Should the English Horn prevail, the other instruments (especially the Alto Flute) must play always* **p** *or* **mp** *instead of* **pp** *and* **f** *instead of* **mf** *(in bars 1 - 14).*

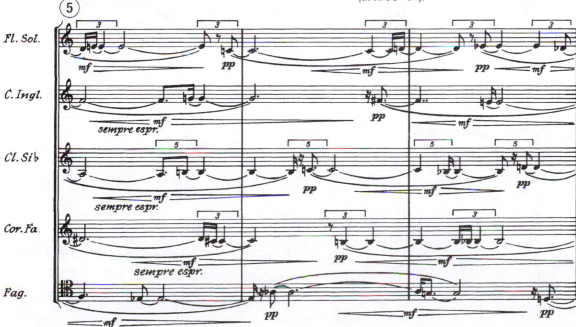

Fl. Sol.

C. Ingl.

Cl. Si♭

Cor. Fa.

Fag.

*)	Quasi legato von Klarinette, Horn, Fagott zu Altflöte und Englischhorn: Es soll weder die mindeste Zäsur noch eine Überlappung entstehen.

**)	*fff* tenuto in Altflöte, Englischhorn, Klarinette, Fagott: Einsätze „flach" ausführen, d. h.: ohne besonderen Akzent, aber mit aller Kraft einsetzen, ohne diminuendo halten, dann schnell nur für einen Atemzug unterbrechen und wieder „flach" mit aller Kraft einsetzen. Hier gibt es keine dynamische Balance mehr: jedes Instrument bläst so laut wie möglich, außer Horn. Die Klarinette bleibt im Hintergrund, sie soll aber ebenfalls so laut blasen, wie es in diesem Register nur möglich ist.

***)	*ff* tenuto im Horn: Ebenfalls „flach", ohne besonderen Akzent einsetzen, ohne diminuendo halten, dann schnell atmen und wieder „flach" einsetzen. Doch spielt das Horn nicht lauter als die anderen Instrumente, so daß es nicht solistisch hervortritt. (Horn *ff* = *fff* der anderen).

*)	"Quasi legato" from Clarinet, Horn and Bassoon to Alto-Flute and English Horn; there should not be the slightest caesura, nor should the instruments overlap.

**)	*fff* tenuto in Alto-Flute, English Horn, Clarinet, Basson: Play the entrances "level", that is, without any special accentuation, but attack with full force, sustain without diminuendo, interrupt quickly to take breath, and re-enter "level" and with full force. There is no balance of dynamics; each instrument plays as loud as possible, except Horn. The Clarinet remains in the background, but must also play as loud as possible in this register.

***)	*ff* tenuto in the Horn: play the entrances likewise "level", without any special accentuation, sustain without diminuendo, breathe quickly, re-enter "level". The Horn should not play louder than the other instruments, so that it does not stand out. Horn *ff* = *fff* in the other instruments.

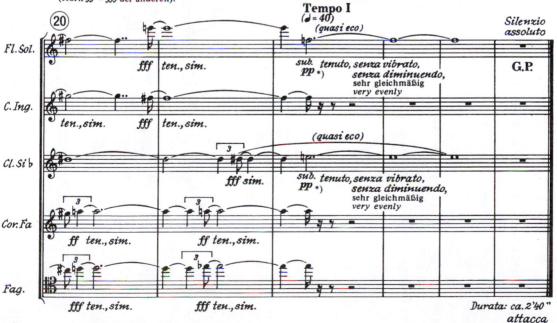

*)	Dynamische Balance: Altflöte *pp* = Klarinette *pp*

*)	Balance of dynamics: Alto Flute *pp* = Clarinet *pp*

¿POR QUÉ NACÍ ENTRE ESPEJOS?

No. 1 of *Madrigals, Book IV* (1969)

Text: Federico García Lorca (1899–1936)

George Crumb (b. 1929)

The American George Crumb composed between 1963–1971 a large body of works based on poetry by the Spanish writer Federico García Lorca. Four of these works are books of madrigals scored for soprano and small ensembles of instruments, with texts that treat the universal themes of love, nature, life, and death. Though each book comprises three madrigals intended to be performed as a group, each madrigal is also a complete composition.

Crumb's work is remarkable for its exploration of unusual and colorful timbres. Listen to the opening chord of the madrigal given here and consider the factors that contribute to its unique sonority. The composer's performance notes state that the glockenspiel ("Glsp.") sounds, as usual, two octaves higher than written. They also state that the sign ⌐⌐⌐ means "approximately 7 seconds," and that ♩. = ♪♪ and ♪ = ♪♪. What is the logic of the latter notation? (Just figuring out the rhythm and the performance directions is a considerable analysis problem.)

Though Crumb seems little interested in compositional systems, he has organized the elements of this piece according to a simple but rigorous scheme. Discover this scheme and consider its meaning.

The original score contains the following translation by J. L. Gili.

Why was I born surrounded by mirrors?
The day turns round me.
And the night reproduces me in each of her stars.

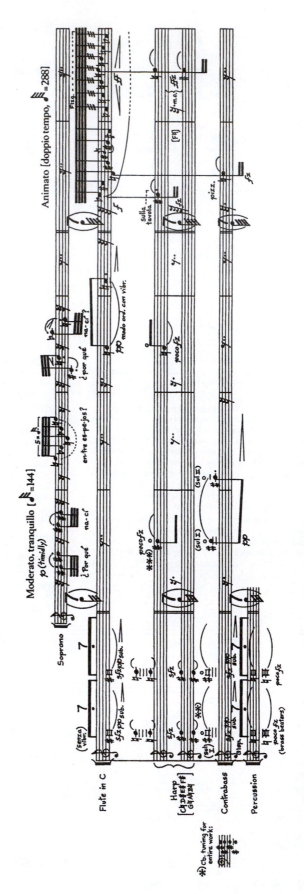

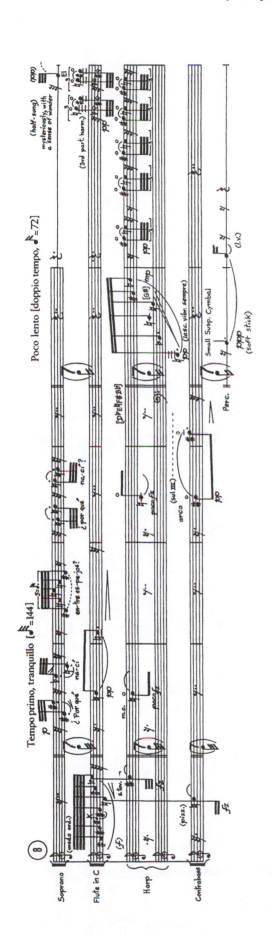

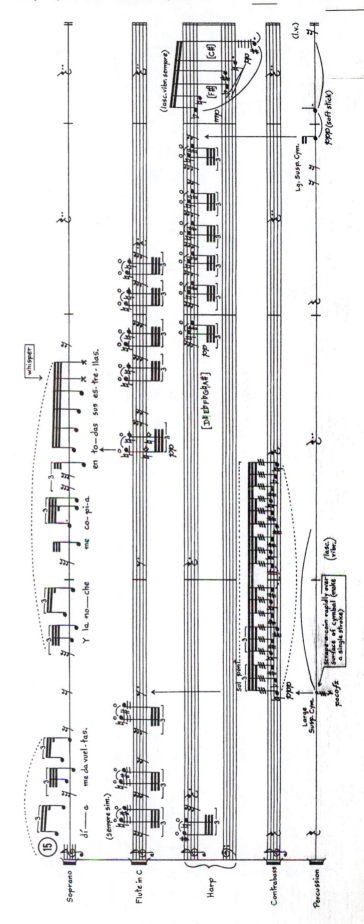

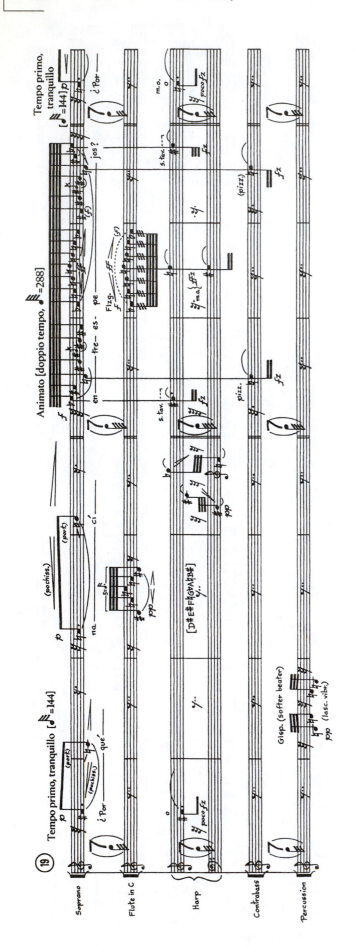
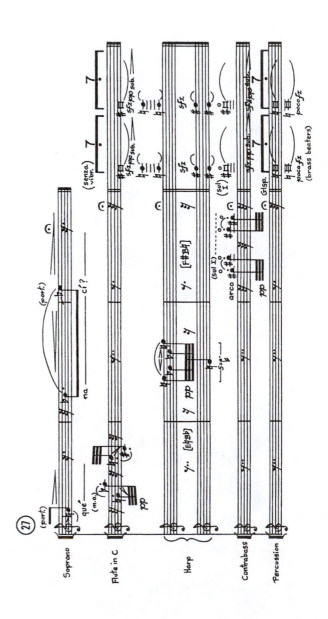

AUTUMN
first movement of *Rocking Mirror Daybreak* for violin duo (1983)

Toru Takemitsu (1930–1996)

The music of Toru Takemitsu, the leading Japanese composer of the twentieth century, brings together aspects of the Eastern and Western musical traditions. Having passed through an extended period of experimental modernism that reached its apogee in the early 1970s, Takemitsu gradually adopted a more simplified style that, particularly in the 1980s, included a turning toward what he himself described as "the sea of tonality."[34]

Rocking Mirror Daybreak, composed at a time of growing international fame, was commissioned by the violinists Ani and Ida Kavafian for their first duo recital at Carnegie Hall. The title of the work and those of its four movements, namely, *Autumn, Passing Bird, In the Shadow,* and *Rocking Mirror,* come from a "linked verse" in four parts (not further quoted in the score), two written by Makoto Ooka and two by Thomas Fitzsimmons. In *Autumn,* can one discover some force or process that influences the transformations of the evocative opening motive?

SYMBOLS AND ABBREVIATIONS:

↕	1/4 tone above
pont. or **s.p.**	sul ponticello
tasto	sul tasto
p.o.	position ordinary
N.V.	without vibration (non vibrato)
(p.o.)——⋯➤s.p.	move gradually from position ordinary to sul ponticello
s.p. ——⋯➤p.o.	move gradually from sul ponticello to position ordinary
s.s.	without mute (senza sordino)
c.s.	with mute (con sordino)

---

[34] For a comprehensive account of Takemitsu's stylistic development, see Peter Burt's *The Music of Toru Takemitsu* (New York: Cambridge University Press, 2001).

IN C
(1964)

Terry Riley (b. 1935)

The early 1960s saw the rise of the musical style known as minimalism. With roots in the work of John Cage, minimalist works at first were generally characterized by constant repetition of one or more short diatonic patterns, with alterations introduced into the pattern very slightly and gradually to produce an effect of kaleidoscopic change. The style arose partly as a reaction to the complexity of serialism and partly as an attempt to reproduce the perceived stasis, or timelessness, of Oriental music. The most important early figures were Terry Riley, Steve Reich, and Philip Glass, all of whom later moved beyond the style of the early, "classical," minimalism as described here.

Riley's *In C* was a landmark in the early development of minimalism. Clearly its score can give little idea of its effect in performance. After listening to one of the recordings,[35] ask yourself if you listen to *In C* any differently from the way you listen to a Haydn quartet, Chopin nocturne, or Stravinsky ballet? Riley has said that he came to realize that "things didn't sound the same when you heard them more than once, and the more you heard them, the more different they did sound."[36] What did he mean? Many minimalist works feature a degree of improvisation. Does the improvisation in *In C* differ from jazz improvisation?

The following directions are provided in the score by the composer:

All performers play from the same part.

There are 53 repeating figures, played in sequence.

They are to be taken consecutively with each performer determining the number of times he repeats each figure before going on to the next.

The pulse is traditionally played by a beautiful girl on the top two octaves of a grand piano. She must play loudly and keep strict tempo for the entire ensemble to follow.

The tempo should be determined by how fast the ensemble can execute the smallest units (16th notes).

All performers must strictly adhere to the tempo of the pulse.

After the pulse has begun to sound, each performer determines for himself when to enter on the first figure.

As a general rule the performers should remain within a compass of 4 or 5 figures of each other, occasionally trying to merge together in a unison. This means that although each performer is essentially free to repeat a figure as many times as he wishes, he must ultimately abide by the pace taken on by the majority in the ensemble.

The ensemble should sit as close together as is comfortably possible, all performers radiating outward from the pulse, who should be in the center.

It is O.K. to amplify instruments that can't naturally play so loud, such as strings, flutes, harpsichords, etc.

All parts should be played at the written pitch. It is generally O.K. to transpose up an octave. Transposing down an octave should be discouraged unless several performers are doing so and even then they should be extremely careful in choosing alignments and try to absorb the tendency to stick out.

Since performances often go over an hour, each figure can easily be repeated for a minute or longer. (Performances could last days, months, a year—a figure for each week, with the closing one to start the new year.)

Don't be in a hurry to move from figure to figure. Stay on your part and keep repeating it, listening for how it is relating to what the rest of the ensemble is playing. If it sounds like everyone is playing in the same alignment of a figure, you may shift yours to create an opposing alignment.

Say that most of the ensemble
is playing figure #12 like this:

you may chose to align like this:

or this:

and so on.

---

[35] The many recordings include ARGO 430380-2ZH and CBS MK-7178. The most recent to date, Cantaloupe Records CA 21004, has been well received.
[36] *New York Times*, October 7, 2001.

In this way you have not 53 figures but literally thousands and it is part of the creative task of the ensemble to explore the different combinations.

Play at a good loud volume but avoid letting your part get isolated from the others. Make all exits and entries as inconspicuous as possible.

In order to play continuously without fatigue, a figure can be repeated in groups of 4 or 5 with a rest included to form an overall pattern consisting of x number of repetitions plus a rest. The duration of the rest may be equal to the duration of the figure being repeated, as illustrated below.

This makes the part more stable and symmetrical and allows it to groove better with the rest of the ensemble, especially if everyone else is stabilized in a pattern formation. However, any number of repetitions and any duration of rest if permitted.

Changes should not be dramatic. The sequence should very gradually unfold.

When each performer reaches figure #53 he should stay on that figure until the entire ensemble has arrived and a unison is achieved. The players can then gradually drop out, the pulse continuing a few moments after the rest of the ensemble has finished. If a performer comes to a figure he cannot play, he may omit it.

The ensemble should learn all figures in unison before attempting any combination. It is essential that every one play the figures correctly.

Any number of instruments can play. In general the more players, the better it goes. Several keyboard instruments should be used as well as percussion instruments that are tuned, such as marimbas, vibraphones, and xylophones.,

In figures #22 to #26 the dotted quarter notes are usually played as three eighth notes.

CLAPPING MUSIC
for two performers
(1972)
Steve Reich (b. 1936)

Steve Reich's chief contribution to the early development of minimalism was his "phase" compositions, wherein two or more identical sound-sources performing a constantly repeated figure begin in unison, then gradually move out of phase with one another, thus producing ever-changing sound-combinations—a process in which improvisation plays no part. *Clapping Music* was the last (and the simplest) of Reich's strictly "phase" compositions, but he continued to develop similar repetitive, pulse-driven procedures in imaginative ways in much more elaborate works, such as, for example, his *Music for 18 Musicians* of 1974–1976, and *Triple Quartet* of 1999 for string quartet and tape or three string quartets live. To what other kind(s) of twentieth-century music does *Clapping Music* bear some relationship?[37]

Directions for Performance

The number of repeats is fixed at 12 repeats per bar. The duration of the piece should be approximately 5 minutes. The second performer should keep his or her downbeat where it is written, on the first beat of each measure and not on the first beat of the group of three claps, so that the downbeat always falls on a new beat of the unchanging pattern. No other accents should be made. It is for this reason that a time signature of 6/4 or 12/8 is not given – to avoid metrical accents. To begin the piece one player may set the tempo by counting quietly; "one, two, three, four, five, six".

The choice of a particular clapping sound, i.e. with cupped or flat hands, is left up to the performers. Whichever timbre is chosen, both performers should try and get the same one so that their two parts will blend to produce one overall resulting pattern.

In a hall holding 200 people or more the clapping should be amplified with either a single omni-directional microphone for both performers, or two directional microphones; one for each performer. In either case the amplification should be mixed into mono and both parts fed equally to all loudspeakers. In smaller live rooms the piece may be performed without amplification. In either case the performers should perform while standing as close to one another as possible so as to hear each other well.

---

[37] Michael Nyman discusses Reich's phase works in detail in *Experimental Music / Cage and Beyond* (New York: Cambridge University Press, 2nd ed., 1999, pp. 151–157). For a comprehensive view of Reich's work through the early 1990s, see K. Robert Schwarz, *Minimalists* (London: Phaidon, 1996).

PSALM 13
from *Four Psalm Settings* (1976–1978)
Bruce Saylor (b. 1946)

After listening to this composition and studying the performance directions and score, consider the role indeterminacy plays in it. Has the composer relinquished control over his material? Is the listener aware that unmetered and metered time simultaneously occur, or that a performer sometimes improvises? In bars 37–39, how are the pitches of the two parts related? Indeterminacy aside, what elements give the work coherence and form?[38]

PERFORMANCE DIRECTIONS

1. The flutist plays in strict time except between bars 37 and 39. The singer, whose part is unmetered, watches the flute part and aligns her part approximately with it.

2. Between bars 37 and 39, where the flutist improvises, the situation is reversed: The flutist now watches the singer's text and interjects the *sf* notes as indicated.

3. Vocal symbols: ●━━━━━━ sustained tone;

    ● short tone;

    |○| reciting tone: Sing the text crisply and rapidly in the rhythm of speech.

4. The symbol + (bar 8, flute) means *slap keys, tonguing sharply*.

---

[38] *Four Psalm Settings* is recorded by Orion (ORS 80368).

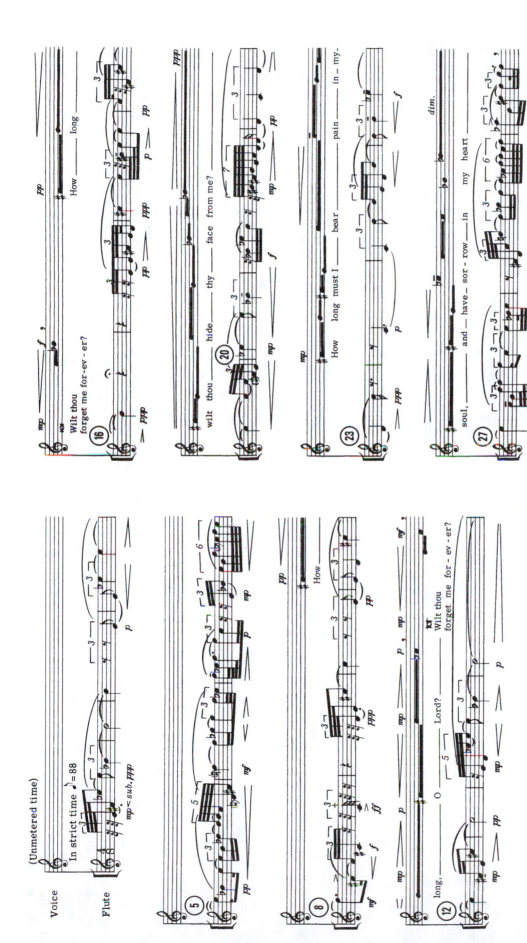

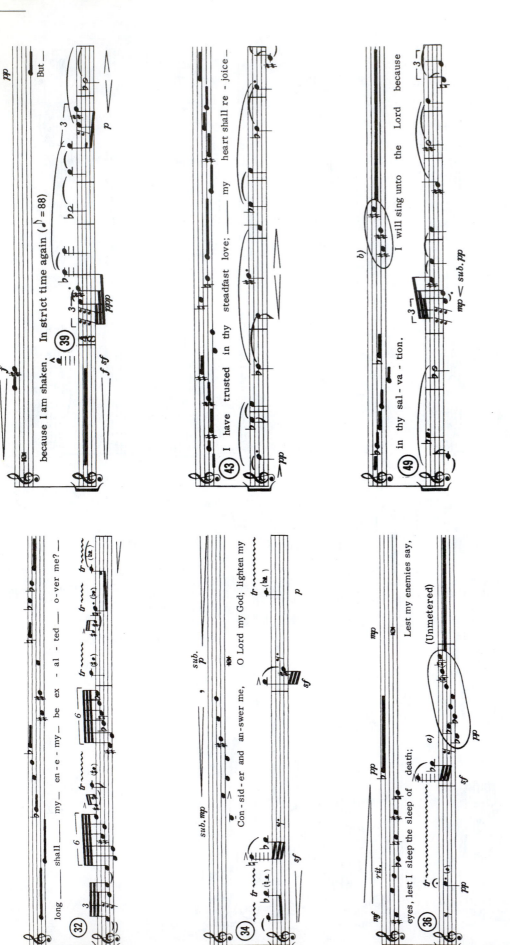

a) Improvise freely and rapidly on these notes, varying the order, the groupings, and the articulations.

b) Sing text slowly, choosing from among these notes.

THIS IS PROPHETIC
from *Nixon in China* (1985–1987)
Libretto by Alice Goodman

John Adams (b. 1947)

In addition to minimalism (see pages 531 and 533), another notable strand in the music of the past four decades has been a "return" to the harmonic materials of the past, a trend sometimes called "The New Tonality." John Adams came to compositional maturity by the time both these strands had been established and has drawn upon both in creating a large body of instrumental and vocal works. He is one of the most widely performed contemporary composers of concert music.

Nixon in China is a three-act opera based on the historic 1972 visit of President Richard Nixon to Chairman Mao Zedong that ended the long stand-off between their two countries and effected a shift in the global balance of power. Despite the contemporaneity of the subject, the work is not primarily satiric, but on a heroic scale, yet touched with humor and compassion. In Act I the leaders meet, discuss issues, then proceed to a banquet that ends with ever more enthusiastic toasts. Act II begins next morning as the First Lady, Pat Nixon, is conducted on an official sight-seeing tour. Pausing before the Gate of Longevity and Good Will, she is moved by a vision of a happy future for all humankind, and in the aria given here expresses her faith in the enduring values of ordinary American life as she sees them. We give the orchestral transition into the aria, which begins at bar 32. At the aria's end, a strong final cadence is avoided, while the orchestra (which includes saxophones and electronic keyboards) continues with a transition into the next scene.

Examine the way Adams uses harmony. Could any one harmony be called a "tonic" or "pitch center?" How do the chords progress one to the next? What is the nature of the vocal line? Does Adams's handling of triadic harmony differ from the procedures of "traditional" harmony? And what do you make of the muted trumpet passage that starts at bar 159?

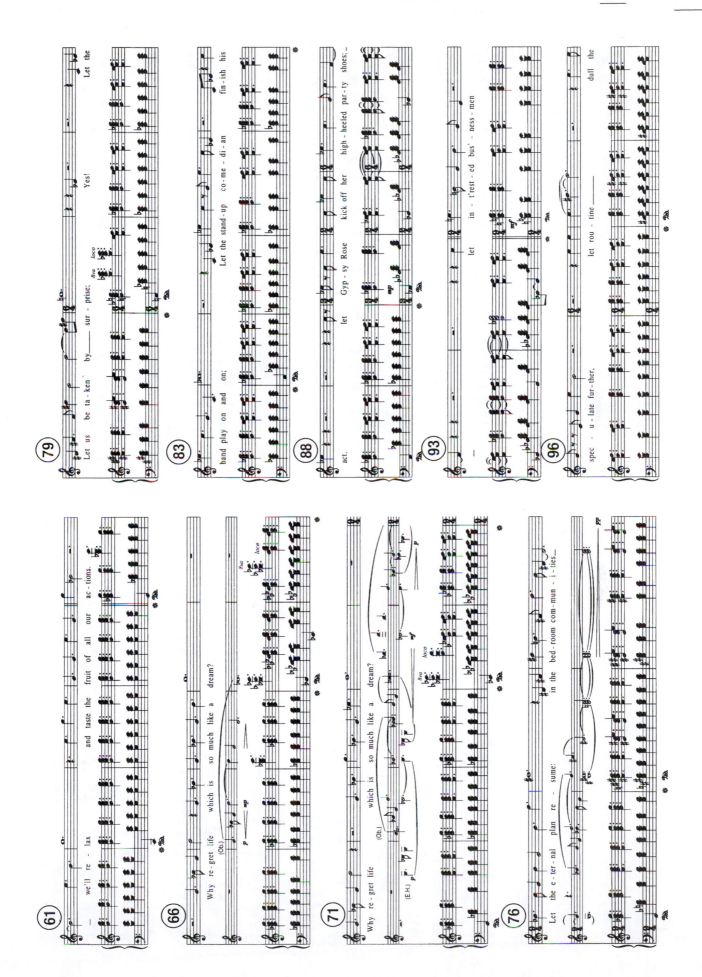

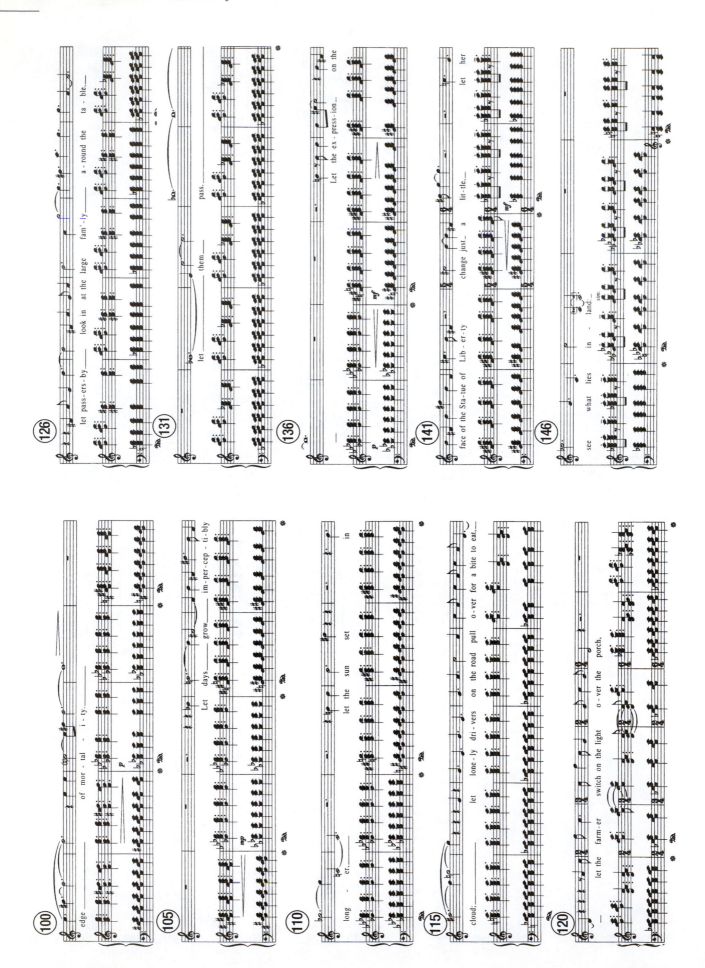

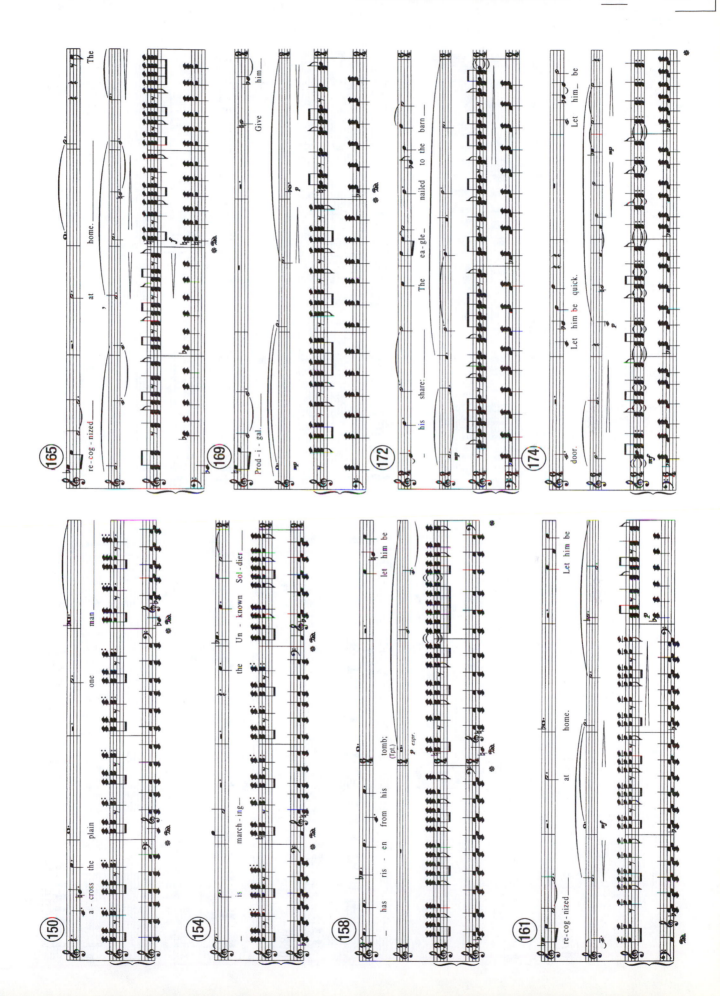

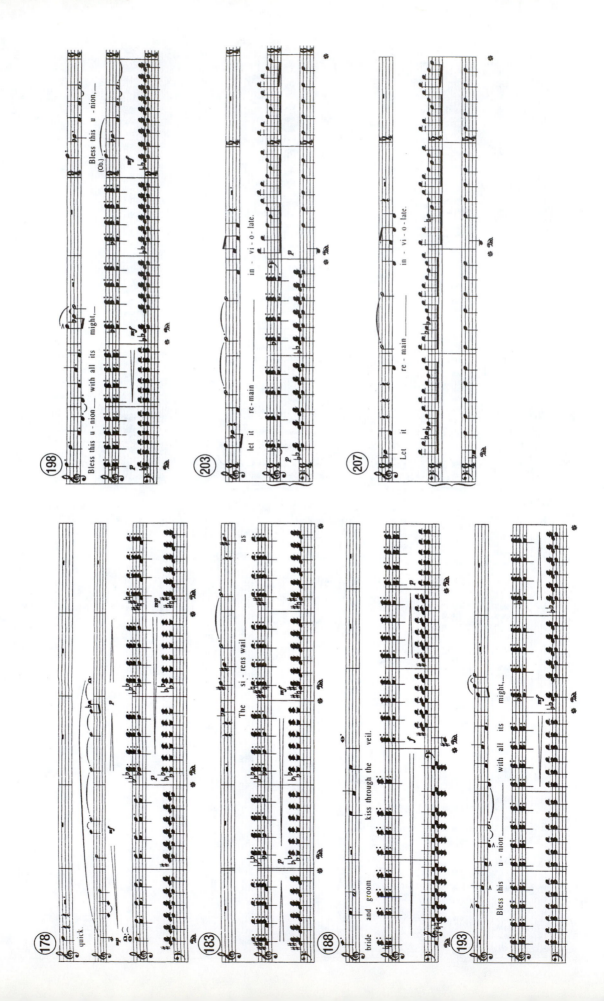

Appendix A

Two Jazz Forms:
Blues and Rhythm Changes

*T*his selection of examples, which focuses on some of the important characteristics of jazz and some of the ways jazz is related to the classical tradition, is primarily designed to illustrate just two standard forms—*blues* and *Rhythm changes*. Both of these forms have figured notably in the eventful history of jazz, and are still used today, their long durability doubtless due to their fruitfulness as vehicles for improvisation—a defining ingredient of most jazz styles. Both are simple rhythmic-harmonic structures that have proved capable of infinite embellishment. (For an interesting historical antecedent, see the late Renaissance pieces founded on "stock basses" that are given on pages 32–36.)

Though the examples that follow are far too few to be a historical survey of either blues or Rhythm changes,[1] they are nonetheless arranged chronologically and may be studied in sequence.

---

[1] For such a survey, see and hear the *Smithsonian Collection of Classic Jazz*, a well-known album of recordings found in many school libraries.

EXAMPLE 1

THE BLUES FORM

The use of the word "blue" to mean low-spirited is recorded as early as 1550. A related early term, "blue devils," was used in the eighteenth century to mean the low spirits themselves (as in Thomas Jefferson's remark: "We have something of the blue devils at times"), and this expression soon got shortened to just "blues."[2] It is this term, "blues," that came to be applied to a large body of late nineteenth- and twentieth-century black American poetry, some of which, though far from all, expressed troubled feelings. Many of these blues were sung, but because few sung blues were recorded before 1923, it is difficult to trace the early history of musical blues in detail. By that date, however, a form had evolved that has remained standard. This form comprises twelve bars divided as three 4-bar phrases and has five basic harmonies, as follows:

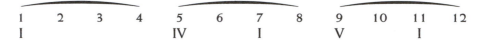

1	2	3	4	5	6	7	8	9	10	11	12
I				IV		I		V		I	

(A common variant adds a IV in bar 10.) The harmonies alone are referred to as the "blues progression."

EXAMPLE 2

WEST END BLUES
First Published Version (1928)
Words by Clarence Williams (1898–1965)

Music by Joseph "King" Oliver (1885–1938)

"King" Oliver, cornetist, band leader, and composer, is one of the great figures of early jazz. In 1923, after his move from New Orleans to Chicago, his Creole Jazz Band, which included his protégé, the young Louis Armstrong, on second cornet, was the first important black group to make an extensive series of jazz recordings. After moving to New York in 1927, Oliver composed "West End Blues" with his friend, Clarence Williams, who also published it. Though Oliver recorded it three times, it became world-famous in a recorded version by Armstrong, who by this time had left Oliver's band and started his own brilliant career (see Example 3).

We give "West End Blues" here in an exact reproduction of the first published version, unedited except for the addition of measure numbers. A piece of "sheet music," it was issued at the time of the first (Oliver's) recording to capitalize on and also boost the record. Unfortunately it contains various misprints (find them), and the musical arrangement is quite crude (can you improve on it?), but it has the virtue of establishing a kind of basic version against which to compare the many arrangements and recordings. (Why do virtually all jazz recordings of a given tune naturally depart, at least to some degree, from a notated score and also differ one from the other?)

How many statements of the blues form are in Example 2? Analyze the various ways these statements elaborate the blues progression. Also locate and describe the "blue notes"—flatted 3rd, 5th, and 7th degrees of the major scale, and intentionally performed out of tune. Is bar 10's D♭ a blue note?

In reading Example 2 (as well as Examples 3 through 5), remember that in jazz, the written rhythms ♪♪ and ♪♪ are virtually always performed more like ♪♪. This has long been a standard notational practice. Hardly ever do jazz performers divide a beat into *equal* values.

---

[2] For many further references to this cluster of terms, see *The Oxford English Dictionary*.

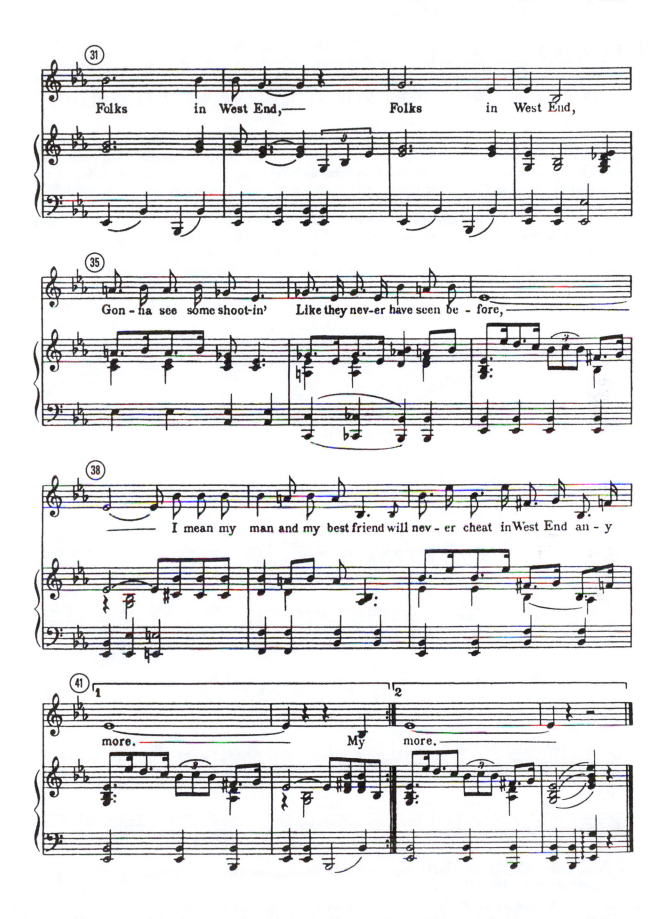

■ EXAMPLE 3

LOUIS ARMSTRONG'S IMPROVISATION ON "WEST END BLUES"

"West End Blues" has always been better known in instrumental than in vocal form. The recording made by Louis Armstrong and his Hot Five on June 28, 1928, has become a jazz classic, much imitated by trumpeters and much discussed by scholars.[3] Reissued many times, it is included in the *Smithsonian Collection of Classic Jazz* (cited earlier). We give from this recording a transcription of Armstrong's solos only.[4]

How would you characterize the remarkable opening section? What is happening rhythmically at the turn of bars 2–3. (Compare with page 509, bars 10–11.) How does the opening relate melodically to the remaining sections? Compare Armstrong's improvisations bar by bar with the relevant section(s) of Example 2 and describe exactly how they relate, noting especially bars 63–66 of the transcription. Also compare the two examples for their treatment of the blues progression.

Words and Music by Joe Oliver and Clarence Williams © Copyright 1928 by Clarence Williams Music Pub. Co. Inc. 1547 Broadway, NYC. Copyright renewed. Used with permission.

---

[3] See, for example, Gunther Schuller's *Early Jazz* (New York: Oxford University Press, 1968; repr. 1986, p. 115f).
[4] The transcription, by H. David Caffey, is from his article, "The Musical Style of Louis Armstrong, 1925–1929," (*Journal of Jazz Studies*, Vol. 3/1, Fall 1975. See pp. 86–88. Reprinted by permission of the Institute of Jazz Studies, Rutgers University, Newark, New Jersey).

Like any lively art, jazz has never stood still. The 1930s saw the rise of "swing," a style that emphasized big-band arrangements of popular songs in 32-bar AABA form. An increasing trend toward commercialization in the late 1930s and early 1940s eventually led to a reaction in the form of "bebop" (or just "bop"), a more sophisticated style, which, initially developing from about 1944 through the 1950s, has continued to the present day as a kind of basic, "common-practice" style. Bop was played by small instrumental groups (combos) and stressed solo improvisation, often at breakneck tempos.

Most of the bop repertory is based on either 12-bar blues or 32-bar popular songs. In working with a popular song, bop improvisers, in order to vary what had grown too familiar, often replaced the original melody with a new one, leaving only the phrase structure and the harmonic structure intact. The new melody could even be given a name and published as a new composition, with the original harmonies shown by chord symbols. (This was not breach of copyright. Why not?) Many well-known popular songs were used as the basis for such new instrumental compositions,[5] but the song that was used far more often than any other was George Gershwin's "I Got Rhythm." So frequently was it used that jazz musicians coined a term to refer to its structure: Because the term "changes" in jazz parlance means a chord progression, and, by extension, the entire series of chords that underlie a piece, the chords underlying "I Got Rhythm" came to be called "Rhythm changes." What is it about this song that made it such a natural starting point for further compositions?[6]

■ EXAMPLE 4

I GOT RHYTHM
(1930)
Lyrics by Ira Gershwin (1896–1983)
Music by George Gershwin (1898–1937)

Apart from its relation to jazz, "I Got Rhythm" merits study on its own. A show-stopping number from Gershwin's *Girl Crazy* (1930), a satire of life on the western frontier, it was first sung by the great Ethel Merman. Its form is very typical of twentieth-century American popular songs: An introductory "verse" is followed by a "refrain" (or "chorus"), which is actually the main body of the song and often performed without the verse. We give only the refrain here. Sing its opening two bars. How would they go with all the syncopation removed? Then analyze its phrase structure and account for the total number of bars.

Popular music notation makes much use of chord symbols written in a more or less standard system. Aside from their practical use to players, these symbols constitute a rudimentary harmonic analysis. Analyze the harmony of the refrain and compare it with the given symbols. How does this system of symbols differ from classical figured bass? Could any of the symbols used here be improved? Notice that the chords are also given here in guitar tablature, another standard feature of much old sheet music. Guitarists, what do you think of these chords? (See also page 34.)

---

[5] An enlightening article on this genre is Frank Tirro's "The Silent Theme Tradition in Jazz" (*Musical Quarterly*, vol. 53, 1967, p. 313).
[6] For a thorough discussion of this subject, including a list of many of the songs based on "I Got Rhythm," see Chapter 7 of Richard Crawford's *The American Musical Landscape* (Berkeley: University of California Press, 1993).

Words by Ira Gershwin. Music by George Gershwin. Copyright © 1930 New World Corporation. Used with permission.

■ **EXAMPLE 5**

ANTHROPOLOGY
(1946)
Charles Parker (1920–1955) and John "Dizzy" Gillespie (1917–1993)

Anthropology, a bebop classic, is one of the many tunes based on the chords of "I Got Rhythm." It was created by the alto saxophonist Charlie Parker and the trumpeter "Dizzy" Gillespie, two pre-eminent figures in the birth and early development of bop style.

5A   This is just the first eight bars of the piano part of an arrangement of *Anthropology* by Gil Fuller, the arranger for Dizzy Gillespie's big band. (The tune, carried by other instruments, is given in small notes.) We give this excerpt because of its very clear use in bar 2 of "tritone substitution," that is, the replacing of a chord, most commonly the dominant seventh, with one whose root is a tritone away, such as B^7 for F^7—a harmonic technique very common in bop (and some other jazz styles) that derives from late nineteenth-century classical music (for other examples see the General Index). What elements of the two chords promote such a substitution? Examine both Examples 5A and 5B for other instances of it.[7]

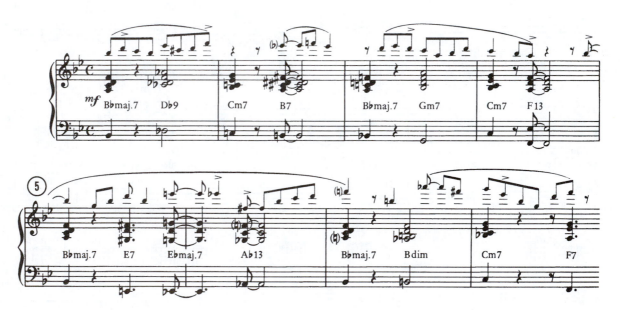

[7] Examples 5A and 5B are both shown and discussed in Leonard Feather's *Inside Be-Bop* (New York: 1949; reprinted as *Inside Jazz* by Da Capo Press, 1977, see p. 60f).

5B   This is the complete *Anthropology* in an arrangement made in 1948 by Frank Paparelli, an associate of Gillespie, who approved it.[8] The style of its harmony richly illustrates Leonard Feather's remark, in speaking of adding a major 7th to a cadential I chord, that "boppers abhor a straight tonic as passionately as nature abhors a vacuum!"[9] The piano part here is something like what a pianist in a small combo might improvise. What relation does this piece have to "I Got Rhythm"? What is noteworthy about the chords in the bridge, both vertically and as a progression?

[8] See Dizzy Gillespie's memoirs (written with Al Fraser), *To Be or Not-to BOP* (Garden City, NY: Doubleday, 1979; repr. Da Capo, 1985, pp. 172 and 354).
[9] Feather, op. cit., p. 65.

5C   When a small jazz combo performs a given title, the performance as a whole usually takes the following three-part form: (1) the entire group plays the tune in its basic (unembellished) form, possibly from a written-out or memorized arrangement; this is followed by (2) a series of improvisations on the tune by one or more solo players, accompanied by the rhythm section; the last soloist is frequently the drummer alone, whose solo signals (3) repetition of No. 1 by the entire group. Jazz musicians call No. 1 the *head*. The head is typically a preexisting popular song (often just the refrain), but can also be newly composed.

Example 5C is a transcription of an improvised solo by Charlie Parker on a recording of *Anthropology* made at the Savoy studios in Newark, New Jersey, on November 26, 1945.[10] At that time the tune was called *Thriving on a Riff* and is so named on the original recording.[11] We give here only Parker's Take 3, which goes through the complete tune twice. Are the harmonies of "I Got Rhythm" observed? Does the melody have internal coherence? Some jazz scholars say Parker's improvisations are typically just a series of repeated formulas; others say they develop motivic ideas from the basic tune. What do you say about Take 3? Does it have a relation to the motives of *Anthropology?* Parker is also famous for his approach to time. What do you make of Take 3's phrase lengths? of its rests?

---

[10] The transcription, reproduced here with permission, is from Henry Martin's *Charlie Parker and Thematic Improvisation*, (Lanham, MD: Scarecrow Press, 2001, pp. 60–63). Martin also gives interesting analytic comments.

[11] *Thriving on a Riff* has been reissued many times, most recently in *The Complete Savoy Studio Sessions*, Savoy CD ZDS-5500. It has also appeared separately in LP and CD collections of Parker's recordings. The tune was early renamed *Anthropology*, and Parker subsequently recorded it many times under that title.

Appendix B

Mostly Chorale Harmonizations

A chorale is a congregational hymn of the German Protestant Church. The early development of the chorale was the work of the great reformer Martin Luther (1483–1546), who considered simple congregational singing in the vernacular an important part of his program to enable all worshippers to understand the liturgy and actively participate in it. A chorale has two components—text and tune. The texts are rhymed metrical poems, usually with many stanzas, on some aspect of Christian belief. (Luther wrote the earliest of these.) The tunes come from various sources: Some were inherited from Catholic practice, both plainchant and vernacular hymns; some were contemporary secular tunes for which new, sacred texts were written; and others were newly composed by Protestant musicians. (Luther also wrote a few of the latter; he was musically quite gifted, and his favorite composer was Josquin Desprez.)

Although the chorales were originally sung in unison and from memory by the congregation (and long continued to be so performed), composers soon began to give them elaborate polyphonic settings intended for trained musicians. These took the form of organ preludes and movements of cantatas and passions—a development of great artistic importance that extended far beyond the period when most of the tunes themselves were produced, reaching its climax in the works of J. S. Bach (1685–1750). In Bach's vocal works, the chorale settings are generally for four-part chorus and range from very elaborate "chorale fantasias" to the simpler, more homophonic type given here. These typically occur as the concluding movement of a cantata. Unlike the other movements, these simpler settings lack independent instrumental parts, each vocal part being merely doubled by instruments. (It should be noted, however, that now and then the vocal *bass* part does diverge from the instrumental bass, in which case the latter is shown here in small notes.)

Chorale harmonizations have long been a staple of music theory study because they provide a wealth of short masterly examples of the techniques of four-part writing. The following selection is drawn chiefly from Bach cantatas, but also includes eight examples in which a setting by an earlier composer is placed side by side with a Bach setting of the same tune. Such comparisons, besides showing changes in musical style, reveal how unchanging structure provides a basis for the infinitely various techniques of elaboration. The selection also includes a few examples that are not chorales to show simple four-part writing in other styles.

When Bach incorporated a chorale into a cantata or other vocal work, he would select the particular stanza that best suited his dramatic purpose, then harmonize the tune so as to express the mood of that stanza, often underlining particularly important words by some vivid musical device such as an accented dissonance or an unusual chromaticism. Therefore, the study of his chorales is not complete without reference to the words. The Bach examples here usually give the exact stanza Bach used (though this is not always possible because some of his harmonizations come to us without text, copied from manuscripts of cantatas that have since been lost). We give some of the texts in German, others in English. The latter, always poetic translations of the original stanza unless otherwise noted, include some that have achieved wide use.

After Bach's death, his son Carl Philipp Emanuel published in 1784–1787 a collection, intended for students, of 371 of his father's chorale harmonizations, each with a title (first line) but otherwise without text. To all of them he assigned numbers that, though wholly arbitrary, have become traditional. In the selection here, the Bach settings are identified by their number in the "371." All the settings, whether by Bach or others, are arranged alphabetically by German title.

Six of the chorales in the selection are given as a melody with figured bass—a common way of notating chorales throughout the seventeenth and eighteenth centuries. Three of these are simple pre-Bach settings. The other three are from the "69 chorale melodies with figured bass" sometimes appended to the 371 in modern editions. The source of these is the *Musicalisches Gesang-Buch* edited by Georg Schemelli and published in Leipzig in 1736. Bach was involved in the production of this book, but, in the opinion of scholars, the precise extent of his contribution cannot be determined. The Schemelli chorales given here are noteworthy in that four-part versions of them exist within the "371." There is no better way to study harmony and voice leading than to compare one's own realizations with Bach's. However, in so doing it is well to remember that, although the figured-bass versions can be realized in four parts, they are actually *vocal solos with continuo accompaniment* and should rightly be realized as such. This fact accounts for some of the occasional discrepancies found between the figured-bass and four-part versions.

ACH GOTT UND HERR

Melody, 1625

Text, 1613

a) This figured-bass version by Christoph Peter (1626–1689) was published at Freiberg in 1655. Because it lacks bar lines, the performer must decide on the best places for downbeats. (We have pitched both versions *a* and *b* a step lower to facilitate comparison of all three settings.)

b) This setting is No. 40 of the "371." Because the work of Bach in which this harmonization occurred is lost, the exact text he used cannot be known. We give the traditional first stanza.

c) No. 279. This setting is from Cantata 48, *Ich elender Mensch (I, wretched man)* of 1723. Note the text-painting: "Punishment *(Straf)* must follow sins; so let me for them suffer *(büssen)*."

ACH, WIE FLÜCHTIG, ACH WIE NICHTIG

Melody and text: Michael Franck, 1652

No. 48. Cantata 26, *Ach, wie flüchtig* (1724) ends with this chorale. "O how fleeting are human concerns! All will fade away. But he who fears God will ever stand." The small notes are the instrumental bass part. Why does it diverge from the vocal bass?

Al - les, al - les was wir se - hen, das muss fal - len

und ver - ge - hen; wer Gott fürcht, bleibt e - wig ste - hen.

Aus tiefer Not schrei ich zu dir

Melody: Martin Luther, 1524

a) The text of this chorale, one of the earliest in the repertoire, is Martin Luther's poetic paraphrase of Psalm 130. This translation is by Catherine Winkworth (1863). The Phrygian tune, possibly also by Luther, is here given in a 1608 setting by Hans Leo Hassler (1564–1612).

b) No. 10. This setting closes Cantata 38, *Aus tiefer Not* (1724)

a) Out of the depths I cry to Thee, Lord, hear me, I im - plore Thee!
Bend down Thy gra - cious ear to me, My prayer let come be - fore Thee!

(continued)

a) If Thou re-mem-b'rest each ____ mis-deed, If each should have its right-ful meed,

a) Who may a - bide ____ Thy pres - ence?

AWAKE, AWAKE, GOOD PEOPLE ALL

Ralph Vaughan Williams (1872–1958)
Melody and text: English folk carol
Four-part setting, 1919

Many English traditional folk songs (as well as those from other countries) exhibit modal elements that pre-date the era of major-minor tonality. One pioneer in the English movement to collect and preserve these songs was the distinguished composer Vaughan Williams, who also incorporated the modality of folk music into his own work. From his *Eight Traditional English Carols*, which he collected and arranged, we give his harmonization of a "May carol" whose text celebrates the return of spring as a symbol of Christian redemption. What is the mode? How do the setting's chordal and cadential usages differ from those of major-minor harmonic practice?

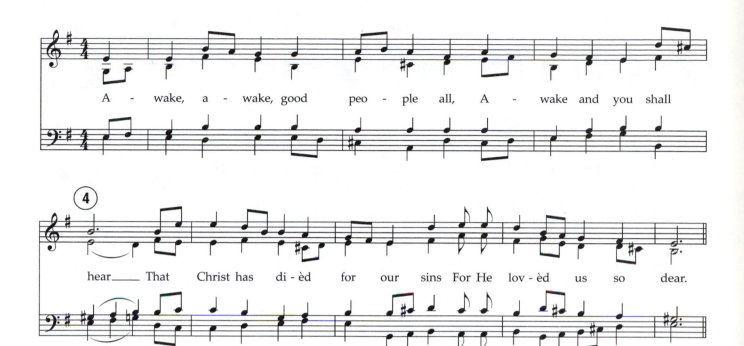

May Day Carol by Ralph Vaughan Williams. Copyright © 1919 by Stainer and Bell Ltd. London, England. Used by permission.

CHRIST LAG IN TODESBANDEN

Melody and text: Martin Luther, 1524

No. 184. The musically and poetically gifted Martin Luther constructed the melody for this chorale from several well-known Gregorian chants and created its text around various scriptural references. Two centuries later Bach chose Luther's by then famous chorale for an Easter cantata, the Cantata No. 4 (*Christ Lay in the Bonds of Death*), in which he based all of its seven movements on the chorale tune. This setting is the seventh movement of the cantata and is sung there to the chorale's seventh stanza. We give the better known first stanza and a translation by Henry S. Drinker. Luther began his Dorian tune thus: A-G♮-A-C-D-C-B-A. How did Bach harmonize that phrase?

(continued)

⑤

dess wir sol-len fröh-lich sein, Gott lo-ben und ihm dank-bar sein und
So now let us joy-ful be and mag-ni-fy Him thank-ful-ly, all

⑨

sin-gen Hal - - le-lu-jah! Hal - - le - -lu - jah!
sing-ing Hal - - le-lu-jah! Hal - - le - -lu - jah!

■ EIN FESTE BURG IST UNSER GOTT

Melody and text: Martin Luther, 1529

a) Luther's famous Reformation chorale (known in English as "A Mighty Fortress Is Our God") is here
given in a harmonization by Hans Leo Hassler (1608). An interesting detail is the use of an E flat
triad at the words *Waffen* and *Gleichen*. Sixteenth-century composers frequently used such a chord to
support the fourth degree of the scale (here B flat) with a *consonant* bass tone. Compare the chord
on the second syllable of *Rüstung*.

b) There are three Bach harmonizations of this chorale melody. This one, No. 273 of the "371,"
closes Cantata 80, *Ein' feste Burg ist unser Gott* (1724), which was composed for Reformation Sunday.

a)
Ein fe-ste Burg ist un-ser Gott, ein gu-te Wehr und Waf - fen.
Er hilft uns frei aus al-ler Not, die uns jetzt hat be-trof - fen.

Burg___ ist un -
frei___ aus al -

b)

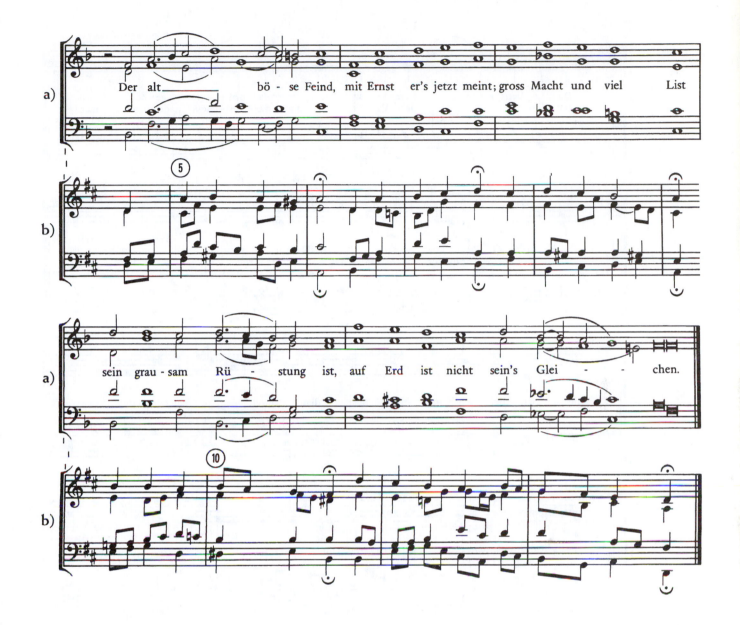

a) Der alt_____ bö - se Feind, mit Ernst er's jetzt meint; gross Macht und viel List

a) sein grau - sam Rü - stung ist, auf Erd ist nicht sein's Glei - - chen.

ERMUNTRE DICH, MEIN SCHWACHER GEIST

Melody: Johann Schop, 1641
Text: Johann Rist, 1641

Both of these harmonizations are by Bach.

a) No. 102. This setting closes Cantata 43, *Gott fähret auf mit Jauchzen* (God ascends amid jubilation), written for the feast of the Ascension in 1726. Both music and text seem to imply that some bars' first beats do not receive a primary stress. What is the best rhythmic interpretation of these places?

b) No. 9. This setting occurs in Part II of the *Christmas Oratorio* (1734) and uses the ninth stanza of the hymn. The translation is by John Troutbeck (1832–1899).

Es ist ein' Ros' entsprungen

Melody and text: Rhenish folk hymn, 15th century

A pre-Reformation Christmas carol, *Es ist ein' Ros' entsprungen* was arranged for four voices by Michael Praetorius (1571–1621) and included in his *Musae Sioniae (The Muses of Zion)*, **Part VI**, of 1609, a collection of simple settings of Protestant hymns for the church year. (See also *Herr Gott, dich loben alle wir,* below.) In the English translation of Theodore Baker (1851–1934), it has gained wide popularity. We give the first of two verses. The tempo should be about 54 to the whole note. Praetorius, following custom, gave no bar lines. Where would you place them?

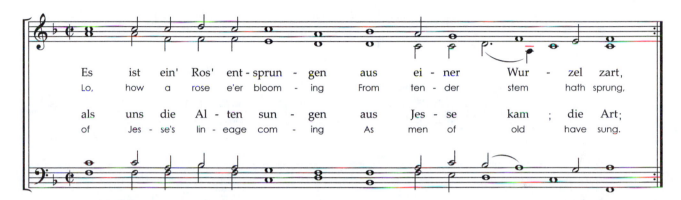

Freuet euch, ihr Christen alle

Melody: Andreas Hammerschmidt, 1646

Text: Christian Keimann, 1646

No. 8. Bach closed Cantata 40, *Dazu ist erschienen der Sohn Gottes* (1723) with this setting, which is sung to the fourth stanza of the hymn. The English text given here is a translation by Catherine Winkworth (1863) of the first stanza.

Herr Gott, dich loben alle wir

Melody: Genevan Psalter, 1551

Text: Paul Eber, ca. 1554

a) This still often sung tune began not as a chorale, but as a French Huguenot psalm tune. The harmonization give here is by the German composer Michael Praetorius (1571–1621), appearing in his *Musae Sionaie* of 1609. (The original is a whole step higher.) In the German church of that time this tune was associated with the Feast of the Archangel Michael. The text praises God for the creation of the angels. (For another Praetorius setting, see page 567).

b) No. 164. The work of Bach in which this harmonization occurred is lost. The elaborated bass particularly requires analysis. Explain the $\frac{4}{2}$ chords in measure 3, 6, and 14.

a) für dein   Ge - schöpf der En - gel schon,

a) die um   dich schwe - ben in deim   Tron. _____

■ HERZLIEBSTER JESU

Melody: Johann Crüger, 1640
Text: Johann Heermann, 1630

a) This is a composition by Johann Crüger (1598–1662), a noted writer of German Protestant church music. Many of Crüger's chorales were published simply as melodies with figured bass. Begin study by writing in the inner voices.

b) No. 59. Bach, who harmonized eleven of Crüger's chorales, made four settings of *Herzliebster Jesu*. This one, which uses the seventh stanza of the text, is from Part I of the *St. John Passion* of 1724. The English translation, from the edition of Arthur Mendel, attempts to preserve Bach's text-painting. Note the treatment of "this vale of tears" (bar 5) and the final word, "perish" (actually "suffer"—*leiden*—in the German).

JESU, JESU, DU BIST MEIN

Schemelli Gesangbuch, 1736

This is No. 53 of the "69 chorale melodies with figured bass" described on page 558. Though it can readily be set for SATB, which small detail in the notes leaves no doubt that it is intended for one vocal part with continuo?

JESU, MEINE FREUDE

Melody: Johann Crüger, 1653

No. 263. This chorale was a favorite of Bach, who set it more than once for organ and used it as the basis of his motet of the same name, BWV 227.

Jesu, my joy, my heart's pasture, my jewel,
Ah, how long, how long the heart is anxious and longs for thee!
Lamb of God, my bridegroom, aside from thee may nothing on earth be dearer to me.

Je - su, mei - ne Freu - de, mei - nes Her - zens Wei - de,
ach, wie lang', ach lan - ge ist dem Her - zen ban - ge,

Je - su, mei - ne Zier, Got - tes Lamm, mein Bräu - ti - gam,
und ver - langt nach dir!

au - sser dir soll mir auf Er - den nichts sonst Lie - bers wer - den.

KOMM, GOTT SCHÖPFER, HEILIGER GEIST

Melody: Gregorian chant

German text: Martin Luther, 1524

No. 187. Some of the chorale tunes that derived from plainchant continued to be sung in modal form well into the major-minor era. An example is the Pentecost hymn *Veni, Creator Spiritus* (**LU 885**):

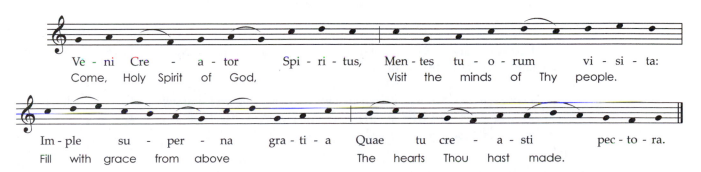

Ve - ni Cre - a - tor Spi - ri - tus, Men - tes tu - o - rum vi - si - ta:
Come, Holy Spirit of God, Visit the minds of Thy people.

Im - ple su - per - na gra - ti - a Quae tu cre - a - sti pec - to - ra.
Fill with grace from above The hearts Thou hast made.

In which mode is this chant? (Compare *Examples of Plainchant*, **page 3**.) In his harmonization Bach has preserved the mode. Is tonality nevertheless manifested in his setting? Does the finalis of the mode feel like a tonic in the modern sense? For other modal chorales see *Aus tiefer Not, Christ lag in Todesbanden*, and *O Haupt voll Blut und Wunden*. (Compare also the Vaughan Williams carol on **page 563**.)

Komm, Gott Schöp-fer, hei-li-ger Geist, be-such das Herz der Men-schen dein; mit

Gna-den sie füll, wie du weißt, daß dein Ge-schöpf vor-hin___ sein.

◼ O Haupt voll Blut und Wunden

Melody: Hans Leo Hassler, 1601
Text of b: Paul Gerhardt, 1656

a) *Mein Gmüth ist mir verwirret* is a composition of Hans Leo Hassler (1564–1612). A secular song, it was published in Hassler's *Lustgarten neuer teutscher Gesäng* in 1601. Twelve years later sacred words were set to the tune and it entered the chorale repertoire. (The original is notated a whole step higher.) Can you suggest a better time signature?

> *My feelings are all mixed up because of a gentle maid, I've quite lost my way, my heart is sick. I have no peace day and night, I complain constantly, I sigh and weep at all times, I simply despair in my grief.*

b) No. 89. This is the last of five appearances of this chorale in the St. Matthew Passion of 1729. It occurs immediately after the death of the crucified Christ.

> *When I must depart (this life), then part Thou not from me! When I must suffer death, then draw Thou near! When deepest sorrows assail my heart, then deliver me from anguish by the strength of Thy anguish and pain!*

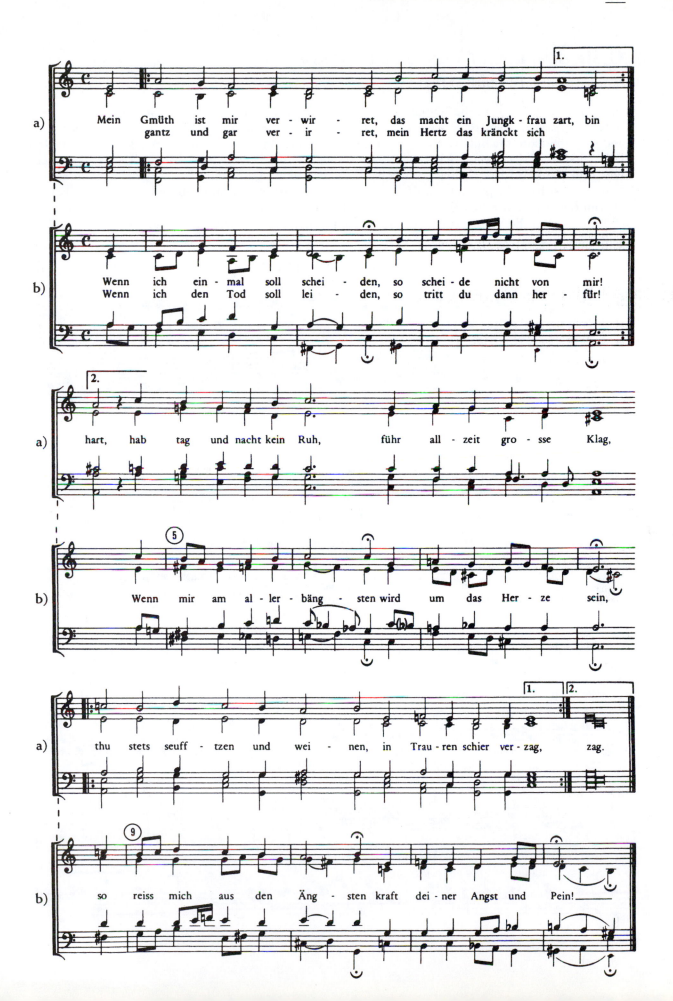

a) Mein Gmüth ist mir ver - wir - ret, das macht ein Jungk - frau zart, bin
gantz und gar ver - ir - ret, mein Hertz das kränckt sich

b) Wenn ich ein - mal soll schei - den, so schei - de nicht von mir!
Wenn ich den Tod soll lei - den, so tritt du dann her - für!

a) hart, hab tag und nacht kein Ruh, führ all - zeit gro - sse Klag,

b) Wenn mir am al - ler - bäng - sten wird um das Her - ze sein,

a) thu stets seuff - tzen und wei - nen, in Trau - ren schier ver - zag, zag.

b) so reiss mich aus den Äng - sten kraft dei - ner Angst und Pein!

■ O Mensch, bewein' dein' Sünde gross

Melody: Matthäus Greitter(?), 1525

No. 201. Though the source of this setting is unknown, it could be a lost cantata Bach composed for Passion week, since the text, which starts "O Man, Bemoan thy Great Sin," is a Passion text and is furthermore the only text the tune ever appears with in Bach's known work (as in, for example, the *St. Matthew Passion*, where a very elaborate setting of this chorale closes Part I.) The setting given here is particularly rich in secondary V and VII chords and in eighth- and sixteenth-note figuration. See in bar 3, first half, the progression IV$_5^6$-V$_5^6$-I, then analyze the chords in the bar's second half. In bar 5, explain the last tenor note (B♭). In bar 13, fourth beat, what justifies the unusual spacing? At the start of 17, how does the V$_2^4$ resolve? What motive runs through bars 1–3? Which phrase strikes you as particularly expressive?

◼ O WELT, ICH MUSS DICH LASSEN

Text for b: Paul Gerhardt, 1647

a) *Isbruck, ich muss dich lassen (Innsbruck, I must leave thee)* by Heinrich Isaac (ca. 1450–1517) was published in 1539. It is uncertain whether Isaac composed or borrowed the tune of this secular *lied.* Sacred words ("O World, I must leave thee") were set to the tune in 1598. Still another sacred text, *Nun ruhen all Wälder,* was set to it in 1633. (The original is notated a minor third lower. We have added the slurs and the naturals in the tenor part.)

b) No. 117. This setting is from Part I of the St. Matthew Passion (1729). Christ has just told his disciples that one of them will betray him. They ask: "Is it I?." Then the chorus, symbolizing the contemporary observer responding to the scene, sings this chorale. Bach chose a stanza starting with the words "It is I."

a) Is - bruck, ich muss dich las - sen, Ich fahr da-hin mein Stra - ssen

b) Ich bins, ich soll - te bü - ssen an Hän - den und an Fü - ssen ge -

a) In fremb - de Land da - hin; Mein' Freud' ist mir ge - nom - men Die

b) bun - den in der Höll. Die Gei - sseln und die Ban - den, und

a) ich nit weiss be - kom - men Wo ich im E - - - - - lend bin.

Wo ich im E - lend, im E - lend bin.

b) was du aus - ge - stan - den, das hat ver - die - net mei - ne _____ Seel.

SO GEHST DU NUN, MEIN JESU, HIN

Schemelli Gesangbuch, 1736

No. 23 of the "69" (see page 558), this chorale is notable for its unusual chromaticism. The text treats of Christ going to his death. How is this subject depicted musically?

SO GIBST DU NUN, MEIN JESU, GUTE NACHT

Schemelli Gesangbuch, 1736

No. 26 of the "69" (see page 558), this Good Friday chorale is worthy of study for its modulations.

VALET WILL ICH DIR GEBEN

Melody: Melchior Teschner, 1615

Text: Valerius Herberger, 1613

No. 108. This setting from the *St. John Passion,* where it is No. 52, is noteworthy for its use of secondary harmonies.

In mei - nes Her - zens Grun - de, dein Nam' und Kreuz al - lein

Fun - kelt all' Zeit und Stun - de, drauf kann ich fröh - lich sein.

Er - schein' mir in dem Bil - de zu Trost in mei - ner Not, wie

du,— Herr Christ, so mil - de, dich hast ge - blut't zu Tod.

WACH' AUF!

from Die Meistersinger von Nürnberg, 1867

Richard Wagner (1813–1883)

Text: Hans Sachs (1494–1576)

This work is not a chorale, but was composed by Wagner in something like chorale style for his great comic opera *The Mastersingers of Nuremberg.* In the final scene of Act III, the Nurembergers, having gathered on a sunny meadow for their traditional Song Contest, greet the entrance of their beloved cobbler-poet Hans Sachs with this chorus, hailing him in the words with which the historical Hans Sachs (see dates above) greeted Martin Luther and the Reformation. The scoring occasionally uses five- and six-note chords. What motivates these departures from strict four-part writing? In what other ways does the style differ from that of the Baroque chorale?

Langsam und feierlich

Wach' auf! es na-het gen den Tag; ich hör' sin-gen im grü-nen Hag ein'
Awake! Day draws nigh; I hear singing in the green wood an

hör' sin - gen im Hag

(Orch.)

6
won - nig-li-che Nach-ti-gal, ihr' Stimm' durch-dring-et Berg und Tal; die
enchanting nightingale; its voice resounds o'er hill and vale;

Stimm'   dringt durch

won - nig - ge   Tal;

10
Nacht neigt sich zum Oc - ci-dent, der Tag geht auf von O - ri - ent, die
night sinks in the west, day rises in the east

Nacht   neigt

Tag   naht   von

der

14
poco rit.   a tempo

- röt   her   durch   die
rot - brün - sti - ge Mor-gen-röt her durch die trü - ben Wol-ken geht.
the ardent glow of dawn breaks through the gloomy clouds

Wol - - ken

WIR CHRISTENLEUT

Melody: Caspar Fuger, 1593
Text of b: Christoph Runge, 1653

a) This setting of *Wir Christenleut,* a **Christmas chorale,** is from the *Cantional* (1627) of Johann Hermann Schein (1586–1630), where it is pitched one half-step higher with a signature of one flat. Though it has four written parts, we give only outer voices plus the figures Schein provided for organ accompaniment.

b) **No. 360.** This setting closes Part III of the *Christmas Oratorio* (1734). Bach uses the text's fourth stanza, given here in a translation by John Troutbeck (1832–1899). The harmony of the last three bars, with upbeat, is unusual in the Bach chorales.

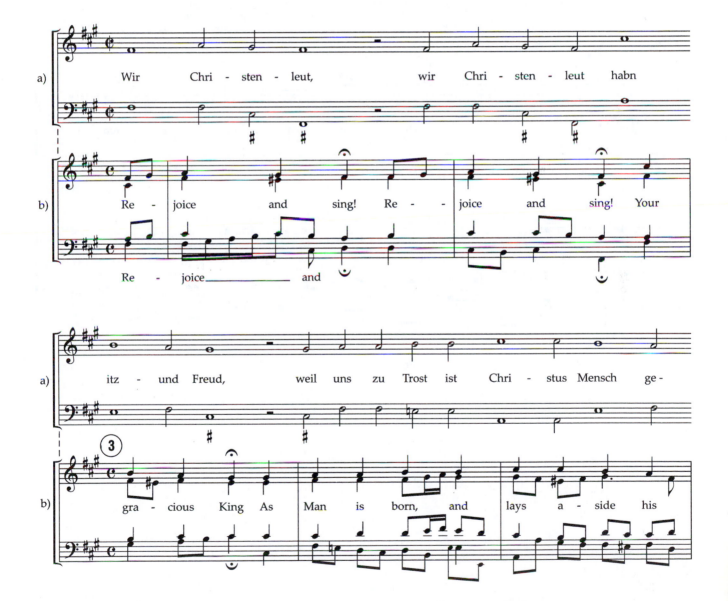

A Note on the Sources

For most of the works of J.S. Bach, Beethoven, Brahms, Chopin, Handel, Haydn, Lassus, Mendelssohn, Schubert, and Schumann, the "critical complete editions" published mainly in the latter half of the nineteenth century by Breitkopf und Härtel of Leipzig have served as sources. (Small corrections have been tacitly made in a few instances.) Sources of the remaining works are given either in a copyright notice (on their first page of music) or in the following list.

BACH, J.S.	*Crucifixus from Mass in B minor* (New York: G. Schirmer, 1899).
BEACH	Masters Music Publications, Inc., n.d.
BRAHMS	*Variations*, Op.9 from *Piano Works*, vol. 1, ed. von Sauer (Kalmus); Opp. *118 and 119* from *Clavierstücke von Johannes Brahms* (Berlin: N. Simrock, 1893).
CLEMENTI	*Sonatinas* (New York: G. Schirmer, 1893).
CORELLI	*Les Oeuvres de Arcangelo Corelli*, ed. J. Joachim and F. Chrysander (London: Augener, 1890).
COUPERIN	*Pièces de Clavecin*, ed. J. Brahms and F. Chrysander (London: Augener, n.d.).
CRÜGER	Zahn, Johannes, *Die Melodien der deutschen evangelischen Kirchenlieder* (Gütersloh, 1889-93).
DEBUSSY	*Prélude à "L'après-midi d'un faune"* (Paris: E. Fromont, 1914); *La cathédrale engloutie* (Paris: Durand, 1910).
DESPREZ	*Baisés moy* edited by Joshua Rifkin from *Canti B. numero Cinquanta* (Venice: Petrucci, 1502). Source for the folk song: *Gérold, Le Manuscrit de Bayeux*, Strasbourg, 1921.
DUFAY	Transcription by Heinrich Besseler in *Die Musikforschung* (Kassel: Bärenreiter Verlag, 1948), p. 109. We have reset. Chant source: *Liber Usualis* (Tournai: 1947), p. 1392.
FISCHER	*Sämtliche Werke für Klavier und Orgel*, ed. E. von Werra (Leipzig, 1901; repr. Broude, 1965).
FRANCK	*Complete Works for Organ*, vol. 4 (Kalmus)
GERVAISE	*Les Maîtres de la Renaissance Française*, ed. H. Expert, *Danceries,1ᵉʳ volume* (Paris: Maurice Senart, 1908).
GORZANIS	Issam El-Mallah, *Tanzzyklus des 16. Jahrhunderts für Laute von Jacomo Gorzanis* (Tutzing: Hans Schneider, 1979). The excerpt of the tablature is reprinted from this publication with permission; transcription by Charles Burkhart.
HANDEL	*Wretched Lovers* from *Acis and Galatea* (Kalmus)
HASSLER	"Aus tiefer Not" from Zahn, *op. cit.*; "Ein feste Burg" and "Mein Gmüth ist mir verwirret" from *Publikationen älterer praktischer und theoretischer Musikwerke*, ed. R. Eitner, 1873. (Reprint: Broude, 1965).
HAYDN	*Symphony No. 101, IV*: Ernst Eulenburg, Leipzig, n.d.; *String Quartet*: Kalmus Miniature Scores, n.d.
ISAAC	*Grove's Dictionary of Music and Musicians*, 3ʳᵈ ed., 1927, p. 741. Reset.
MONTEVERDI	*Tutte le opere di Claudio Monteverdi*, ed. G.F. Malipiero (Asolo: 1930), vol. 6.
MOZART	Piano works from the "Urtext" edition published by Breitkopf und Härtel in 1895 with an introduction by Ernst Rudorff; *Clarinet Concerto*: Ernst Eulenburg, n.d.
PALESTRINA	The chant source is an edition of the mass edited by Henry Washington (London: J. and W. Chester, 1953). [Cf. *Liber Usualis* (1947), p. 235, "On Solemn Feasts."]
PETER	*Generalbass-Choräle*, ed. C. Mahrenholz (Kassel: Bärenreiter, 1948). Reset.
PRAETORIUS	*Gesamtausgabe der Musikalischen Werke* (Wolfenbüttel: Möseler Verlag, n.d.).
SCHEIN	*Neue Ausgabe sämtlicher Werke*, ed. A. Adrio (Kassel: Bärenreiter Verlag, 1965). We have reset.
SCHUMANN, C.	*Pianoforte-Werke zu zwei Händen*, Volksausgabe 27 (Leipzig: Breitkopf & Härtel, 1879). A photocopy was kindly furnished by the publisher. A few errors have been corrected.
WAGNER	*Tristan und Isolde*, Vollständiger Klavierauszug von Hans von Bülow (Leipzig: Breitkopf & Härtel, n.d.); "Wach' auf!" from *The Mastersingers of Nuremberg* (New York: G. Schirmer, 1904).
ZELTER	*Gedichte von Goethe in Compositionen seiner Zeitgenossen*, ed. Frielaender (Weimar, 1896).

Translations of Foreign Terms

The German terms and phrases in the works by Wagner, Mahler, and Schoenberg, and the French ones by Debussy, Ravel, and Messiaen, are translated on the scores themselves. The foreign terms (except the most common) in the remaining scores are translated below.

accompagnando	*It.*	accompanying
ad libitum (ad lib.)	*Lat.*	at will, freely
adagio	*It.*	slow
affetuoso	*It.*	tenderly
al	*It.*	at the, to the
allmählich	*Ger.*	gradually
am Steg	*Ger.*	*see* sul ponticello
anima	*It.*	feeling, soul, spirit
animato	*It.*	animated
animé	*Fr.*	animating
Anmut	*Ger.*	grace
appassionato	*It.*	impassioned
appena	*It.*	scarcely, hardly
arco	*It.*	bow
ascendat Gloria Regis	*Lat.*	may the glory of the king ascend
assai	*It.*	very, much
assoluto	*It.*	absolute
attacca	*It.*	attack, begin at once
au mouvement	*Fr.*	in tempo
auf dem G	*Ger.*	on the G string
äusserst	*Ger.*	extremely
belebt	*Ger.*	brisk, animated
ben	*It.*	well
bewegter	*Ger.*	faster
Bogen (Bog.)	*Ger.*	(play with) bow
breit, -er,	*Ger.*	broad, broader
brio	*It.*	spirit, brilliance
calando	*It.*	gradually diminishing in pace and dynamic
calmando	*It.*	calming
calmo	*It.*	calm
cantabile	*It.*	lyrical, song-like
cantando	*It.*	singing
capriccoso	*It.*	capricious, lively
circa	*Lat.*	approximately
col	*It.*	with the
con	*It.*	with
Dämpfer	*Ger.*	mute
divisi (div.)	*It.*	divided
dolce (dol.)	*It.*	sweetly, gently
dolcissimo (dolciss.)	*It.*	very sweetly, gently
doppio	*It.*	double
doppio movimento	*It.*	twice as fast
doux	*Fr.*	sweetly, gently
drängend	*Ger.*	pressing on, quickening
e, ed	*It.*	and
egal	*Ger.*	equal, uniform
ein	*Ger.*	one, a
erste	*Ger.*	first

espressione	*It.*	expression
et	*Fr.*	and
etwas	*Ger.*	somewhat
expressif	*Fr.*	expressive
feierlich	*Ger.*	with solemnity
Flageolet (Flag.)	*Fr.*	(play as) harmonics
Flatterzunge	*Ger.*	flutter tongue
flessibile	*It.*	flexible
fliessend, -er,	*Ger.*	flowing, more flowing
flüchtig	*Ger.*	fleeting
Flzg.		*see* Flatterzunge
forza	*It.*	force, strength
frisch	*Ger.*	fresh, brisk
fuggevole	*It.*	fleeting, transient
fuoco	*It.*	fire
gayement	*Fr.*	gaily, happily
geteilt	*Ger.*	divided
giocoso	*It.*	jocose, playful
giusto	*It.*	just, precise
gli altri	*It.*	the others
glissando (gliss.)	*It.*	sliding
G.P. (Generalpause)	*Ger.*	General Pause
grave	*It.*	serious
grazioso	*It.*	graceful
il	*It.*	the
inferiore	*It.*	lower
innig	*Ger.*	intimate, heartfelt, fervent
innigster	*Ger.*	most heartfelt
kräftig	*Ger.*	strong, vigorous
lang	*Ger.*	long
langsam, -er	*Ger.*	slow, slower
languido	*It.*	languid
largo	*It.*	slow, broad
lasc. vibr. (l.v.)	*It.*	let vibrate
lebhaft, -er	*It.*	lively, livelier
leggiero (legg.)	*It.*	light, nimble, quick
leise	*Ger.*	soft, gentle
lent	*Fr.*	slow
lento	*It.*	slow
ligato	*It.*	variant of *legato*
l'istesso tempo	*It.*	(at) the same pace
ma	*It.*	but
ma non troppo	*It.*	but not too (much)
maggiore	*It.*	major
marcato (marc.)	*It*	marked, emphasized
marqué	*Fr.*	*see* marcato
m.d.	*Fr.*	*main droite*, right hand
même	*Fr.*	same

meno	*It.*	less
mezza voce (m.v.)	*It.*	(with) half voice
m.g.	*Fr.*	*main gauche*, left hand
mit	*Ger.*	with
modéré	*Fr.*	moderate in tempo
modo ordinario (m.o.)	*It.*	ordinary manner
möglich	*Ger.*	possible
moins	*Fr.*	less
molto	*It.*	very
morendo	*It.*	dying away
mosso	*It.*	*see* più mosso
moto	*It.*	movement, motion
m.s.	*It.*	*mano sinistra*, left hand
mutandi i deti	*It.*	changing the fingers
nicht	*Ger.*	not
niente	*It.*	nothing
opus posthumous (op. posth.)	*Lat.*	work published after author's death
ordinario	*It.*	ordinary, normal
oscuro	*It.*	obscure
ossia	*It.*	or, as an alternate
ôtez	*Fr.*	remove
pesante	*It.*	heavy, weighty
peu	*Fr.*	little
peu à peu	*Fr.*	little by little
più	*It.*	more
più mosso	*It.*	faster
piuttosto	*It.*	rather, somewhat
pizzicato (pizz.)	*It.*	plucked (string)
plus	*Fr.*	more
pochissimo (pochiss.)	*It.*	very little
poco	*It.*	a little
poi	*It.*	then
ponticello (pont.)	*It.*	bridge (of string inst.)
portamento (port.)	*It.*	gliding between pitches
près de la table	*Fr.*	near the soundboard
pressez	*Fr.*	hurry, press on
rallentando (rall.)	*It.*	slowing down
rilievo	*It.*	(in) relief
rinforzando (rinf.)	*It.*	becoming louder
risoluto	*It.*	resolute
ritenuto (riten.)	*It.*	held back
rubato	*It.*	"stolen" (time), with flexible pulse
ruhig	*Ger.*	calm
sanft und frei	*Ger.*	softly (gently) and freely
sans	*Fr.*	without
scherzando (scherz.)	*It.*	playful, humorous
schnell, -er	*Ger.*	fast, faster
schneller	*Ger.*	faster
schwächer	*Ger.*	weaker
schwer	*Ger.*	heavy
scorrevole	*It.*	flowing, gliding
secco	*It.*	dry
sehr	*Ger.*	very

semplice	*It.*	simple
sempre	*It.*	always
senza	*It.*	without
simile (sim.)	*It.*	similarly
sin' al	*It.*	until the
smorzando (smorz.)	*It.*	dying away
sopra	*It.*	above
sordino (sord.)	*It.*	mute
sostenuto (sost.)	*It.*	sustained
sotto	*It.*	below
sotto voce	*It.*	"below the voice," in an undertone
sourdines	*Fr.*	mute
soutenu	*Fr.*	sustained
spielen	*Ger.*	to play
stretto	*It.*	accelerate pace
Strich	*Ger.*	stroke (of bow)
subito (sub.)	*It.*	suddenly, immediately
sul (A)	*It.*	on the (A string)
sulla tavola	*It.*	on the fingerboard
sul ponticello	*It.*	(bow close) to the bridge
suoni reali	*It.*	actual pitches
tasto	*It.*	fingerboard
t.c.	*It.*	*tre corde* (cancels *una corda*)
teneramente	*It.*	tenderly, gently
tenuto (ten.)	*It.*	held (full value)
tempo primo	*It.*	(return to) first tempo
toujours	*Fr.*	always
tranquillo	*It.*	tranquil
tremolo	*It.*	rapid repetition of one or more notes
trés	*Fr.*	very
tutta, tutto	*It.*	all
u.c.		*see* una corda
uguale	*It.*	equal, uniform
un, une	*Fr.*	one, a
un	*It.*	a
una corda	*It.*	soft pedal
und	*Ger.*	and
verklingend	*Ger.*	dying away
Verschiebung	*Ger.*	soft pedal
viel	*Ger.*	much, many
vivace	*It.*	lively, animated
vivo	*It.*	lively, animated
voce	*It.*	voice
wehmütig	*Ger.*	sad, melancholy
weich	*Ger.*	soft, tender
wenig	*Ger.*	little
wie zu Anfang	*Ger.*	as at the beginning
wieder	*Ger.*	again
zart	*Ger.*	delicately
ziemlich	*Ger.*	rather
Zeitmass	*Ger.*	pace
zögernd	*Ger.*	hesitating
zu 2	*Ger.*	both play
zurückhaltend	*Ger.*	held back
zweite	*Ger.*	second

Complete Short Pieces Suitable for First- and Second-Year Courses

Teachers of harmony courses can locate through the indexes at the end of this book many examples of chords and passages appropriate to such courses. In addition, the following list is offered as an aid in locating pieces that may be usable *in their entirety*. The list is cumulative, proceeding systematically from simple to complex, each new category limited—as much as possible—to the chords and usages named up to that point. Examples of traditional forms, likewise progressing in complexity, are also noted. The list is not intended as a complete syllabus. Items particularly recommended are preceded by an asterisk. Each title is followed by a page number, with measure numbers, where needed, in parentheses. Some titles are followed by suggested assignments.

$\frac{5}{3}$ CHORDS ONLY

"Wir Christenleut," **581,a.** Play in various keys.

*"Greensleeves," **36.** Discover the implied stock bass, then write a chordal accompaniment; sing and play; transpose.

MOSTLY $\frac{5}{3}$

Praetorius, "Es ist ein' Ros,'" **567.** (Complex cadences await study of $\frac{6}{4}$).

"Herr Gott dich loben," **569,a.**

Gervaise, *Pavane,* **33.**

$\frac{6}{3}$ CHORDS; SIMPLE MODULATION; INCREASING FIGURATION

Dufay, *Communio,* **14.** Add middle voice. Perform.

*"Ach Gott und Herr," **559,a.** Realize in keyboard style and play.

*"Herzliebster Jesu," **571,a.**

Vaughan Williams, "Awake," **563.** (In modal style.)

Gorzanis, *Saltarello,* **35.** (Can be followed by the more elaborate *Passamezzo,* **35.**)

*Mozart, *Bird-catcher's Song,* **199.** (I, V, and IV only.)

SPECIAL PROJECT IN SCORE READING

Mozart, *Andantino* from *Divertimento 14 for winds,* **193.**

Write an arrangement for piano, or for piano 4 hands, leaving room for harmonic analysis beneath each system.

III and VII IN MINOR MODE

"Wir Christenleut," **581,a.**

*Schumann, *Poor Orphan Child,* **312** (1-8). (The A-section is a parallel period; the B-section prolongs V. How?)

FURTHER DIATONIC MODULATION

"Ermuntre dich," **566,a.** (Bar form.)

*"So gibst du nun," **578.** Realize, analyze, and play.

Anna Magdalena Book, *Aria,* **65.** Realize unfigured bass. (Binary form.)

*"Jesu, Jesu, du bist mein," **572.** (More elaborate figured bass.)

Couperin, *Les Moissonneurs,* **61.** (Rondeau form.)

Jacquet de la Guerre, Prelude, **58.** Write a reduction showing only essential outer-voice tones, with figured bass to account for inner voices.

PRE-CADENTIAL II $\frac{6}{5}$

*"Freuet euch," **568.** (Also rich in modulations.)

"Christ lag," **563.** (Modulation to minor V; deceptive cadence.)

$\frac{6}{4}$ USAGES

*Schumann, *Wild Rider,* **313.** (Simple ternary form.)

Zelter, "Der König in Thule," **291.**

Haydn, *C-major Menuetto,* **143.** (Rounded binary form; minuet and trio.)

CONTINUO ACCOMPANIMENT. Write out realizations and perform.

Corelli, *Adagio,* **49.**

Corelli, *Allemanda,* **53.** (Many II $\frac{6}{5}$'s; binary form.)

Corelli, *Allegro,* **51.** (Rich in $\frac{4}{2}$ positions and chordal sequences.)

SECONDARY (APPLIED) DOMINANTS

Beethoven, *Scherzo,* Op. 28, III, **261** (1–70). (Chromatic 6-5 sequence; rounded binary form.)

"Wir Christenleut," **581,b**. (A richer example of the 6-5 sequence.)

*"Valet will ich dir geben," **579**. (Besides various secondary dominants, contains the IV^6 – passing $^6_4$ – II $^6_5$ progression.)

Haydn, *D-major Sonata*, III, **140**. (Rondo form, with one retransition.)

SECONDARY (APPLIED) DIMINISHED SEVENTHS

Beethoven, *F-minor Menuetto*, **223** (1–40). (Subtler example of rounded binary form.)

*"So gehst du nun," **578**. (Chromatic descending bass from I to V.) Realize figures and play.

*"O Mensch, bewein," **576**. (Rich in secondary V and VII; also contains the IV$^6_5$ – V$^6_5$ progression.)

MODE MIXTURE

Brahms, "Wie Melodien," **362**. (And note V$^7_{\sharp5}$'s.)

^{b}II^6 ("NEAPOLITAN SIXTH")

*Handel, "Thy Rebuke," **88**. Realize; sing while playing accompaniment.

AUGMENTED SIXTH CHORDS

Standard resolution
  *Mozart, *Variation* VII, K. 284, **169**.
  Schubert, A^b *waltz*, Op. 9/2, **303**.

Schubert, "Der Doppelgänger," **294**.

*Haydn, *Quartet*, Op. 74/3, II, **144**. Play from score, esp. bars 1-22. (Note the common-tone ^{0}7's.)

*Schubert, *Moment Musical No. 6*, **304**.
  Beethoven, *F-minor Sonata*, Op. 2/1, I, **219**. (Sonata form.)

Common-tone resolution
  Beach, "Dark is the Night," **394**.
  Wolf, "In der Frühe," **386**. (Also features chromatic mediants.)

CHROMATIC MEDIANTS; EQUAL DIVISIONS OF THE OCTAVE

Franck, *Organ Chorale No. 1*, **354**.

EXTENDED CHROMATIC MOTIONS

Chopin, *Prelude in E minor*, **326**.

Chopin, *Mazurka 49 in F minor*, **338**.

Chopin, *Db-major Nocturne*, Op. 27/1, **339**. (See bars 22–25, 38–46, 62–66.)

Wolf, "Das verlassene Mägdlein," **383**. (Features augmented triads.)

Indexes

The following two indexes—more accurately, *example-finders*—refer not to words in the text but to elements in the music. The alphabetical INDEX I—or General Index—locates examples of forms, procedures, genres, media, and many tonal and post-tonal techniques. INDEX II—an Index of Chords, Sequences, and Modulations—is limited mainly to examples from tonal music, and lists the material systematically under "Diatonic" and "Chromatic."

These indexes are designed to aid teachers. A harmony teacher might use INDEX II to locate passages employing the particular chord or usage under study for either class-room presentation or assignment. Since most of the chord-types are illustrated by a *group* of examples, one might assign students to look up some or all the examples in such a group, compare them, and select one or more for performance or discussion at the next class. Such study not only deepens understanding of detail, but promotes a more comprehensive view of a subject by enabling the student to see it worked out in a variety of styles. INDEX I similarly isolates many items suitable for various kinds of presentation and assignment. See, for example, entries such as "Cadences," "Chromatic progressions," "Enharmonic spellings," "Fortspinnung," "Exchange of voices," "Imitation, real and tonal," "Hypermeasure," "Parallel fifths," "Phrase," "Syncopation," or "Twelve-tone series." The same index also lists examples of the various musical forms—the heart of the *Anthology*. For a summary of these, see the entry "Forms."

When an entry is followed by more than one example, the examples are always listed in *page* order. Therefore the first one will not necessarily be the simplest or the most suitable for one's purpose. The asterisks and plus signs (explained on the next page) provide some distinction between levels of difficulty.

In subjects of large scope, such as forms and genres, the indexes are intended to be complete. Smaller subjects, such as individual chords, are naturally illustrated by only a selection chosen for clarity and variety. Teachers and students will discover many more.

How to Find the Examples

Numbers in **bold** type refer to pages; numbers in parentheses ( ) refer to measures.

A *page number standing alone* refers to a complete work or movement, and is the page on which measure 1 of that work begins, thus:

Fantasia, **190**

first page
of the work

A *page number followed immediately by a measure number (or numbers)* gives the exact page and measure(s) where the example will be found, thus:

Hemiola, **100**   (255-256)

page   measures

In cases where *several* examples of a particular item are found within a *single* work, all the measure locations are given together within a single parenthesis. Here the page number is that of the *first* of the several examples, the rest of which can readily be found from their measure numbers only. For example:

V$_3^4$, **225**   (5, 9, 42)

page   measures of the
of the first example   3 individual
(the one in m. 5)   examples

Further help in finding an example is occasionally given in brackets [ ].

Index I: General Index

SEE "HOW TO FIND THE EXAMPLES" ON THE PREVIOUS PAGE

Index II: Chords, Sequences, and Modulations

SEE "HOW TO FIND THE EXAMPLES" ON PAGE 588

As in Index I, the simpler and more typical examples are preceded by an asterisk (*), the more advanced or unusual by a plus sign(+).

DIATONIC

CHORDS

I, V, and V^7 in root position, +160 (274ff., strings), 164 (39ff.), *199 (1–4), +270 (153–156), *313 [No. 8] (1–8)

IV in root position,

With I and V(^{7}) only, +35 [Saltarello] (1–5), *61 (1–8), +332 (1–4), *436 [hymn] (2, 10), *566 [a] (17–19), *567 (at "rose")

Followed by the cadential $^6_4$, *114 (42–43), 165 [Var. I] (3), +198 (175), +572 (15)

VI and II in root position, +149 (123–127), *566 [a] (1, 7), *567 (at "bloom-ing"), 568 (5–6), *569 [a] (2nd phrase, 4th phrase), *577 [a] (2nd system)

see also "Cadences, deceptive" in INDEX I

III and minor-mode VII, 33 (2, 5–6), 291 (5–6), *312 (1–4), +365 (1–8), *371 (41–44), *560 (2), 563 [Awake] (2, 3, 7), 563 [Christ lag] (3, 6, 11), *571 [a] (13), *581 [a] (entire)

Sixth chords

I^{6}and II^6 only, +66 (3, 10, 11), +167 [Var. IV] (1–4), *436 (1, 3), *572 (10)

V^6–I, +76 (1–2, 21, 33), *161 (3), *578 [So gibst] (7–9, 13–15)

VII^6–I, +23 (9), +182 (52), 559 [b] (2, *5), *571 [b] (2), *572 (1), *577 [b] (1, 5), *581 [b] (3)

IV–II^6, +66 (11), +79 (42), *171 [Var. XI] (3), +181 (158), *229 (14)

IV^6–V$^\sharp$ ("Phrygian cadence"), 50 (43–44), +68 (20), +572 (14)

6–6–6 (consecutive sixth chords), *15 (6, 18), *224 (59–64)

Pieces or passages consisting largely of $^5_3$ and $^6_3$ chords, +14, +85 57ff.), *559 [a], *571 [Herzliebster, a]

see also the $^6_3$ usages under SEQUENCES, below

VII as a diminished triad, 49 (12), +67 (4), 107 (10 [last 8th]), +114 (25, 31, 32, 33, 38), +560 [Ach wie] (3), *565 [a] (last line: at "Rü–stung")

Cadential $^{6-5}_{4-3}$, *38 (15), 76 (*6, +26, 42), *114 (43), +125 (48), 132 (97), *165 [Theme] (4), +168 [Var. VI] (4), *181 (159), +187 (158ff.), 200 (23), 219 (8), 229 (8, 15), 293 (+4, *8), +389 (30ff., 95ff.), +567 (final cadence), *572 (8, 16), *575 [b] (3)

Other $^6_4$ usages

The consonant $^6_4$ (including $^6_4$ caused by arpeggiation in the bass), 143 (27–28), +194 (83 [see also 76–83]), *313 [No. 8] (9, 10, 11, 12), 319 (+1–2, *4), *343 (76), +355 (38, 40), +392 (72), +580 (2, 11)

$^6_4$ caused by neighbor tones and/or passing tones in upper voices over stationary bass, 23 (21), +152 (57ff., 149ff.), *185 (66–67), *291 (8–9), *313 [No. 8] (2, 3), +314 [No. 14] (2), +319 (1–2), +334 (1)

$^6_4$ occurring over a passing tone in the bass voice, *91 (25 [4th beat]), 114 (24), 353 (+44, *54), *573 (12), *579 (7, 11)

599

Sequences

(The following are not one-voice but chordal sequences: *All* voices proceed sequentially. Such passages, in addition to being very common voice-leading techniques, provide useful first steps in the study of reduction. In each case the student should discover the basic voice leading by removing the elaboration, and also discover from whence the sequence comes and whither it goes—how it fits into the phrase that contains it.)

CHROMATIC

NOTE

In addition to the items indexed below, see the entries in INDEX I starting at "Chromatic." See also the preface to Part Four (page 289) for pieces and passages relevant to the study of chromatic harmony.

MODULATIONS

To diatonically related keys, but with salient chromatic embellishment, e.g., secondary chords, mixture, *152 (52–65), *233 (1–5), *298 (32–58), +306 (1–12, 12–17), +365 (8–16), *571 [Herzliebster, b] (4–6)

To key of ♭VI, *226 (24–25), 279 (67–2nd ending–70 [compare 1st ending])

Achieved by various chromatic techniques
    (Modulations to both diatonically and chromatically related keys are represented.)
Via ♭II as pivot, 374 (25–38)
Via chromatic sequences, *54 (17–24, 24–29), *138 (44–51), +156 (172–189), *223 (14–20 [and see 27–28!]), 234 (35–51), +254 (94–116)
Via an augmented-6th or diminished-3rd chord, +125 (49–53), *144 (1–10), *169 [Var. VII]

(5–8), +205 (75–103), +251 (1–33–38), *263 (14–22–35, 174–183–196), *329 (9–16), *352 (19–25)

Via V⁷ enharmonically changed to augmented 6th (diminished 3rd), *137 (37–43), +378 (130–138)

Via enharmonically changed °7, *88 (4–8), 236 (133–137)

Via free (non-sequential) chromatic voice leading (Exchange of voices occurs in some examples), 233 (5–11), *241 (47–51), 328 [Prelude 9] (5–8 [3rd beat]), +391 (68–72)

Pieces containing several modulations between chromatically related keys, 88, 297, 354 (1–16–37), 357 [Var. III] (61–84)
see also 550 (6ᵇ–8ᵃ)